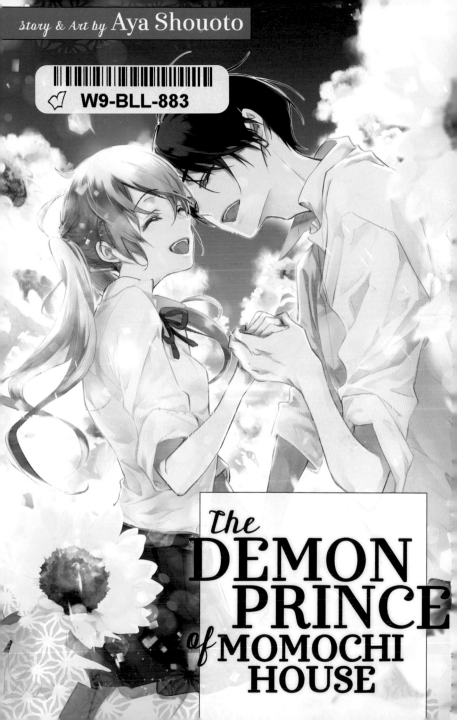

Story & Art by **Aya Shouoto**

The
DEMON
PRINCE
of MOMOCHI
HOUSE

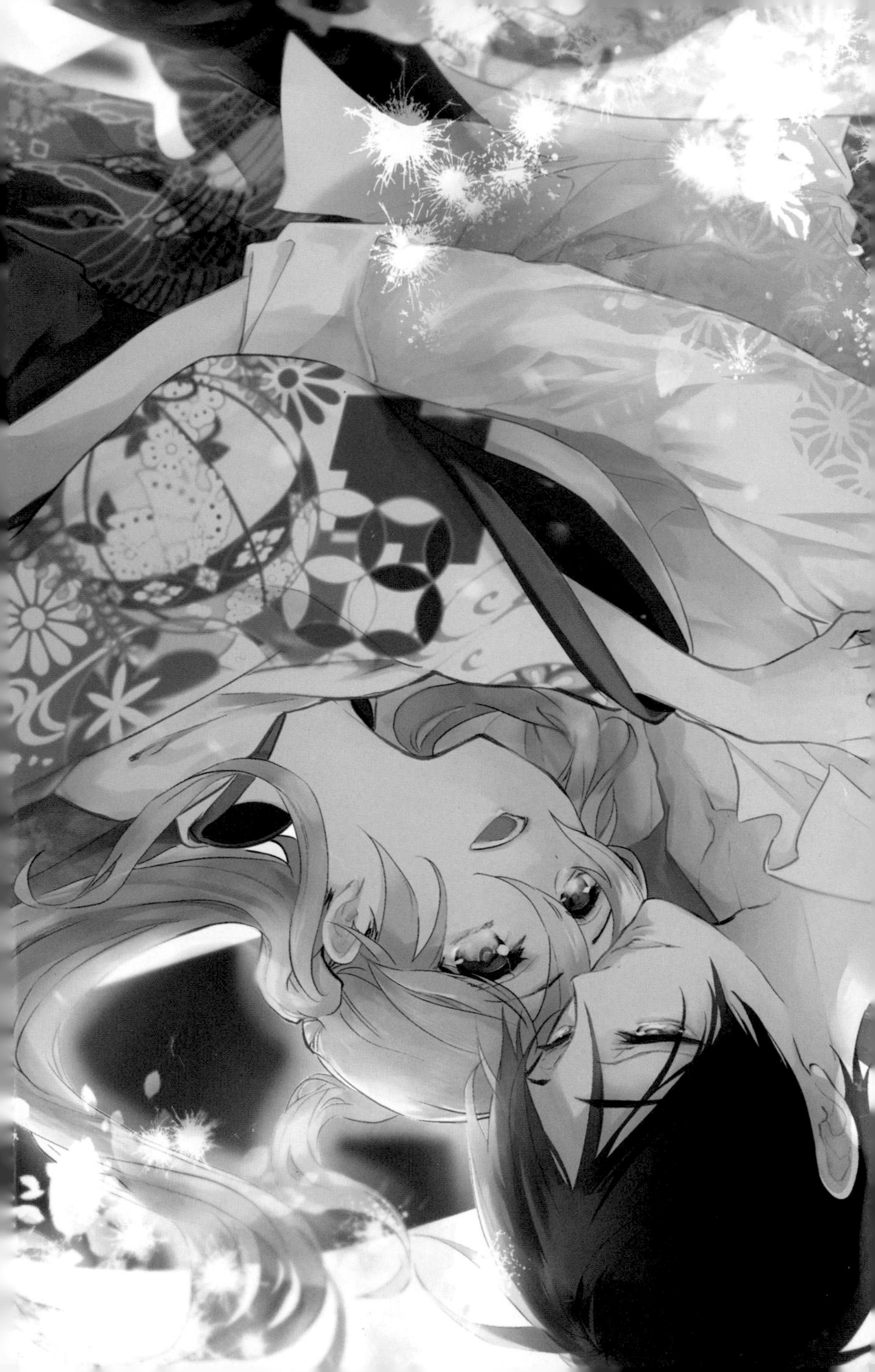

CHAPTER 61
Spirited Away

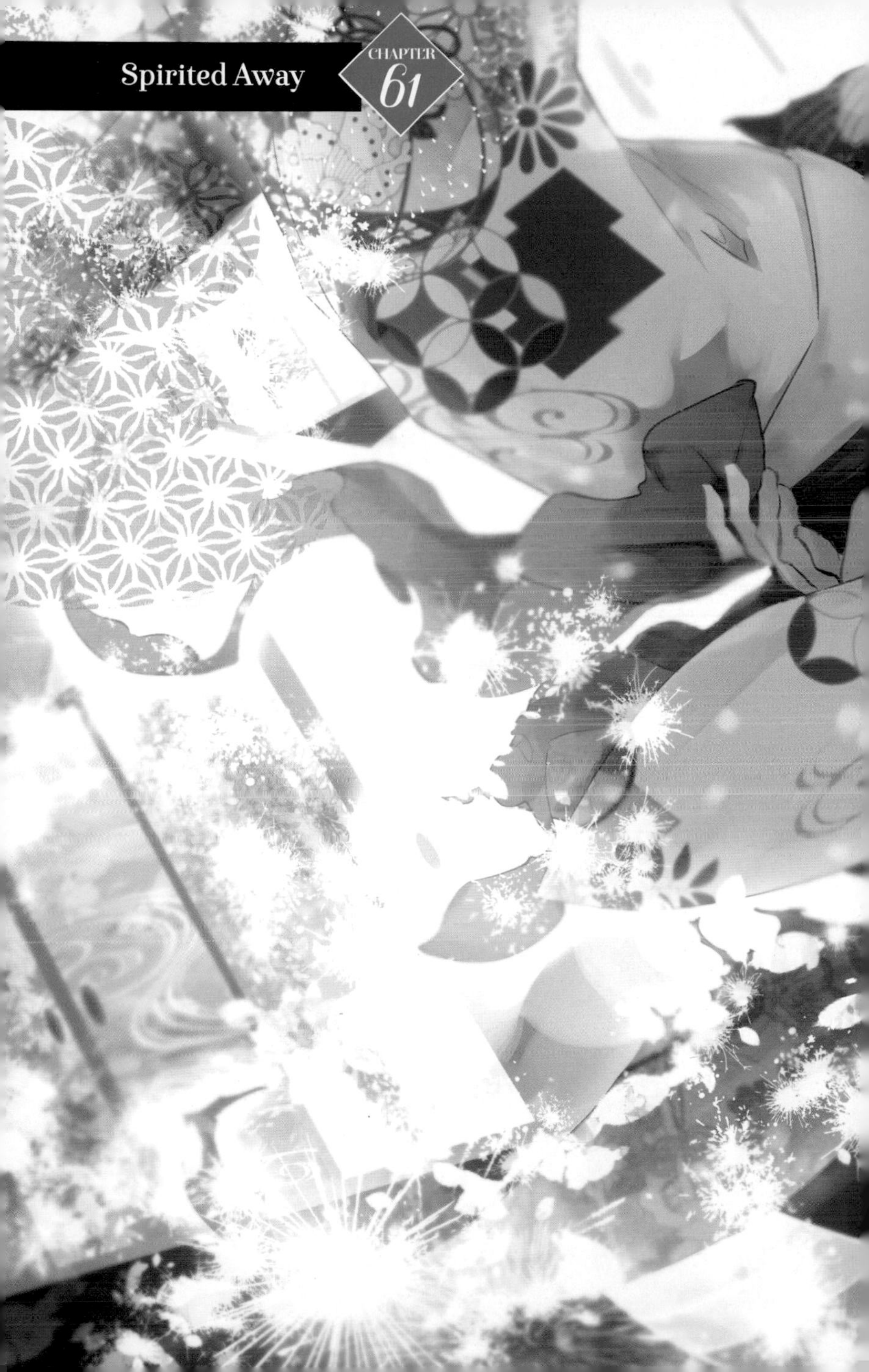

The DEMON PRINCE of MOMOCHI HOUSE

16

Contents

The Mysterious Residents of Momochi House

Aoi Nanamori

When he was 10 years old, he wandered into Momochi House and was chosen as the Omamori-sama. He transforms into a nue to perform his duties, but it seems this role was meant for Himari.

Omamori-sama (Nue)

An ayakashi, or demon, with the ears of a cat, the wings of a bird, and the tail of a fox. As the Omamori-sama, the nue protects Momochi House and eliminates demons who make their way in from the spiritual realm.

Yukari

One of Omamori-sama's shikigami. He's a water serpent.

Ise

One of Omamori-sama's shikigami. He's an orangutan.

Himari Momochi

A 16-year-old orphan who, according to a certain will, has inherited Momochi House. As rightful owner, she has the ability to expel beings from the house.

Lesser Yokai

EVERYONE IS HERE!

Momochi House: Story Thus Far

Aoi's fierce battle in the spiritual realm against Kasha, his greatest enemy, has come to an end. Himari and Aoi's summer together flies by. One day, when Himari wakes, Aoi is suddenly nowhere to be seen, but he has left behind a letter telling her goodbye. Around the same time, Momochi House begins to collapse. Aoi has been absorbed by the house and is trying to release Himari and the shikigami. Will Himari be forced to leave the house without saving Aoi?

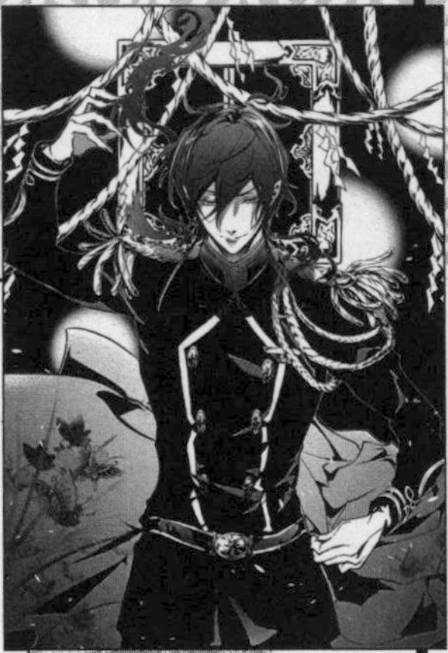

Kasha

The highest level of ayakashi. He reigns over all others. He constantly gives Nue (Aoi) a hard time.

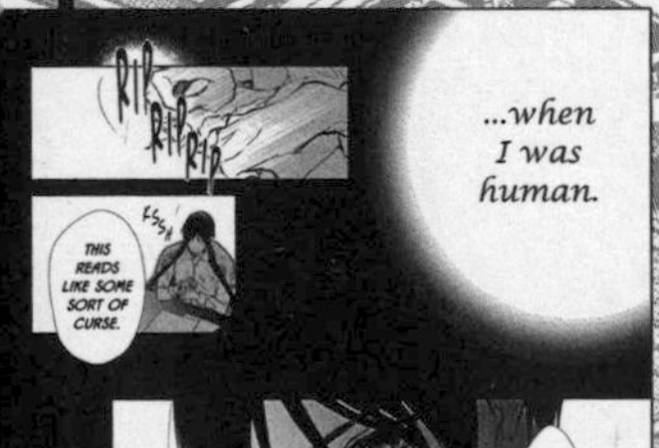
...when I was human.
RIP RIP RIP
THIS READS LIKE SOME SORT OF CURSE.
"GOOD-BYE."
KREK
That was all I could say to you.

Hakka

Omamori-sama's newest shikigami. His identity is Shuten Douji.

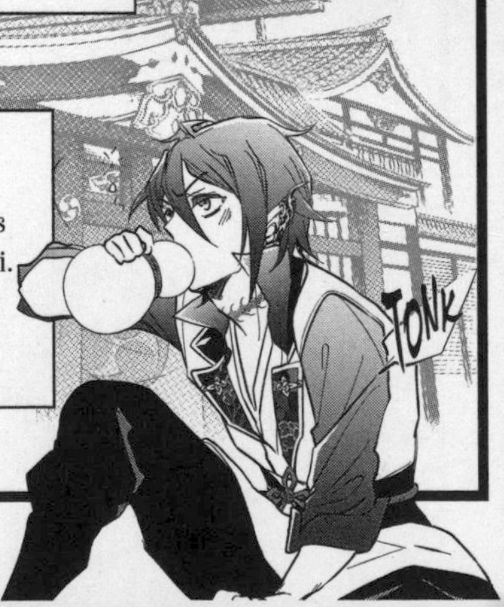
TONK

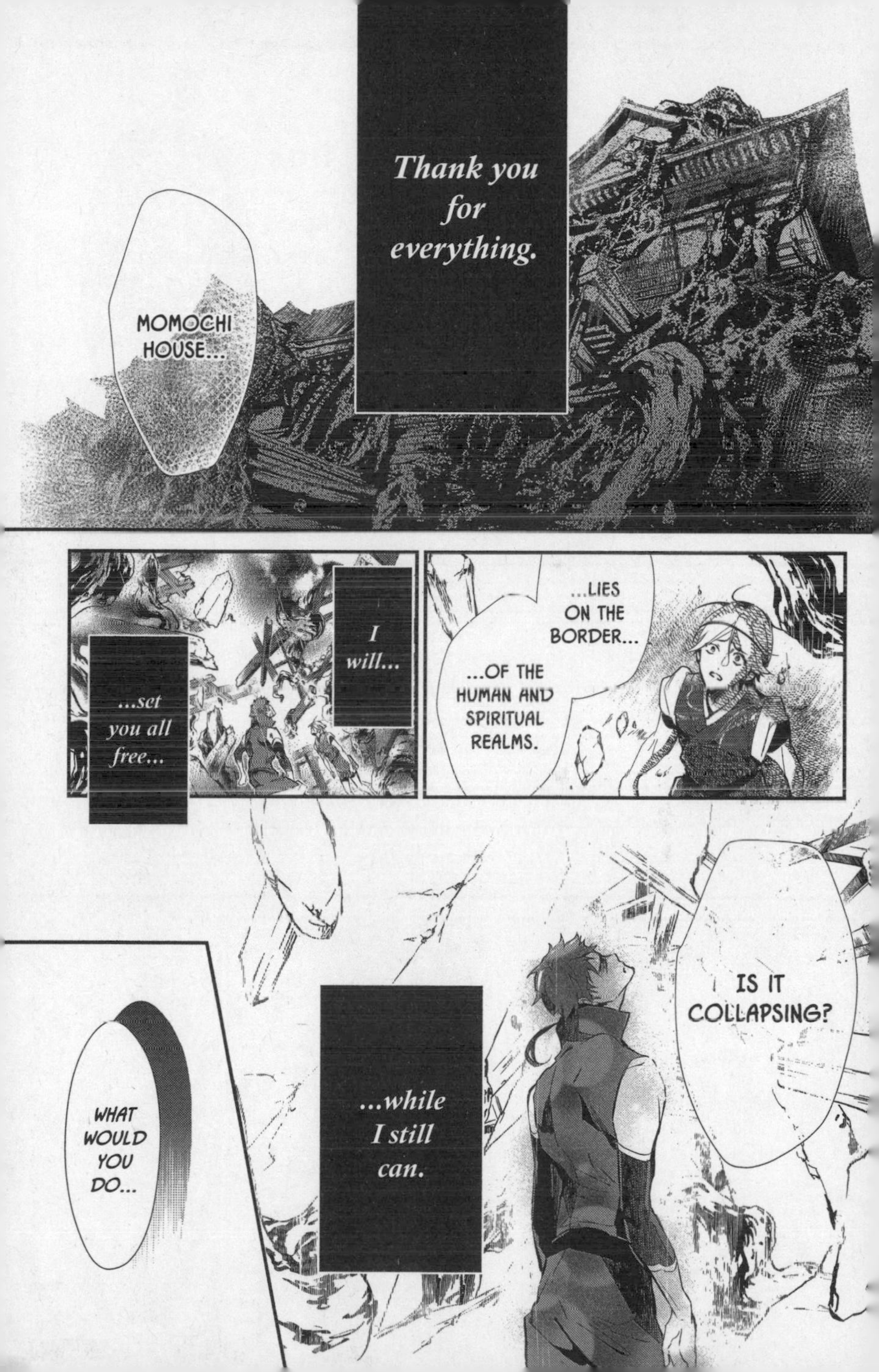
Thank you for everything.
MOMOCHI HOUSE...
...LIES ON THE BORDER...
...OF THE HUMAN AND SPIRITUAL REALMS.
I will...
...set you all free...
IS IT COLLAPSING?
...while I still can.
WHAT WOULD YOU DO...

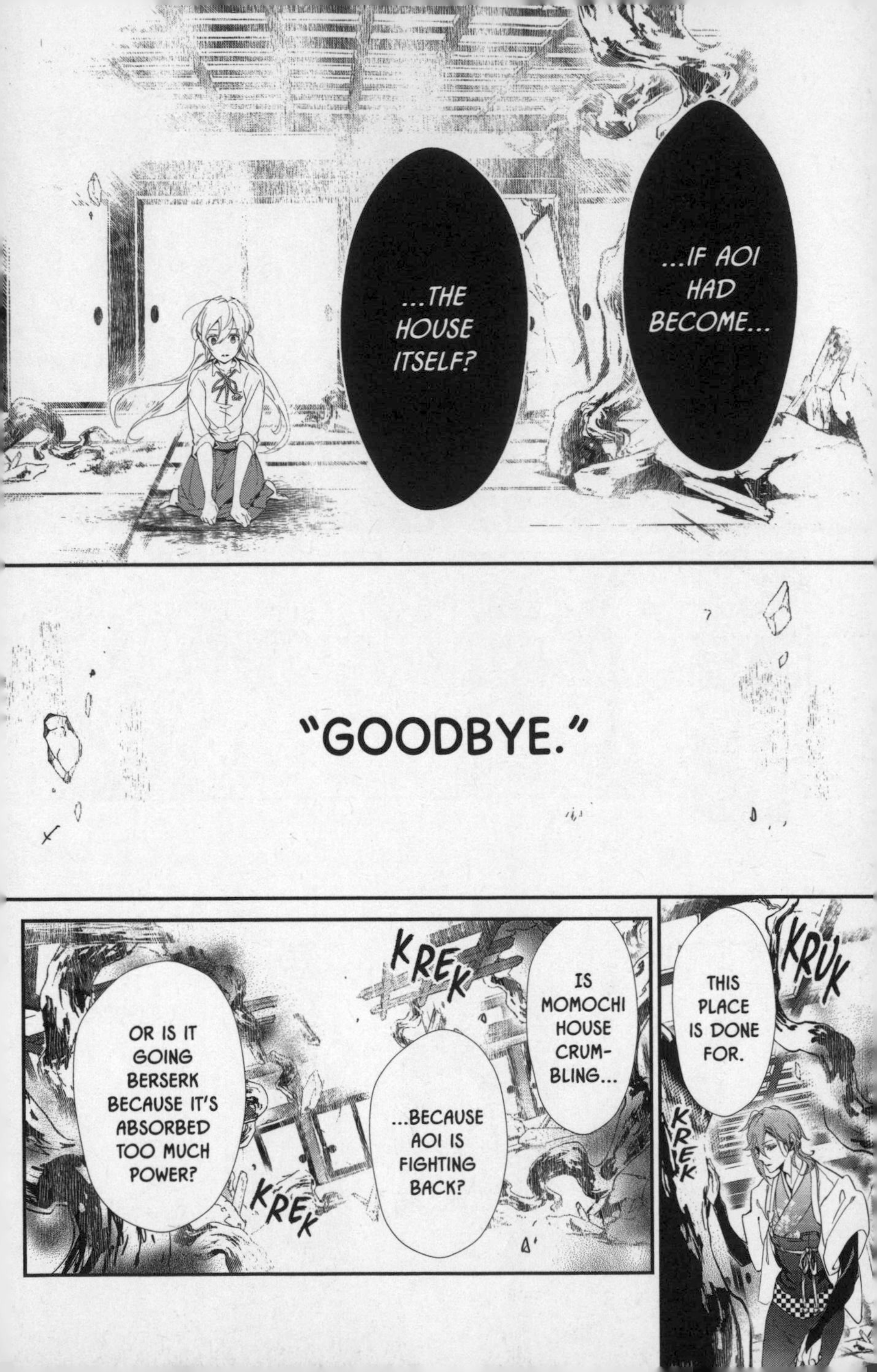
...IF AOI HAD BECOME...
...THE HOUSE ITSELF?
"GOODBYE."
KRUK
THIS PLACE IS DONE FOR.
KREK
KREK
IS MOMOCHI HOUSE CRUMBLING...
...BECAUSE AOI IS FIGHTING BACK?
OR IS IT GOING BERSERK BECAUSE IT'S ABSORBED TOO MUCH POWER?
KREK

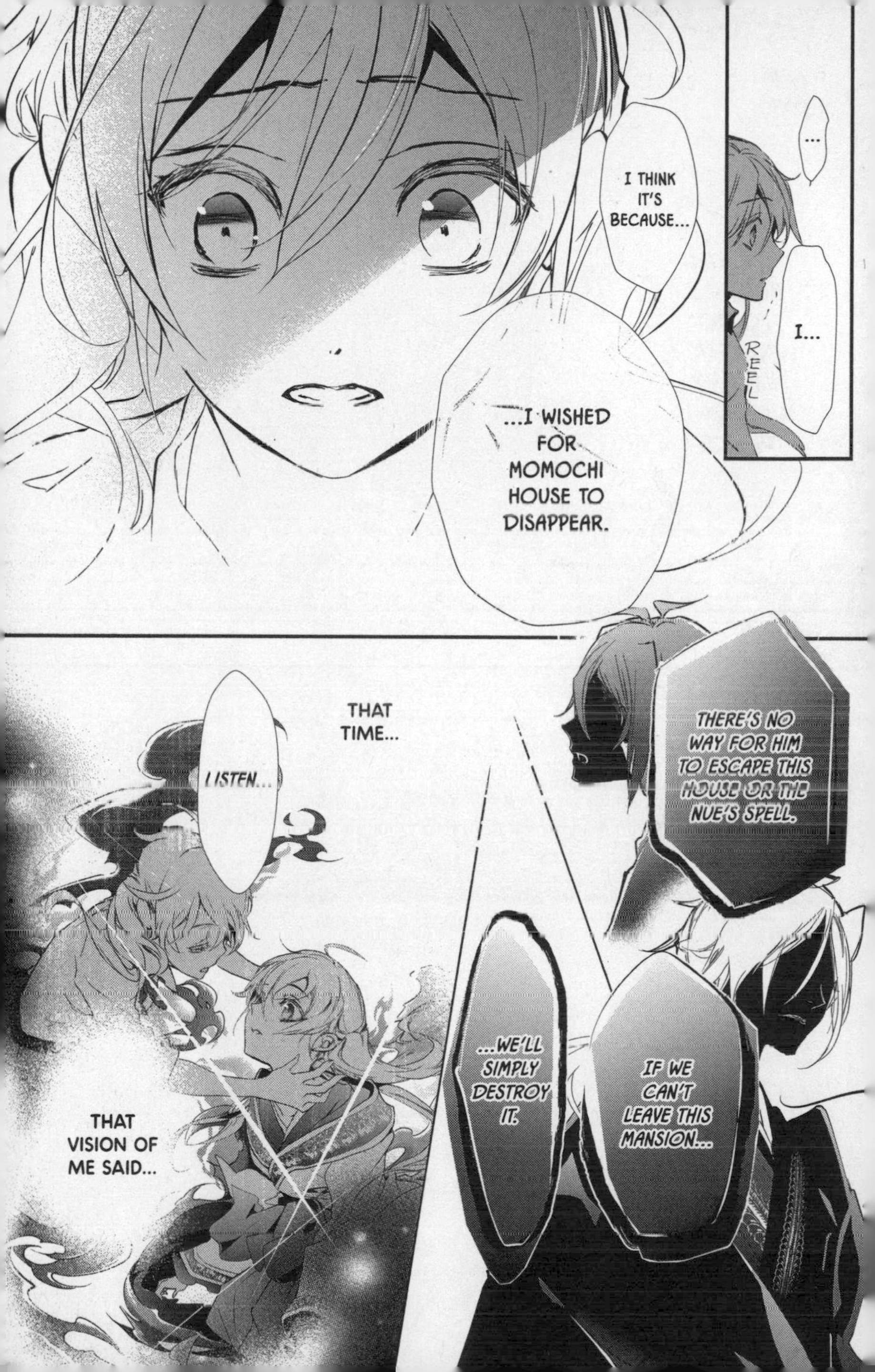
...
I...
REEL
I THINK IT'S BECAUSE...
...I WISHED FOR MOMOCHI HOUSE TO DISAPPEAR.
THAT TIME...
LISTEN...
THERE'S NO WAY FOR HIM TO ESCAPE THIS HOUSE OR THE NUE'S SPELL.
IF WE CAN'T LEAVE THIS MANSION...
...WE'LL SIMPLY DESTROY IT.
THAT VISION OF ME SAID...

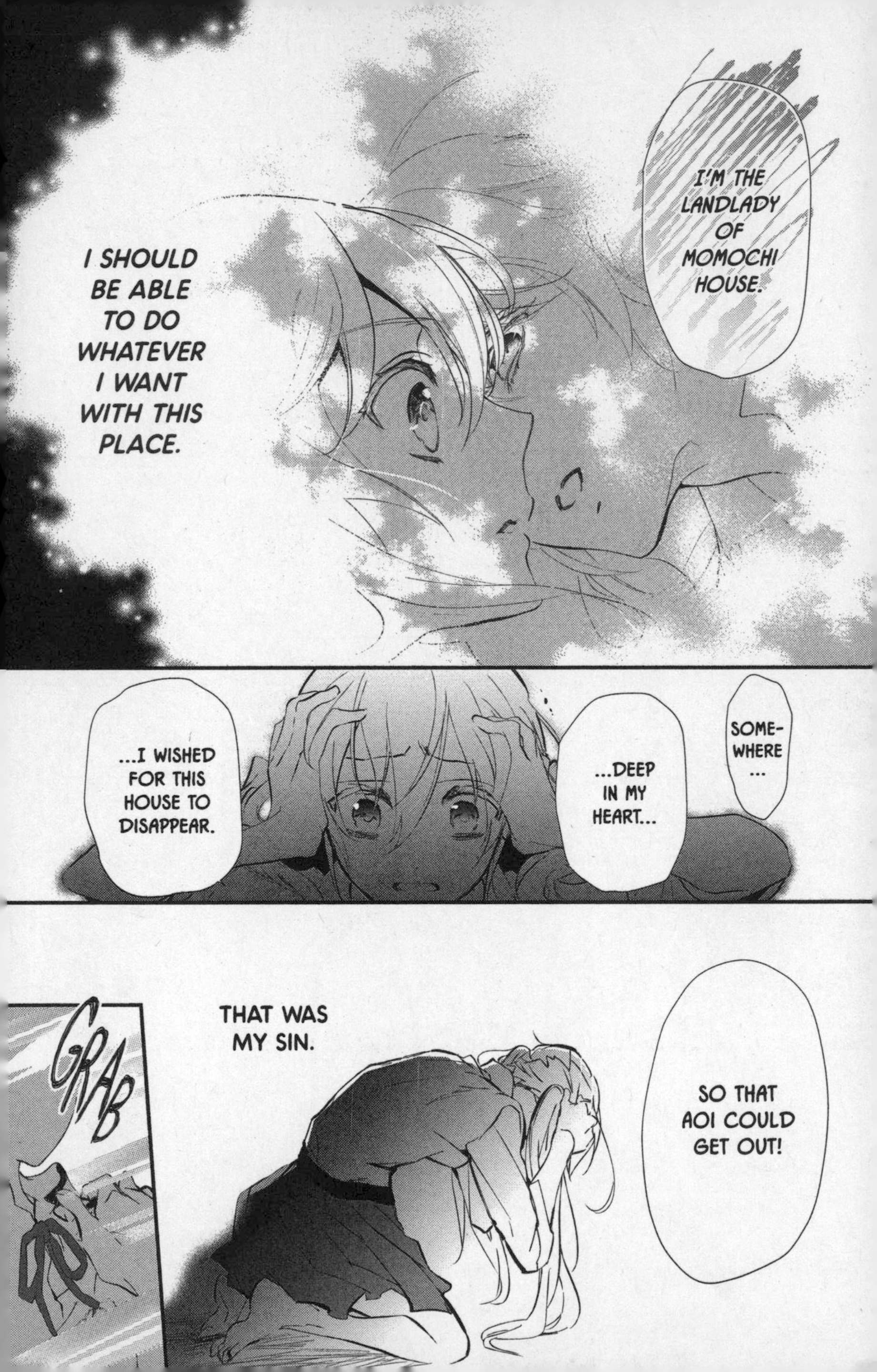
I'M THE LANDLADY OF MOMOCHI HOUSE.
I SHOULD BE ABLE TO DO WHATEVER I WANT WITH THIS PLACE.
SOME-WHERE...
...DEEP IN MY HEART...
...I WISHED FOR THIS HOUSE TO DISAPPEAR.
SO THAT AOI COULD GET OUT!
THAT WAS MY SIN.
GRAB

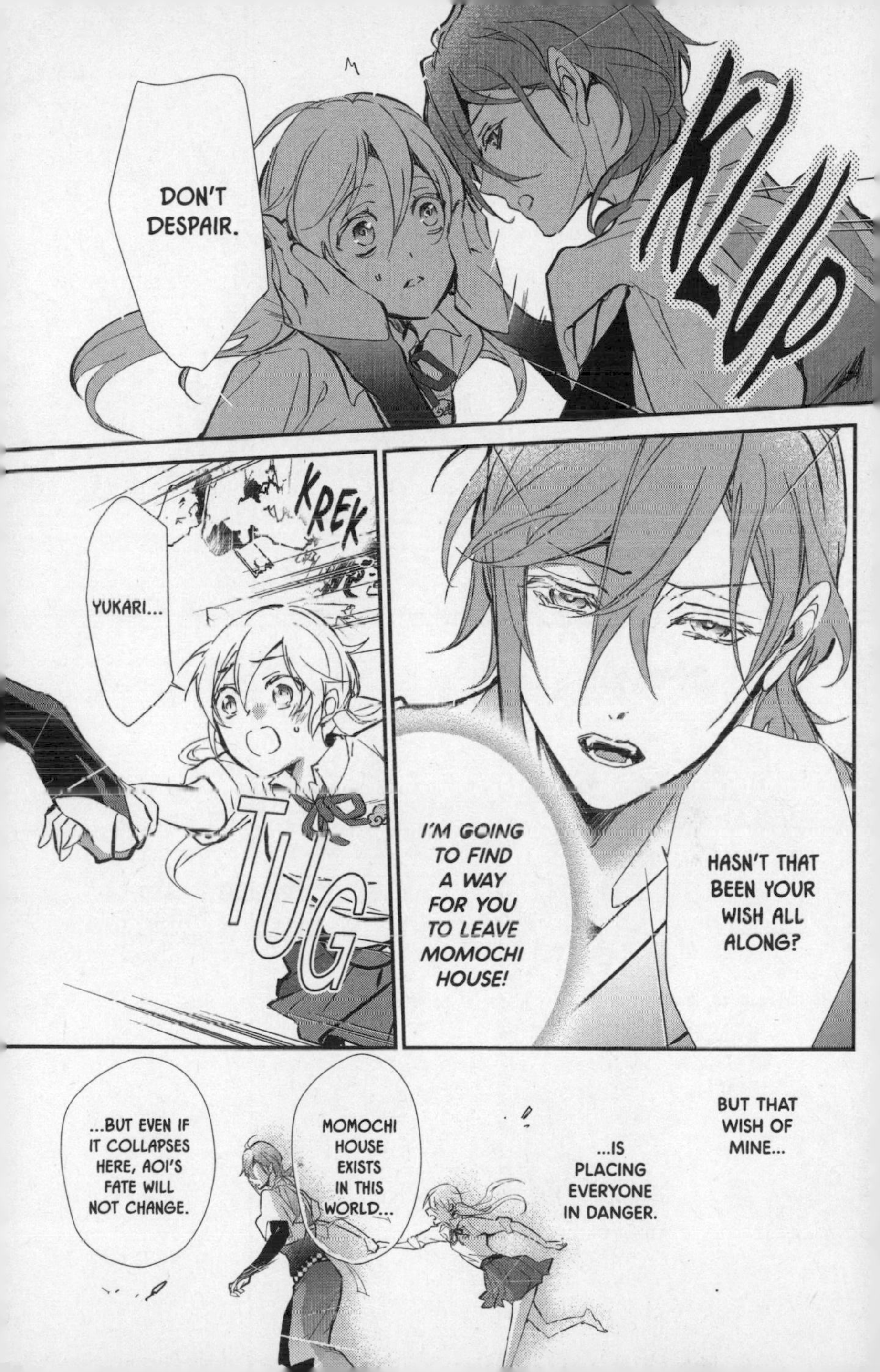
KLUP
DON'T DESPAIR.
HASN'T THAT BEEN YOUR WISH ALL ALONG?
I'M GOING TO FIND A WAY FOR YOU TO LEAVE MOMOCHI HOUSE!
KREK
YUKARI...
TUG
BUT THAT WISH OF MINE...
...IS PLACING EVERYONE IN DANGER.
MOMOCHI HOUSE EXISTS IN THIS WORLD...
...BUT EVEN IF IT COLLAPSES HERE, AOI'S FATE WILL NOT CHANGE.

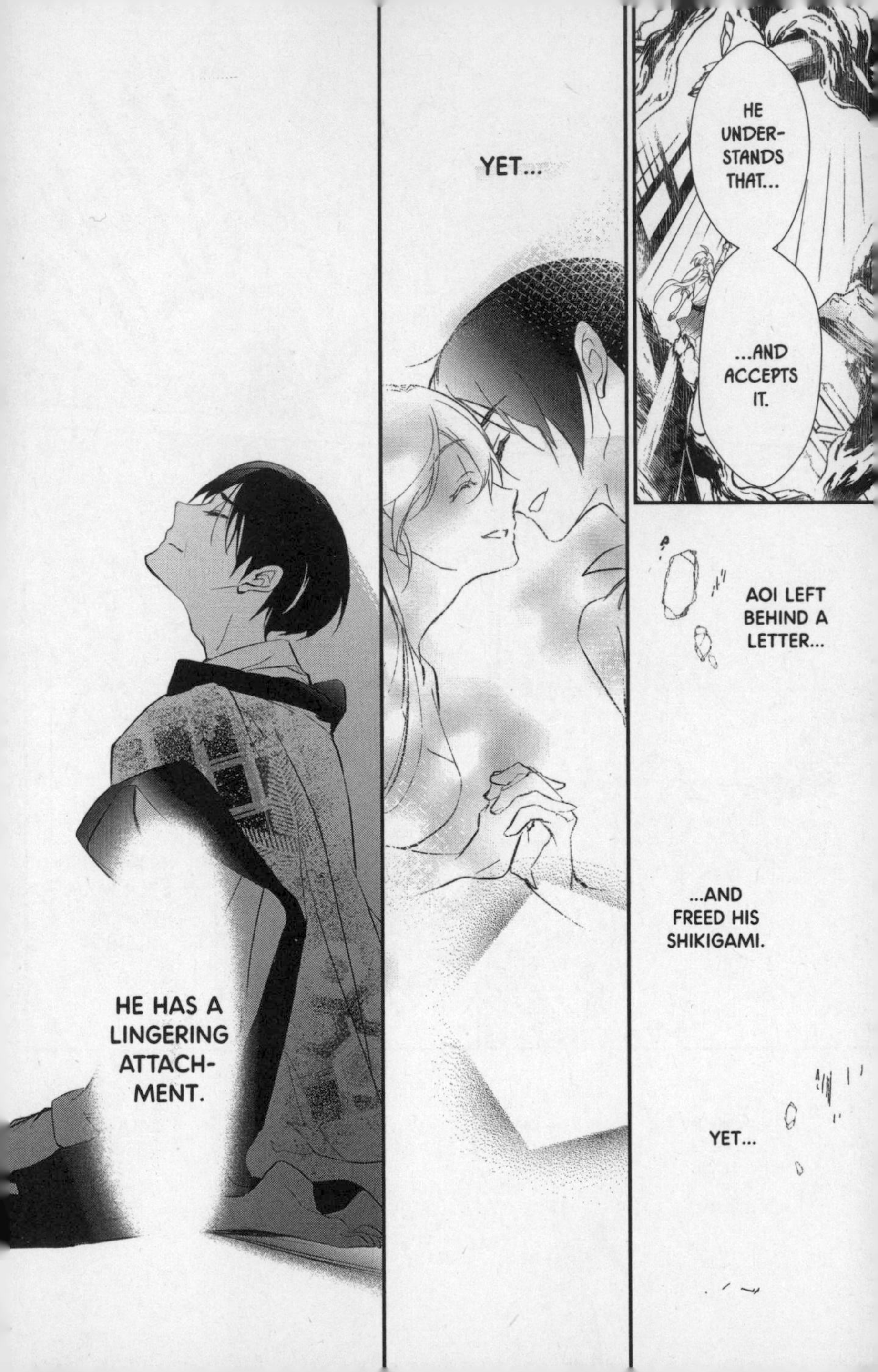
HE UNDER-STANDS THAT...
...AND ACCEPTS IT.
AOI LEFT BEHIND A LETTER...
...AND FREED HIS SHIKIGAMI.
YET...
YET...
HE HAS A LINGERING ATTACH-MENT.

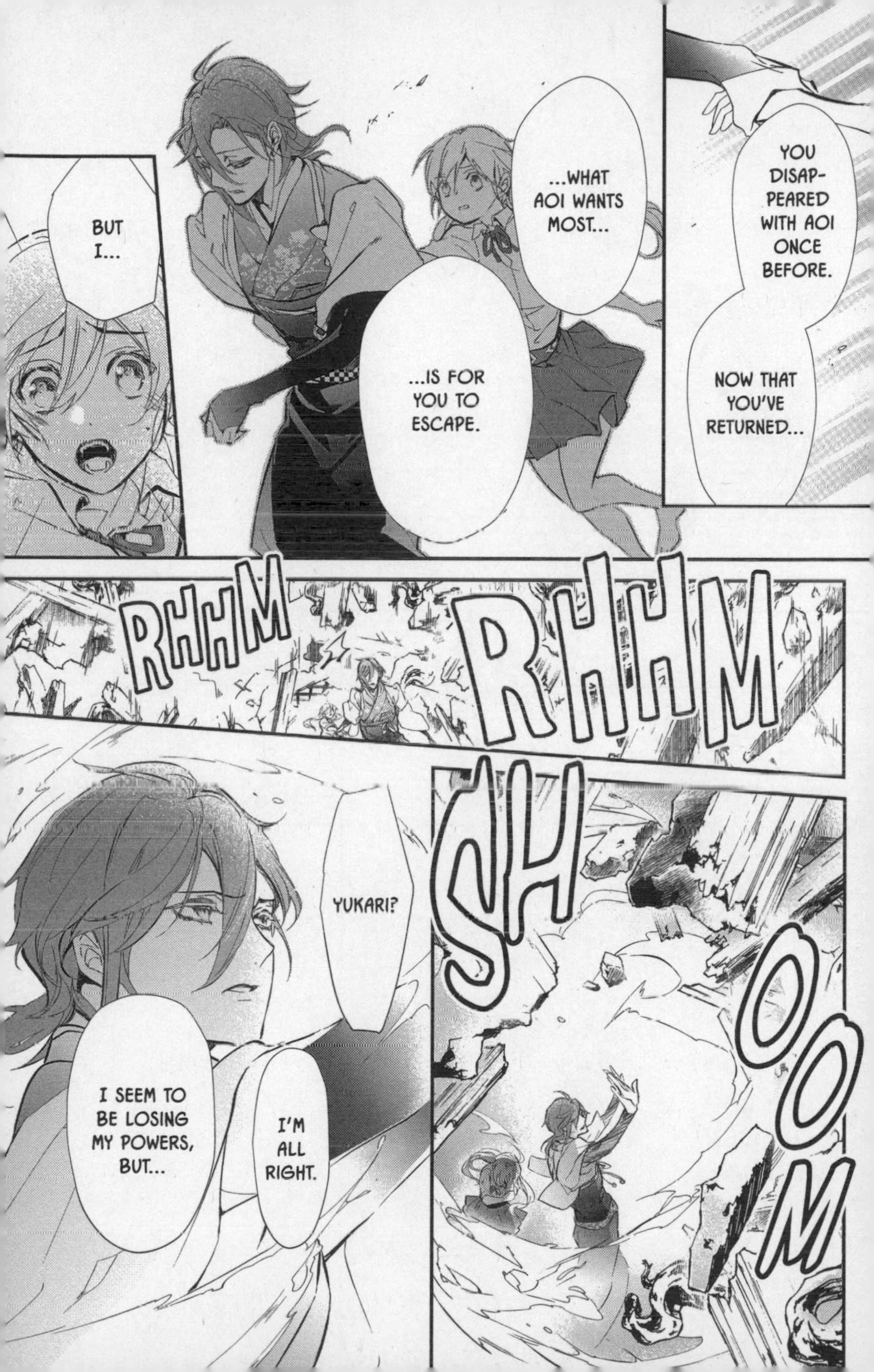
YOU DISAPPEARED WITH AOI ONCE BEFORE.
NOW THAT YOU'VE RETURNED...
...WHAT AOI WANTS MOST...
...IS FOR YOU TO ESCAPE.
BUT I...
RHHM
RHHM
SHOOOM
YUKARI?
I SEEM TO BE LOSING MY POWERS, BUT...
I'M ALL RIGHT.

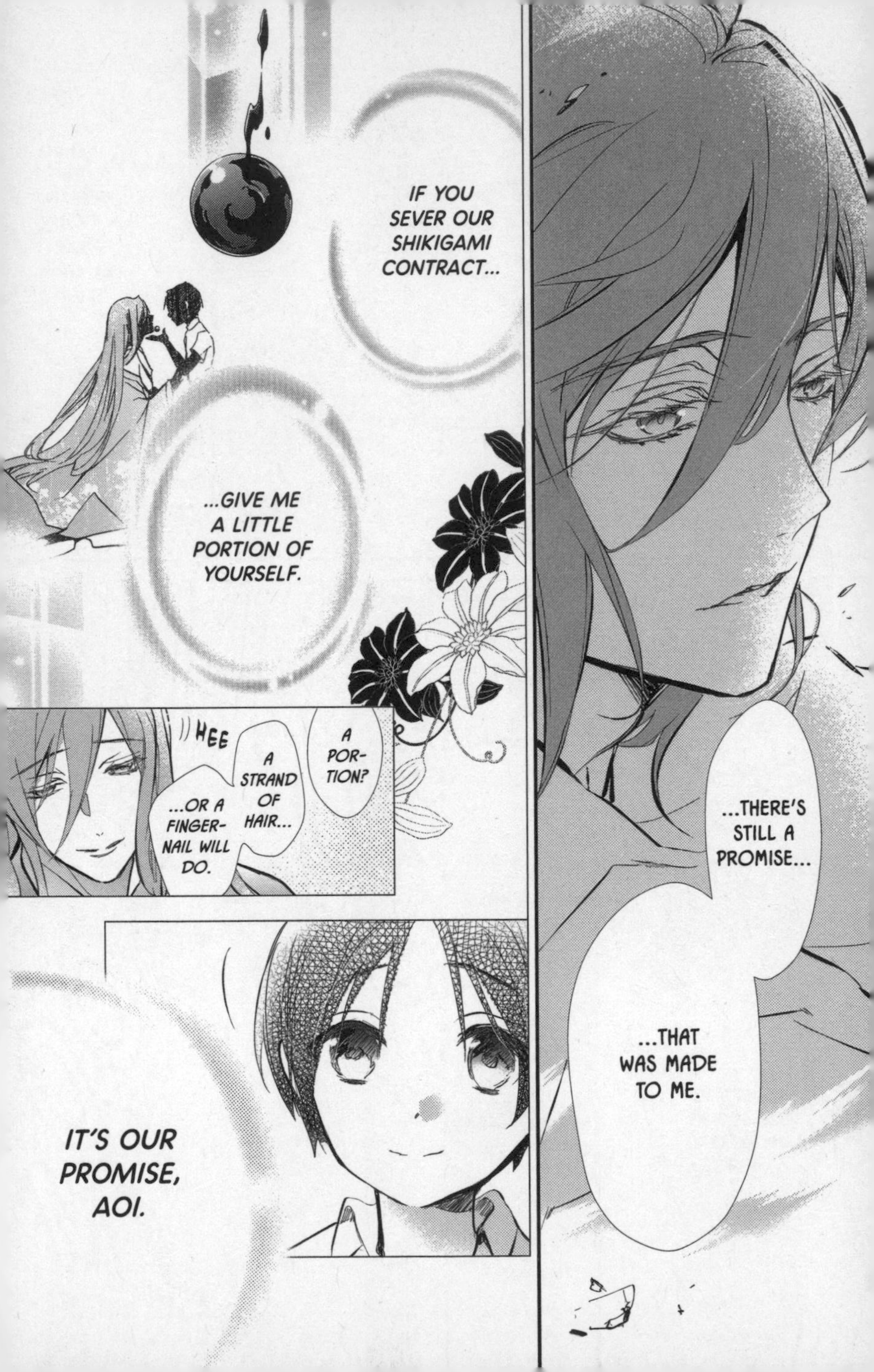
...THERE'S STILL A PROMISE...
...THAT WAS MADE TO ME.
IF YOU SEVER OUR SHIKIGAMI CONTRACT...
...GIVE ME A LITTLE PORTION OF YOURSELF.
A POR-TION?
A STRAND OF HAIR...
...OR A FINGER-NAIL WILL DO.
HEE
IT'S OUR PROMISE, AOI.

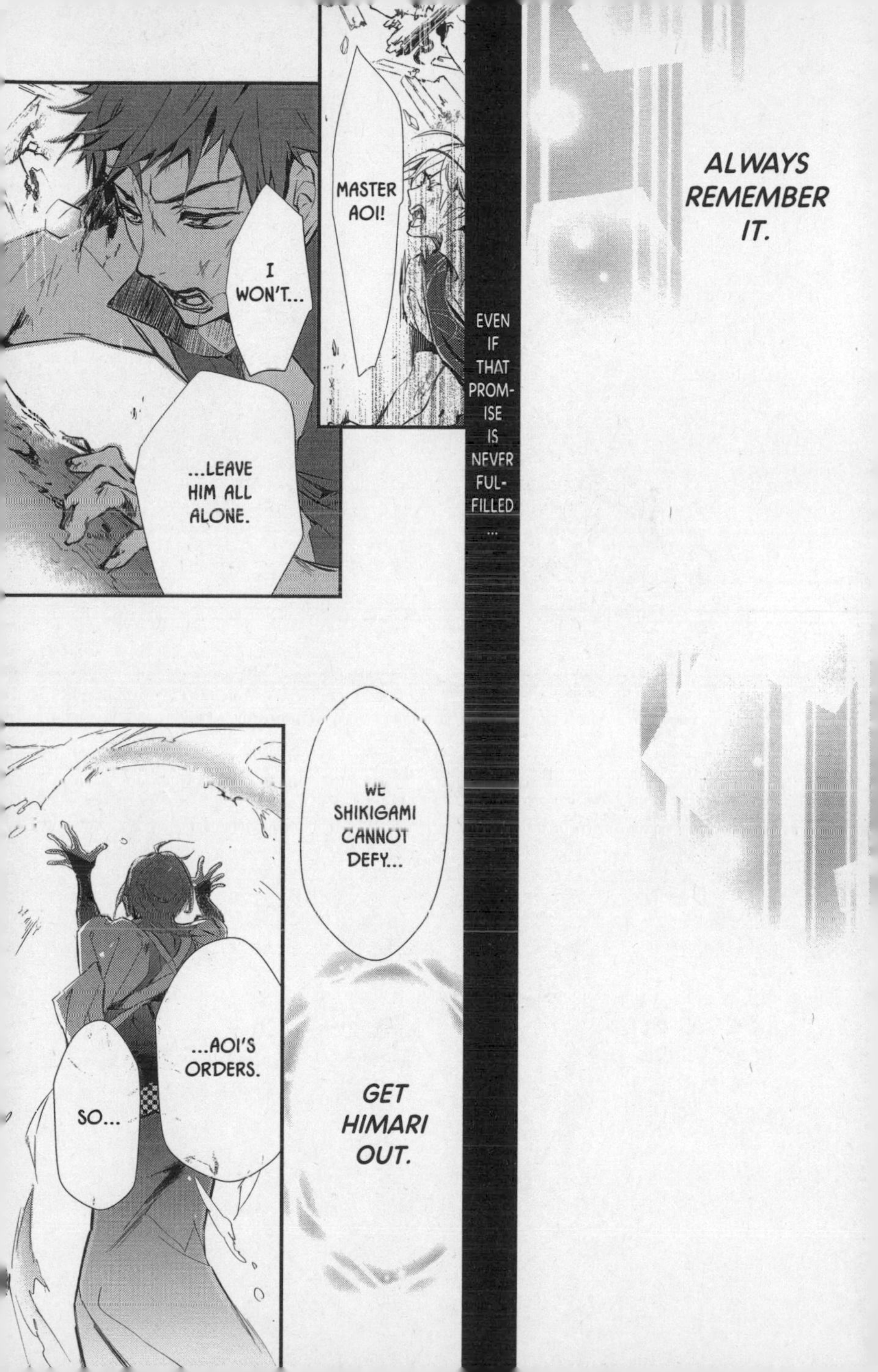
EVEN IF THAT PROMISE IS NEVER FULFILLED...
ALWAYS REMEMBER IT.
MASTER AOI!
I WON'T...
...LEAVE HIM ALL ALONE.
WE SHIKIGAMI CANNOT DEFY...
...AOI'S ORDERS.
SO...
GET HIMARI OUT.

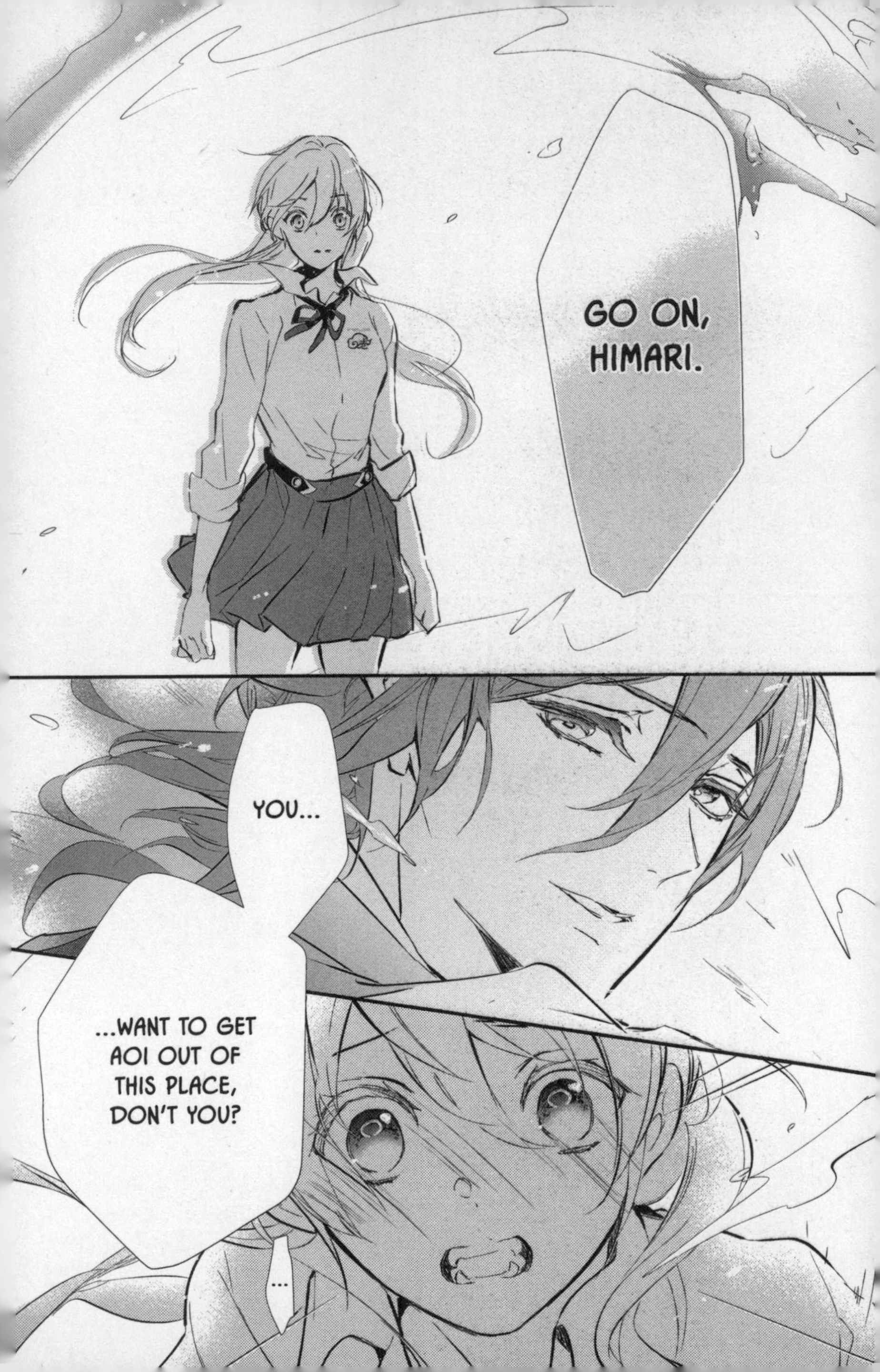
GO ON, HIMARI.
YOU...
...WANT TO GET AOI OUT OF THIS PLACE, DON'T YOU?
...

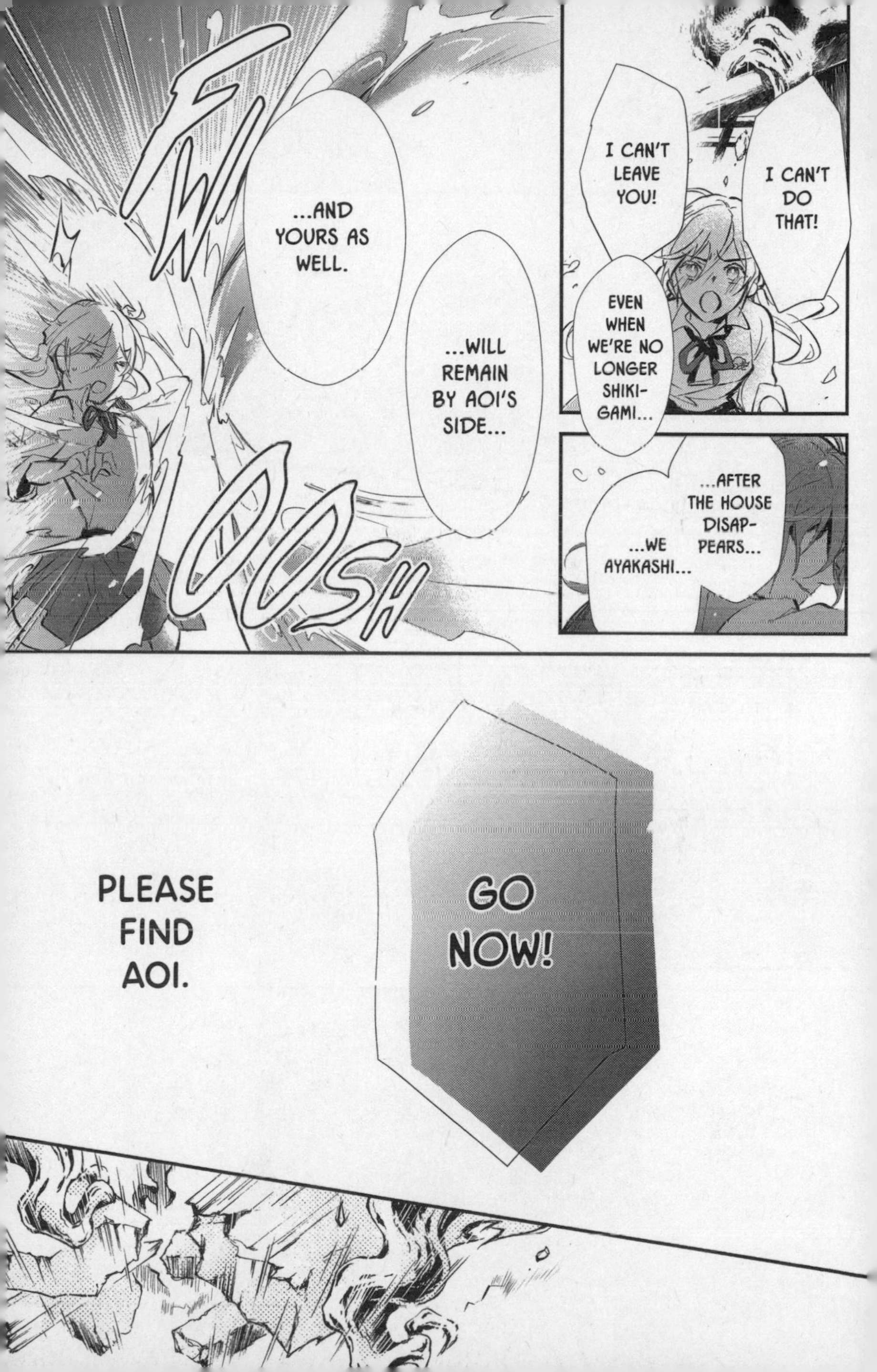
I CAN'T DO THAT!
I CAN'T LEAVE YOU!
EVEN WHEN WE'RE NO LONGER SHIKI-GAMI...
...AFTER THE HOUSE DISAP-PEARS...
...WE AYAKASHI...
...WILL REMAIN BY AOI'S SIDE...
...AND YOURS AS WELL.
FWOOSH
GO NOW!
PLEASE FIND AOI.

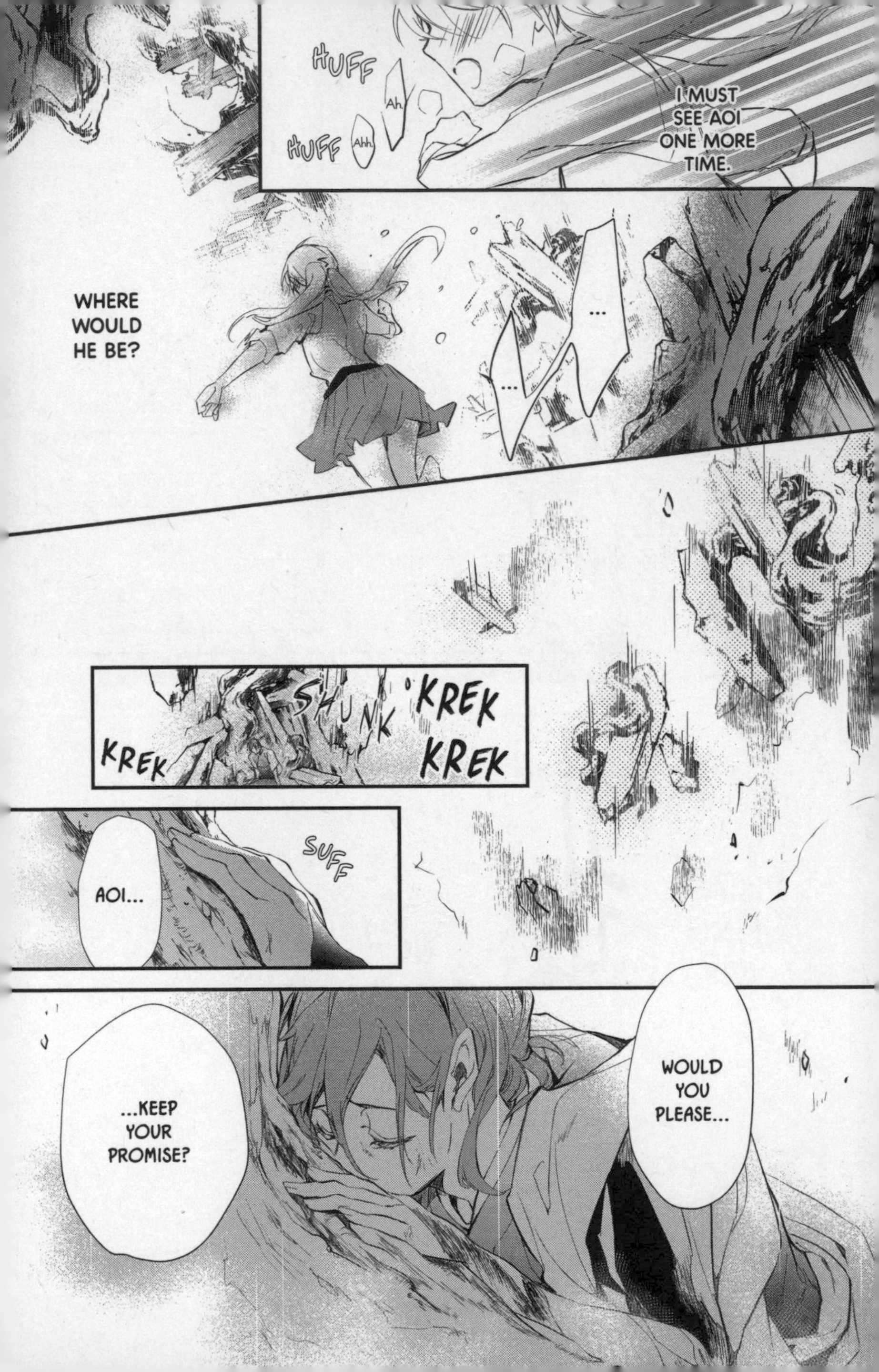
I MUST SEE AOI ONE MORE TIME.
HUFF
Ah.
HUFF
Ahh.
...
...
WHERE WOULD HE BE?
KREK
KREK
SHUNK
KREK
SUFF
AOI...
WOULD YOU PLEASE...
...KEEP YOUR PROMISE?

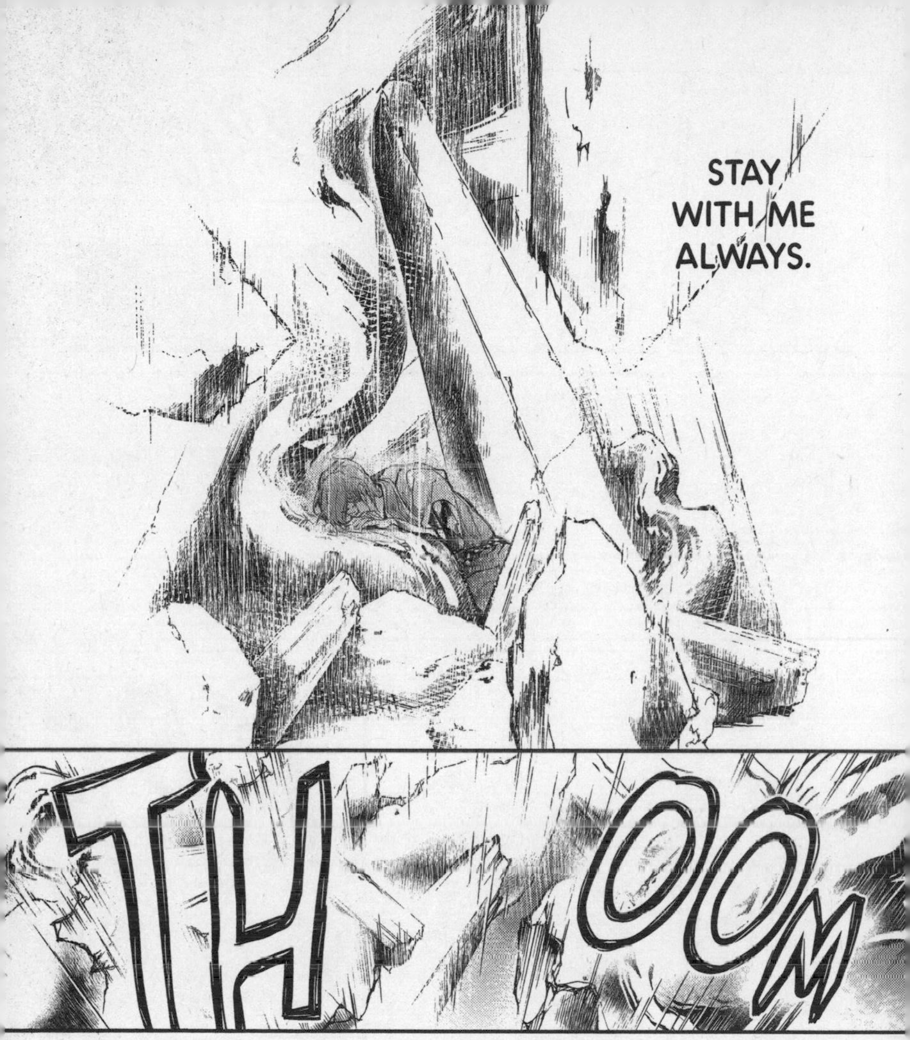
STAY WITH ME ALWAYS.
THOOM

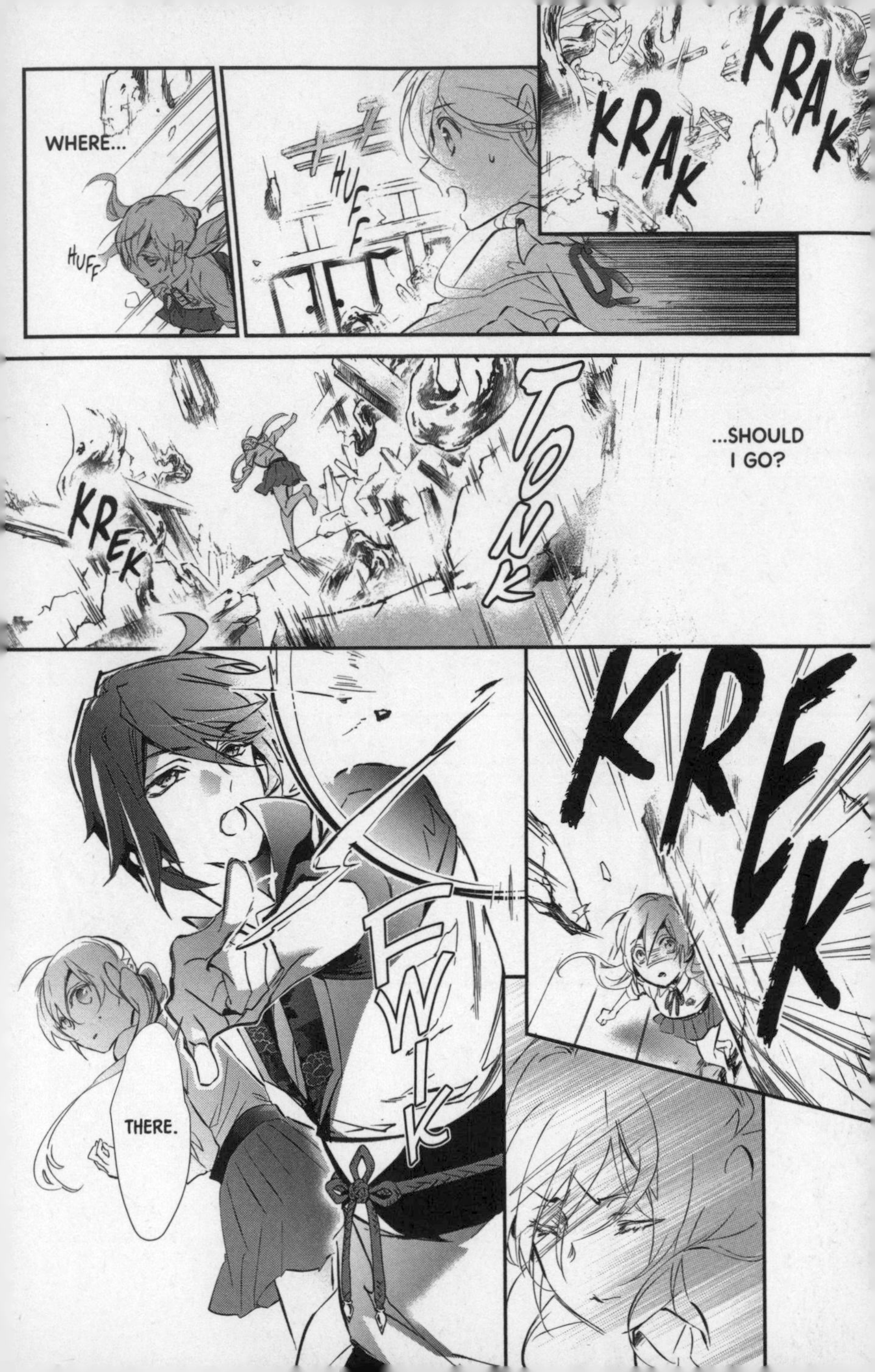
KRAK
KRAK
HUFF
WHERE...
HUFF
...SHOULD I GO?
TONK
KREK
KREK
FWIK
THERE.

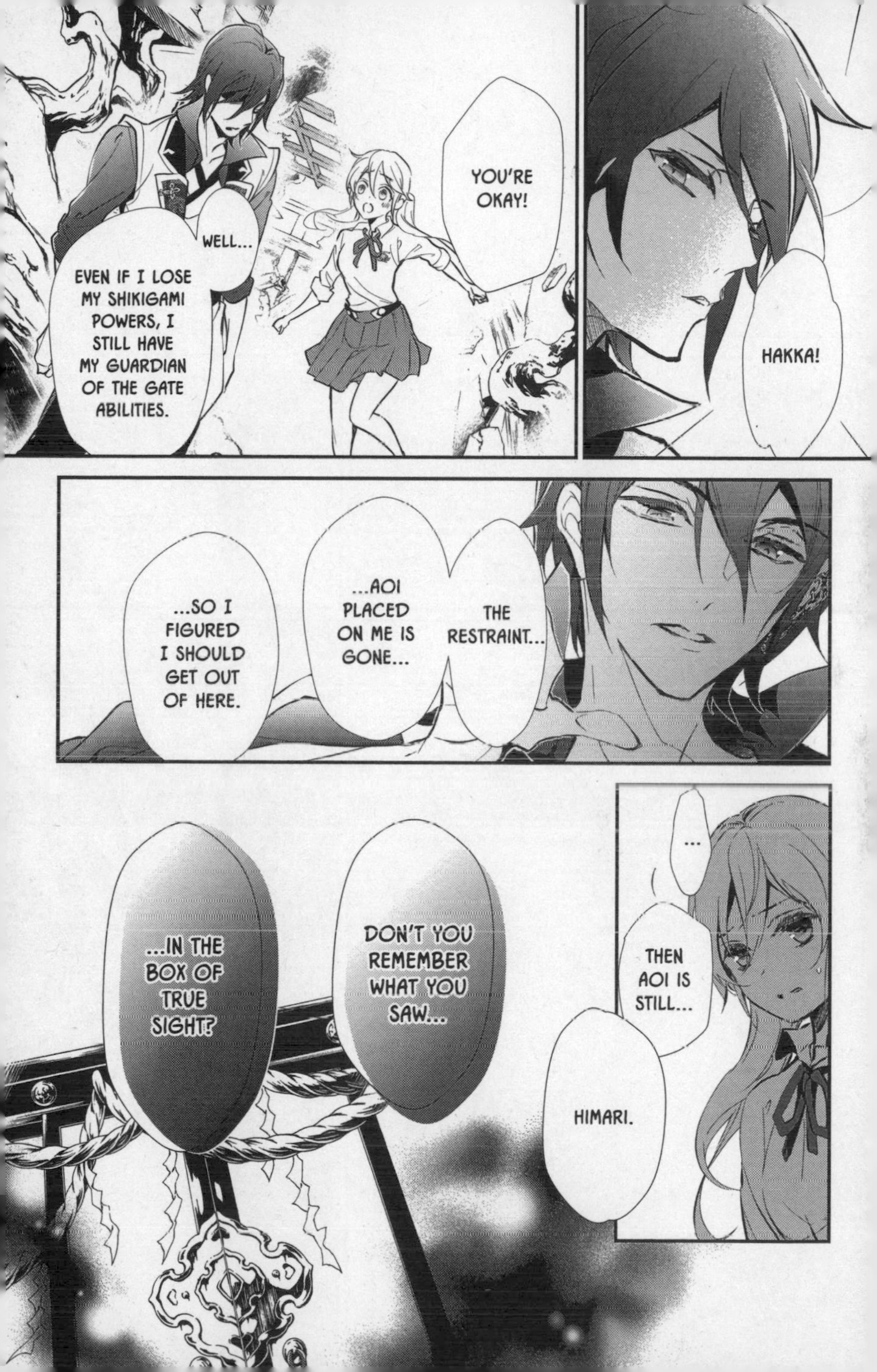
HAKKA!
YOU'RE OKAY!
WELL...
EVEN IF I LOSE MY SHIKIGAMI POWERS, I STILL HAVE MY GUARDIAN OF THE GATE ABILITIES.
THE RESTRAINT...
...AOI PLACED ON ME IS GONE...
...SO I FIGURED I SHOULD GET OUT OF HERE.
...
THEN AOI IS STILL...
HIMARI.
DON'T YOU REMEMBER WHAT YOU SAW...
...IN THE BOX OF TRUE SIGHT?

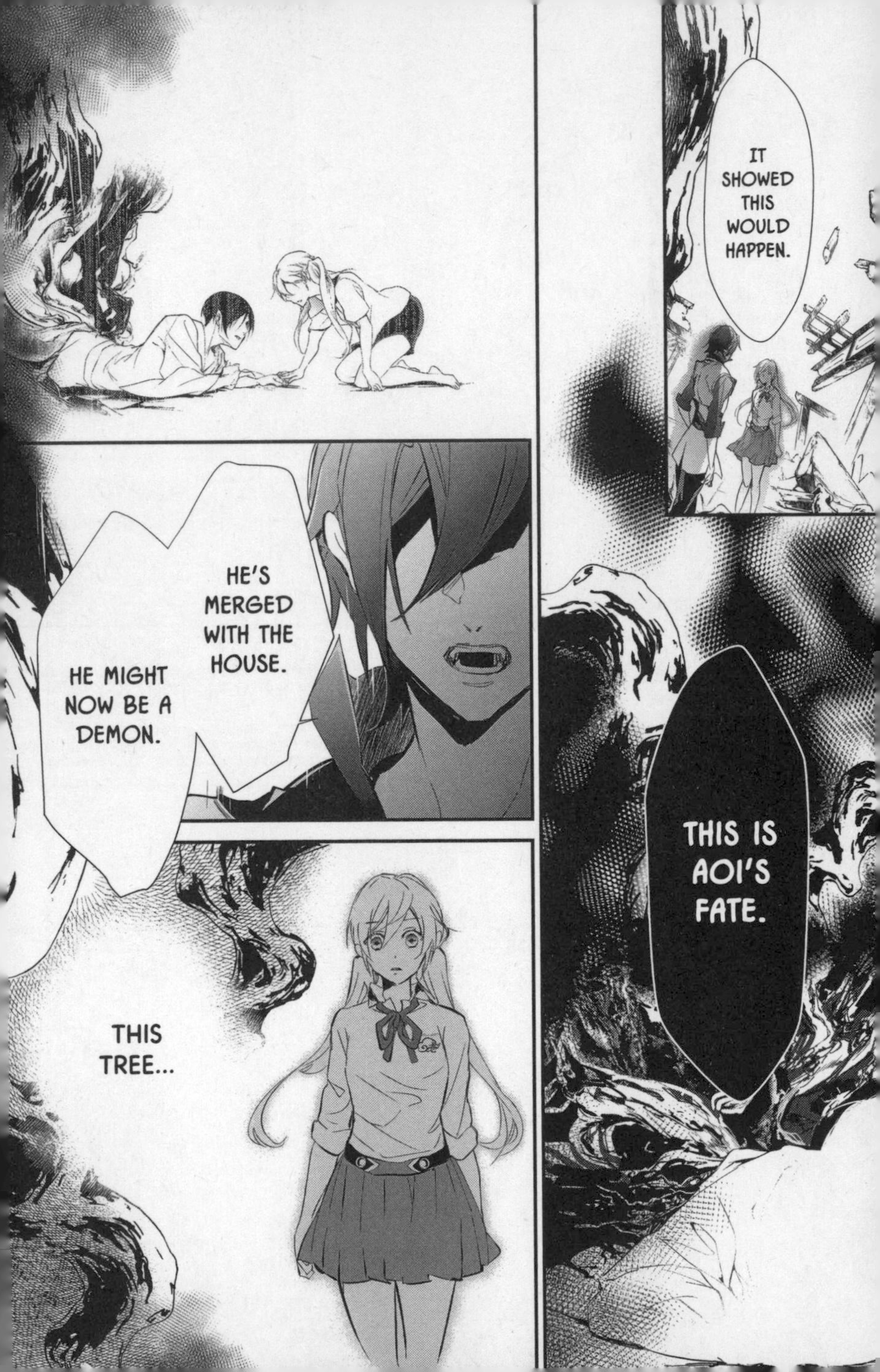
IT SHOWED THIS WOULD HAPPEN.
THIS IS AOI'S FATE.
HE'S MERGED WITH THE HOUSE.
HE MIGHT NOW BE A DEMON.
THIS TREE...

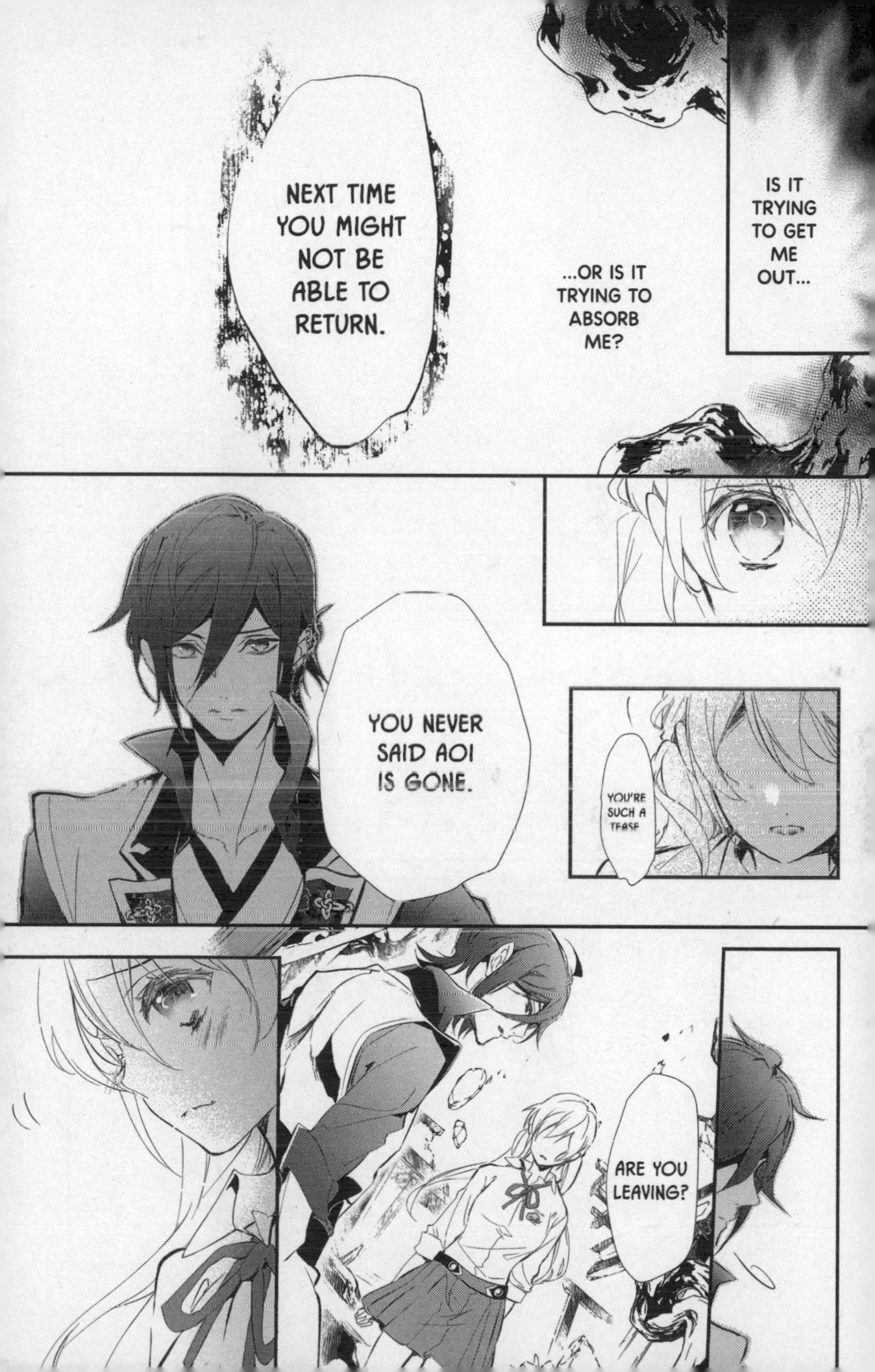
IS IT TRYING TO GET ME OUT...
...OR IS IT TRYING TO ABSORB ME?
NEXT TIME YOU MIGHT NOT BE ABLE TO RETURN.
YOU'RE SUCH A TEASE
YOU NEVER SAID AOI IS GONE.
ARE YOU LEAVING?

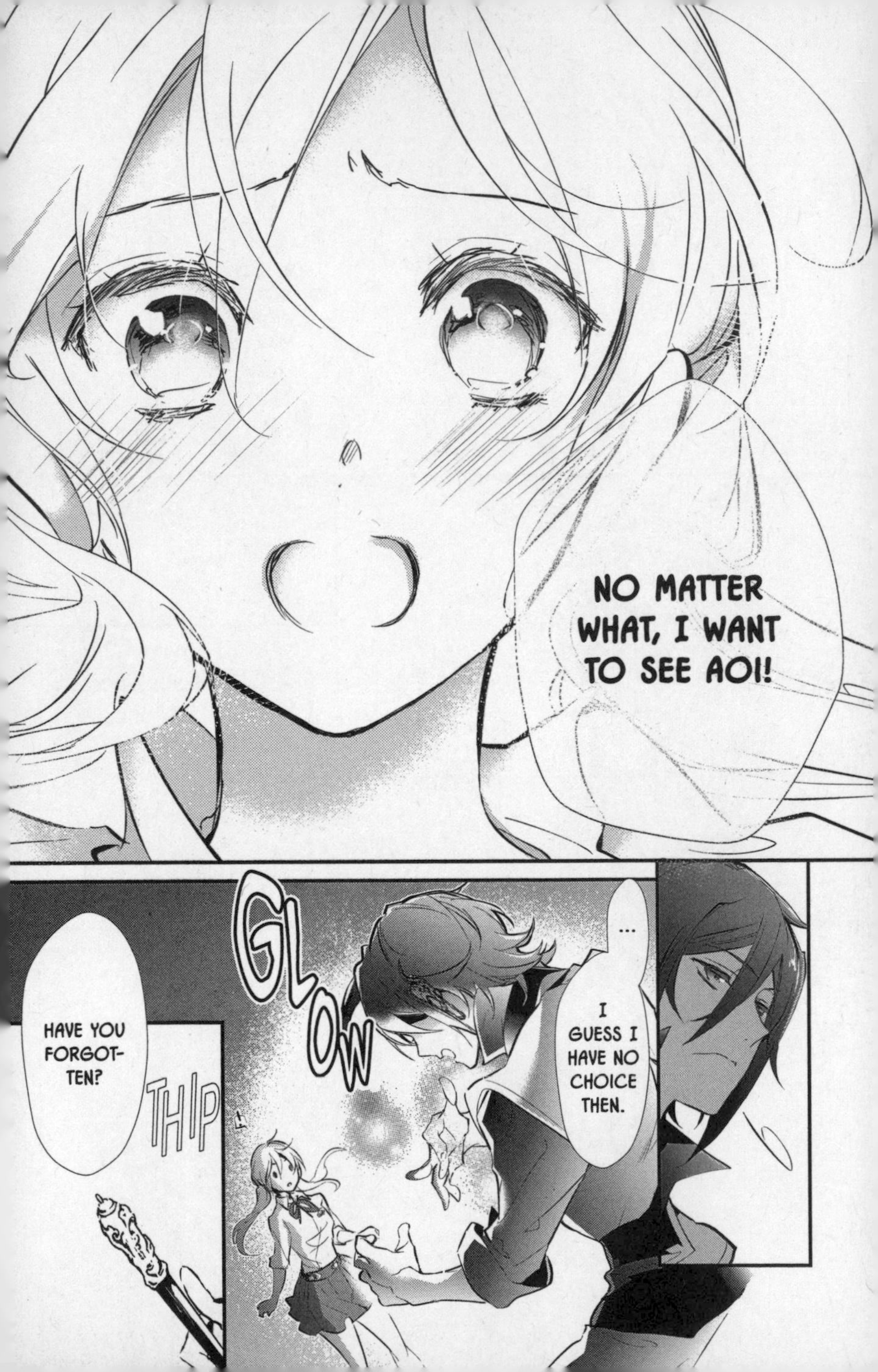
NO MATTER WHAT, I WANT TO SEE AOI!
...
I GUESS I HAVE NO CHOICE THEN.
GLOW
THIP
HAVE YOU FORGOT-TEN?

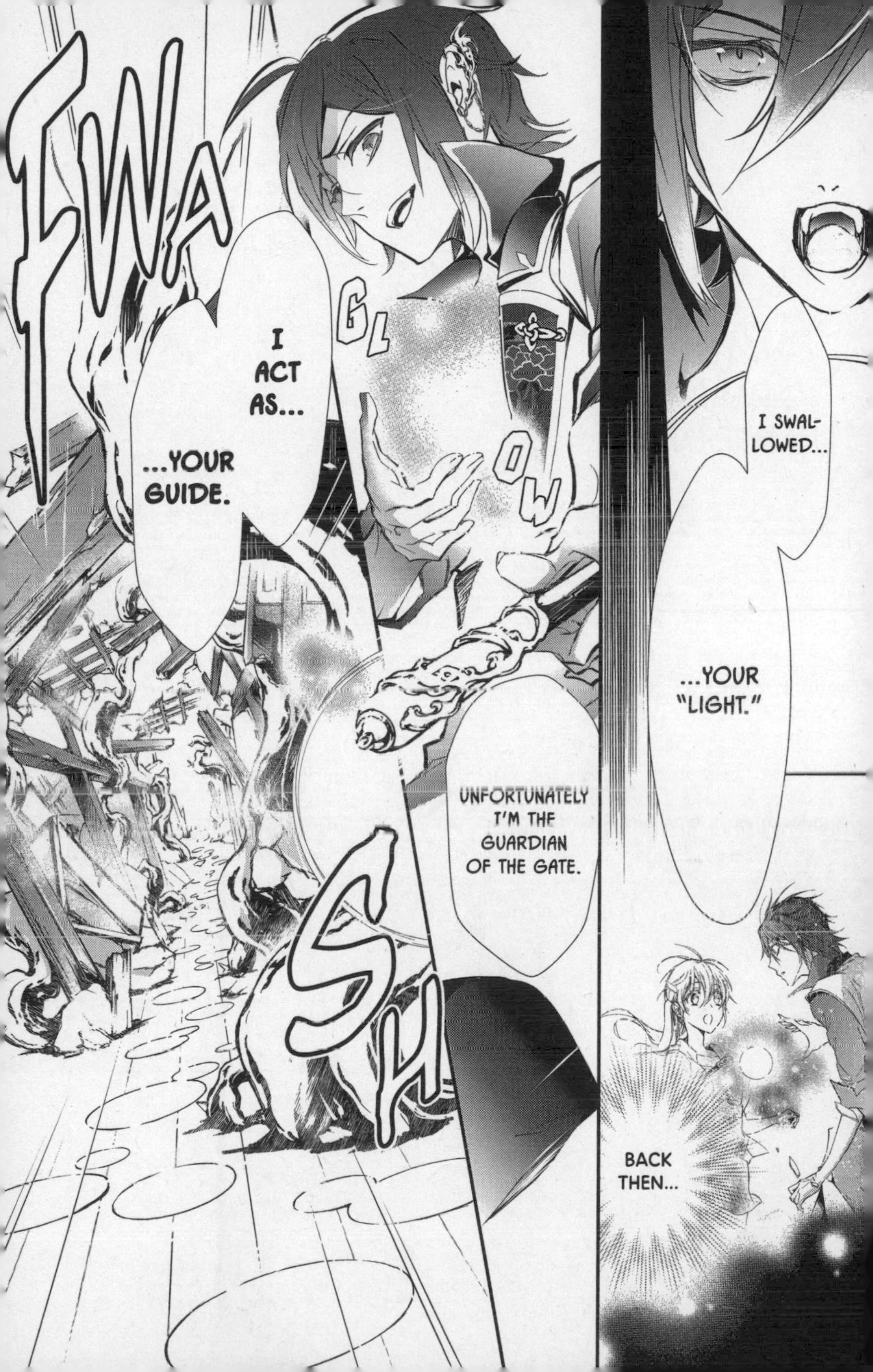
I SWAL-LOWED...
...YOUR "LIGHT."
BACK THEN...
GLOW
FWA
I ACT AS...
...YOUR GUIDE.
UNFORTUNATELY I'M THE GUARDIAN OF THE GATE.
SH

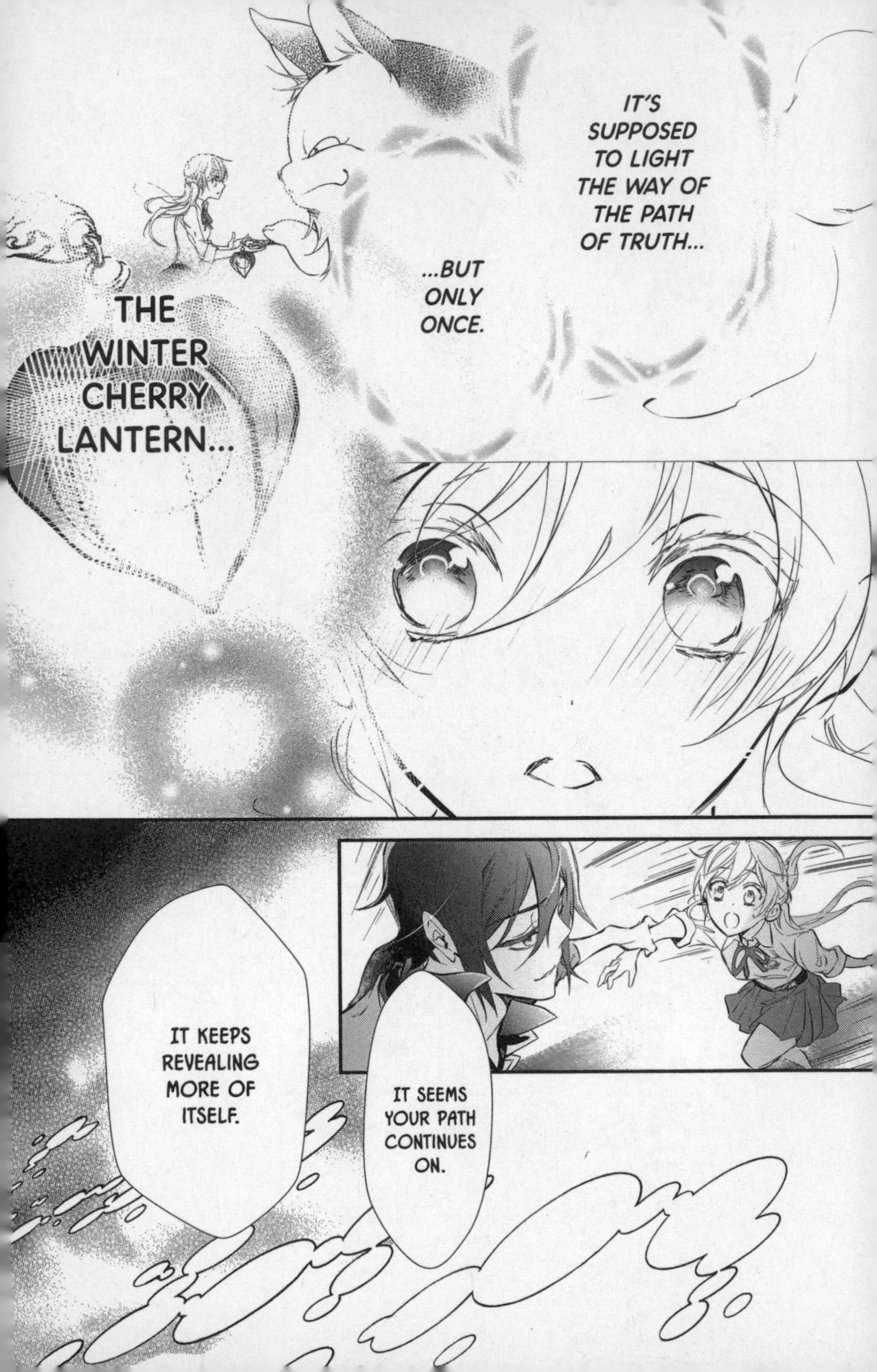
IT'S SUPPOSED TO LIGHT THE WAY OF THE PATH OF TRUTH...
...BUT ONLY ONCE.
THE WINTER CHERRY LANTERN...
IT SEEMS YOUR PATH CONTINUES ON.
IT KEEPS REVEALING MORE OF ITSELF.

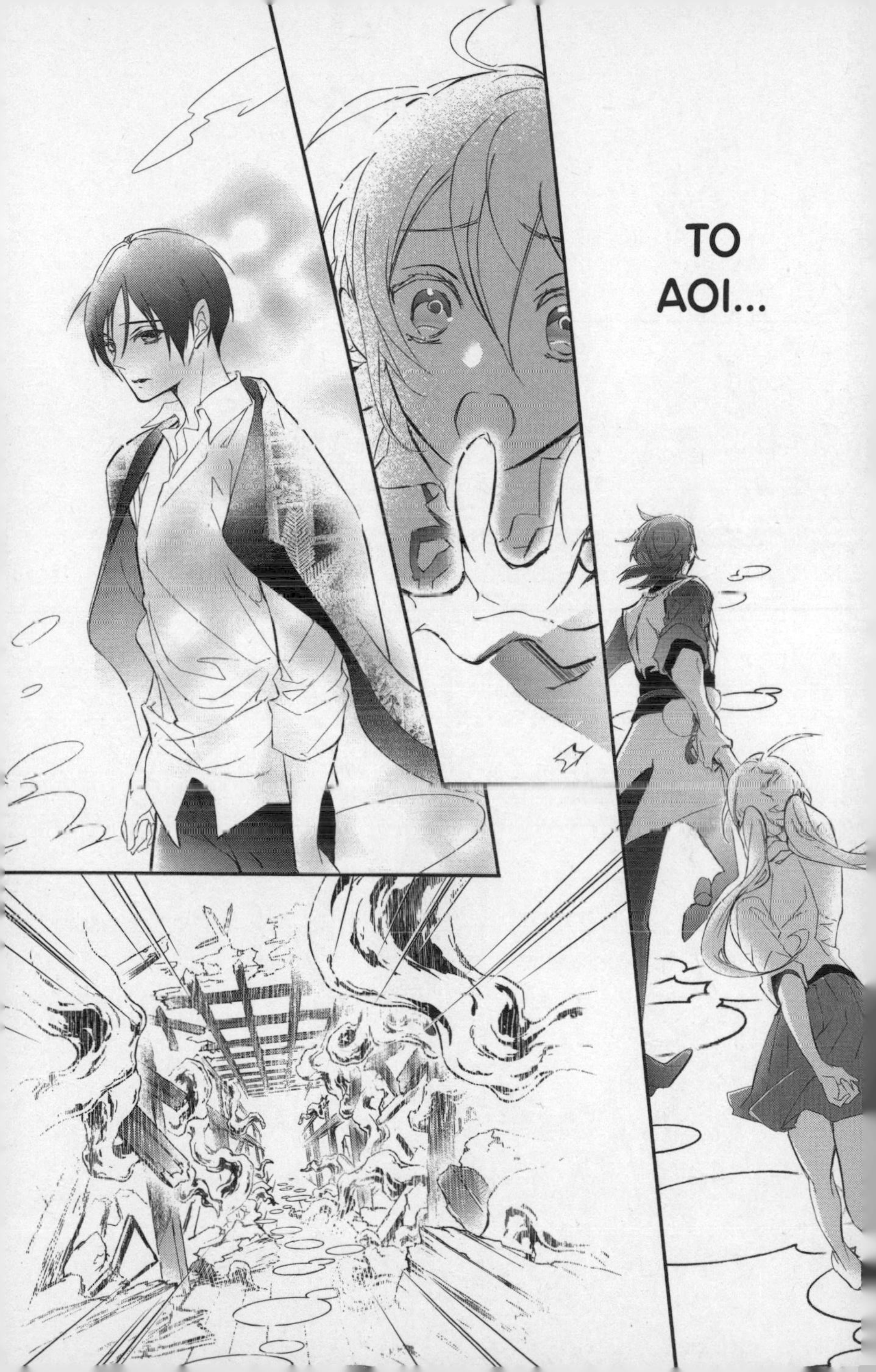
TO
AOI...

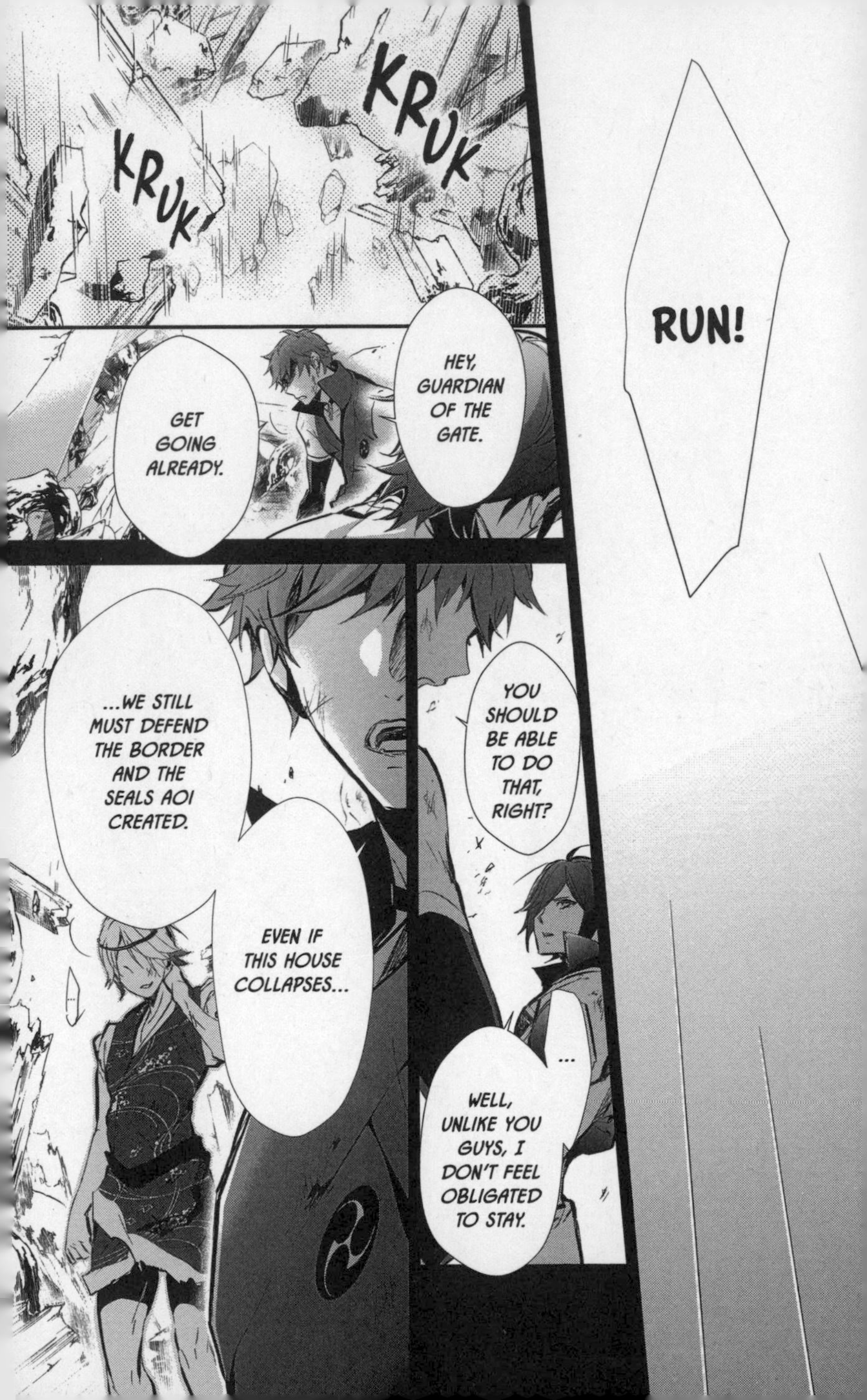
RUN!
KRUK
KRUK
HEY, GUARDIAN OF THE GATE.
GET GOING ALREADY.
YOU SHOULD BE ABLE TO DO THAT, RIGHT?
...
WELL, UNLIKE YOU GUYS, I DON'T FEEL OBLIGATED TO STAY.
EVEN IF THIS HOUSE COLLAPSES...
...WE STILL MUST DEFEND THE BORDER AND THE SEALS AOI CREATED.
...

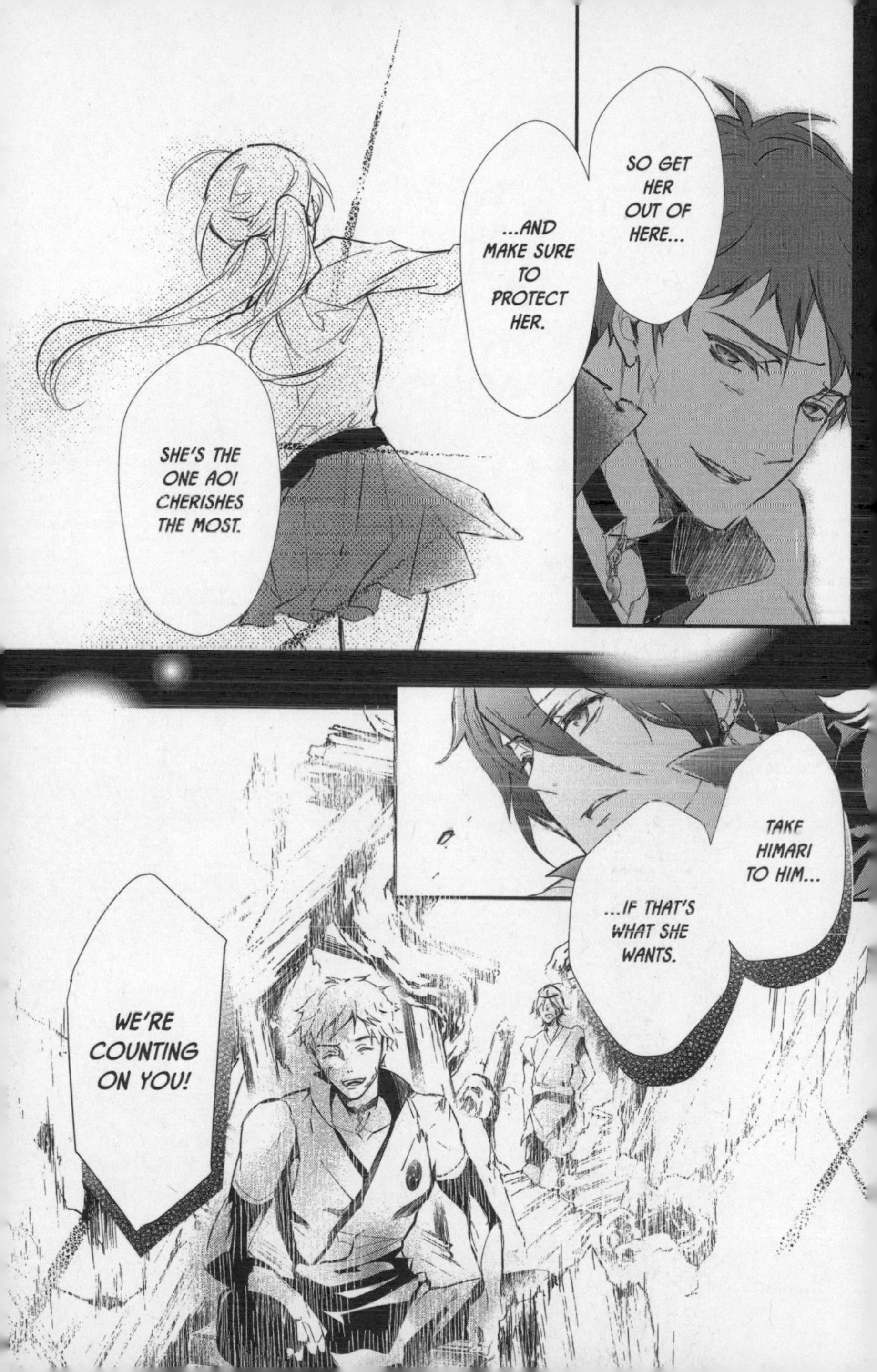
SO GET HER OUT OF HERE...
...AND MAKE SURE TO PROTECT HER.
SHE'S THE ONE AOI CHERISHES THE MOST.
TAKE HIMARI TO HIM...
...IF THAT'S WHAT SHE WANTS.
WE'RE COUNTING ON YOU!

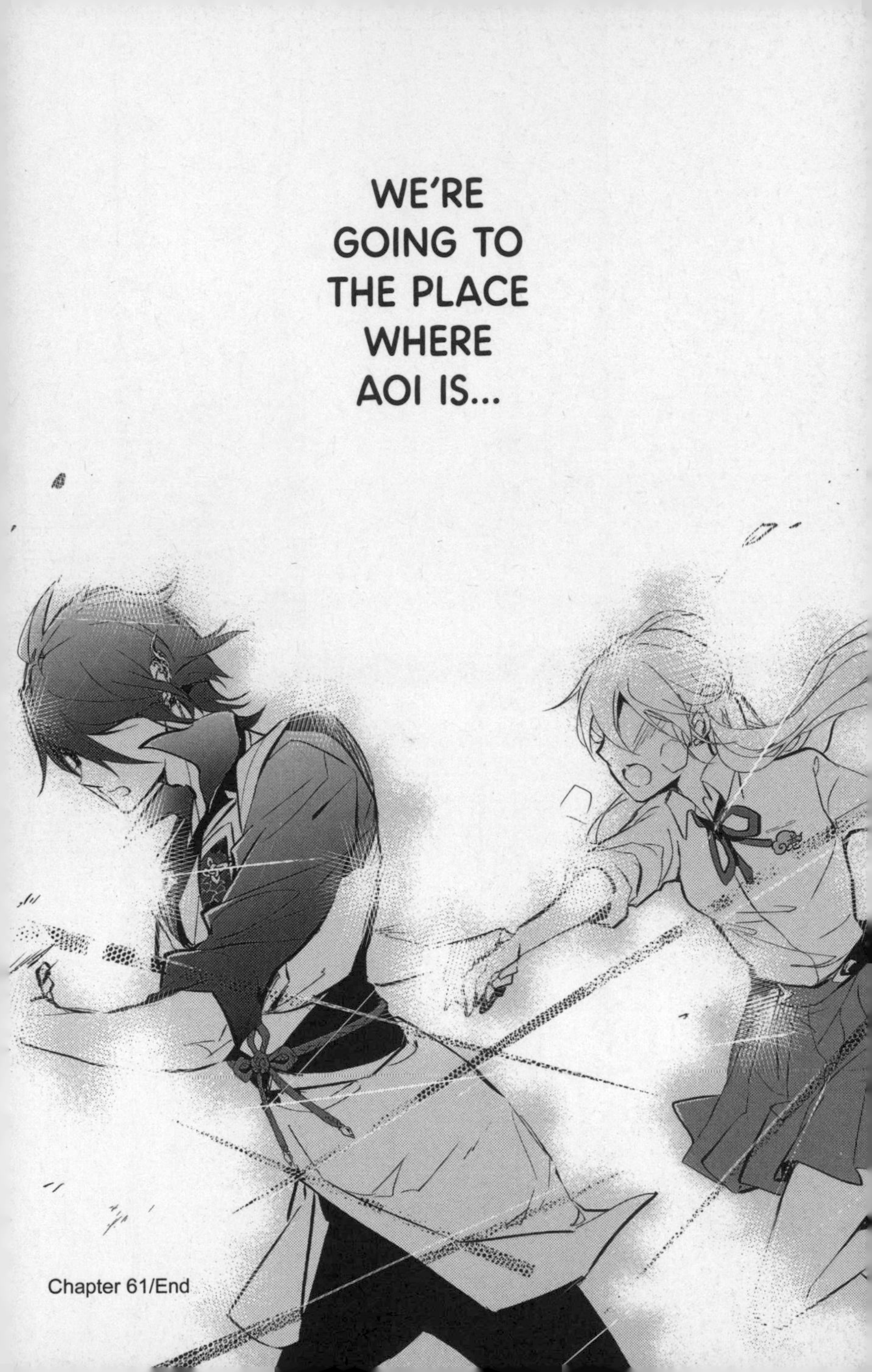
WE'RE GOING TO THE PLACE WHERE AOI IS...
Chapter 61/End

The
DEMON
PRINCE
of MOMOCHI
HOUSE

the
DEMON
PRINCE
of MOMOCHI
HOUSE

CHAPTER 62

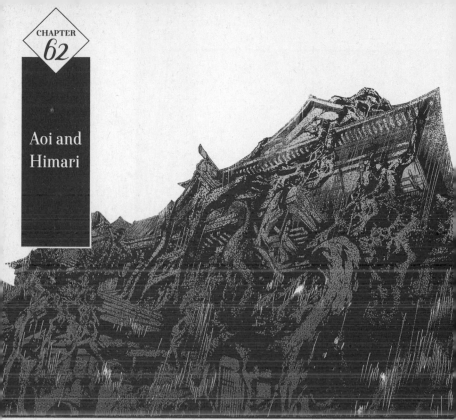

Aoi and Himari

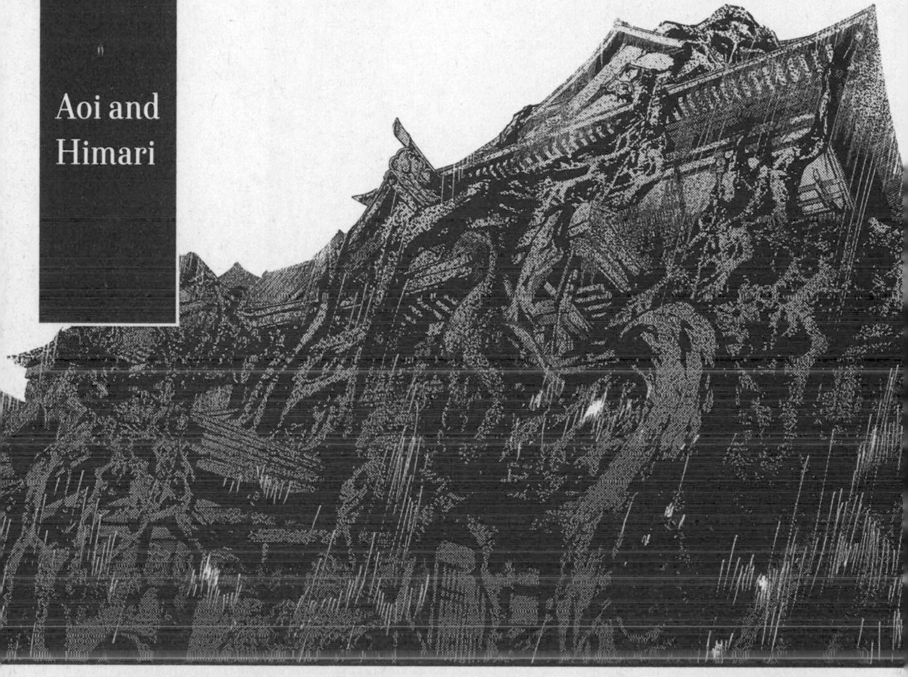

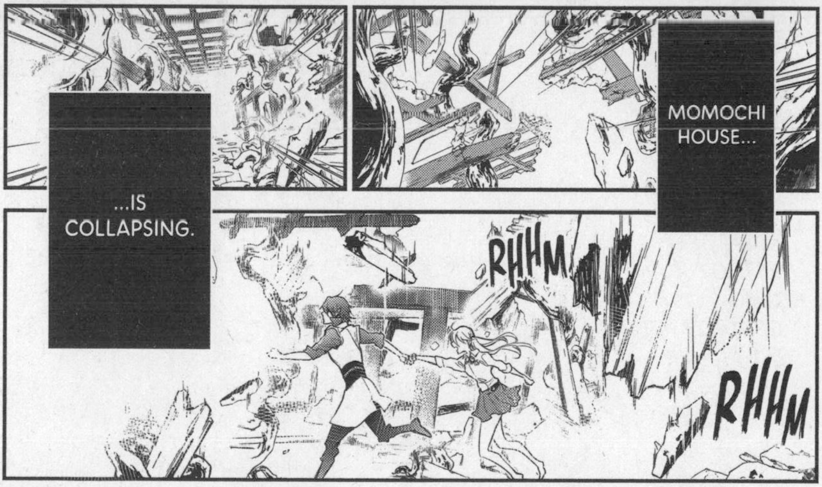
MOMOCHI HOUSE...
...IS COLLAPSING.
RHHM
RHHM

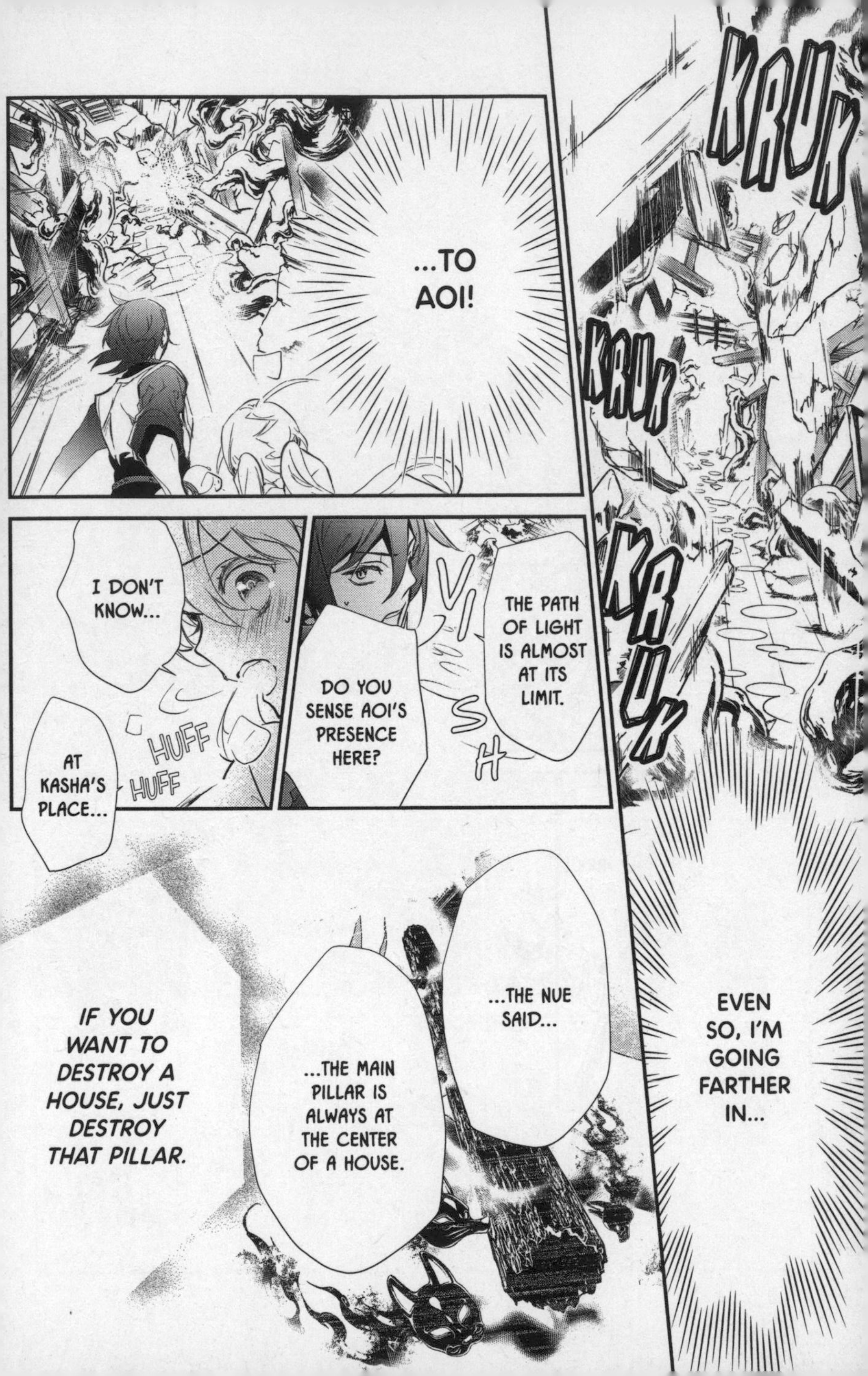
KRUK
KRUK
KRUK
EVEN SO, I'M GOING FARTHER IN...
...TO AOI!
THE PATH OF LIGHT IS ALMOST AT ITS LIMIT.
VISH
DO YOU SENSE AOI'S PRESENCE HERE?
I DON'T KNOW...
HUFF HUFF
AT KASHA'S PLACE...
...THE NUE SAID...
...THE MAIN PILLAR IS ALWAYS AT THE CENTER OF A HOUSE.
IF YOU WANT TO DESTROY A HOUSE, JUST DESTROY THAT PILLAR.

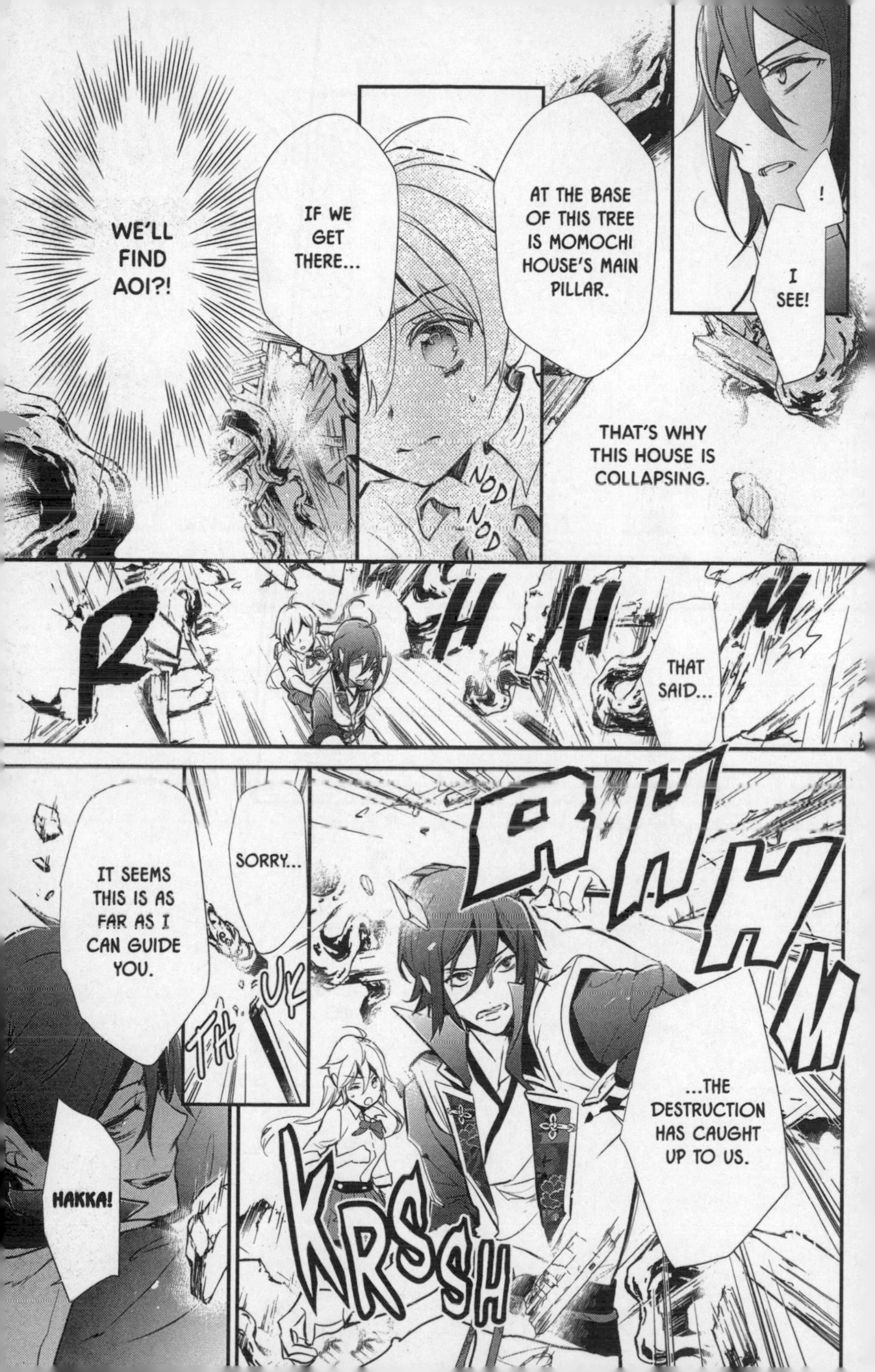
!
I SEE!
AT THE BASE OF THIS TREE IS MOMOCHI HOUSE'S MAIN PILLAR.
THAT'S WHY THIS HOUSE IS COLLAPSING.
IF WE GET THERE...
NOD NOD
WE'LL FIND AOI?!
RHHM
THAT SAID...
AHHM
...THE DESTRUCTION HAS CAUGHT UP TO US.
SORRY...
IT SEEMS THIS IS AS FAR AS I CAN GUIDE YOU.
THUK
KRSSH
HAKKA!

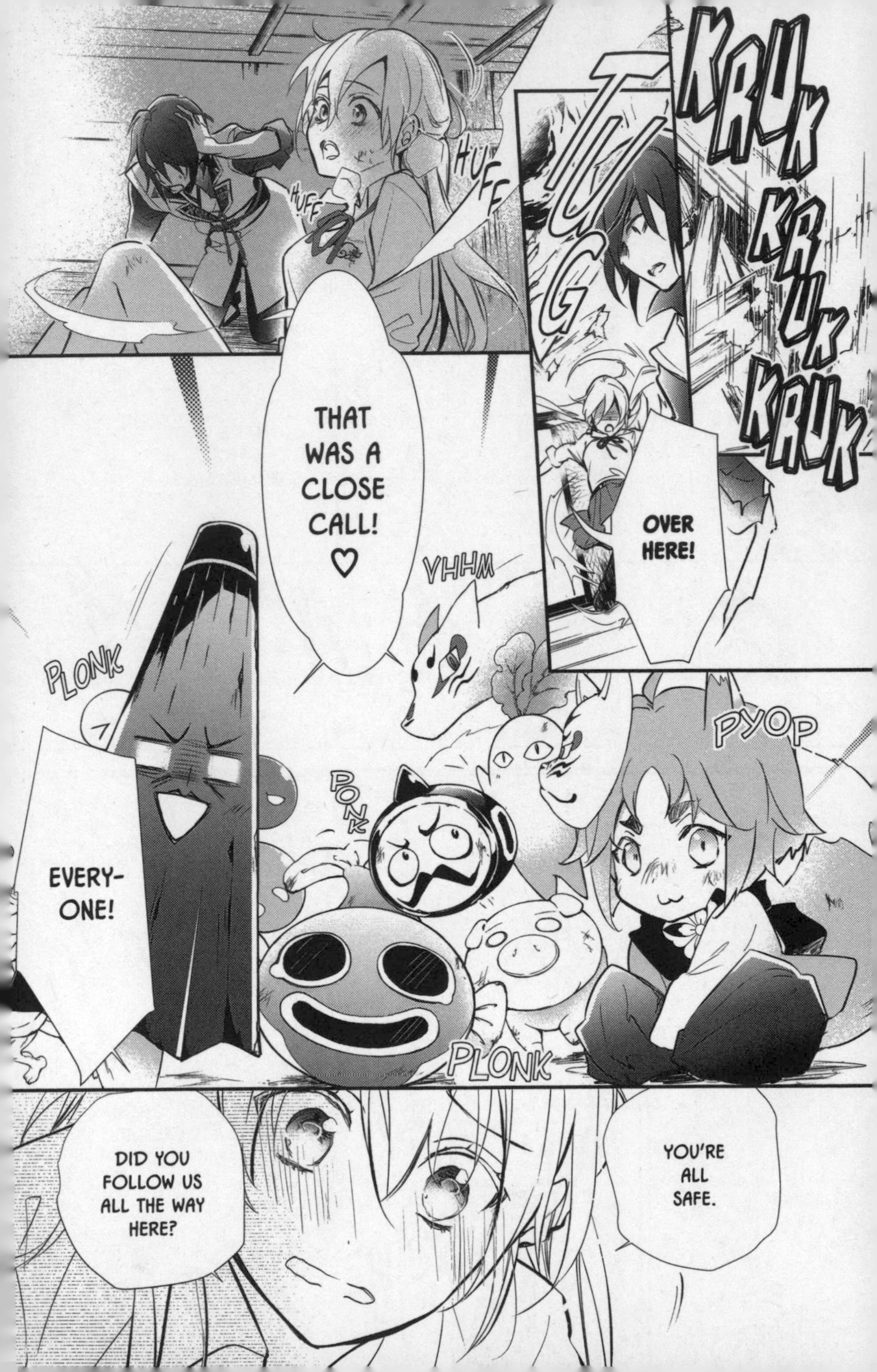
KRUK KRUK KRUK KRUK
TUG
OVER HERE!
HUFF
HUFF
THAT WAS A CLOSE CALL! ♡
VHHM
PYOP
PONK
PLONK
EVERY-ONE!
PLONK
YOU'RE ALL SAFE.
DID YOU FOLLOW US ALL THE WAY HERE?

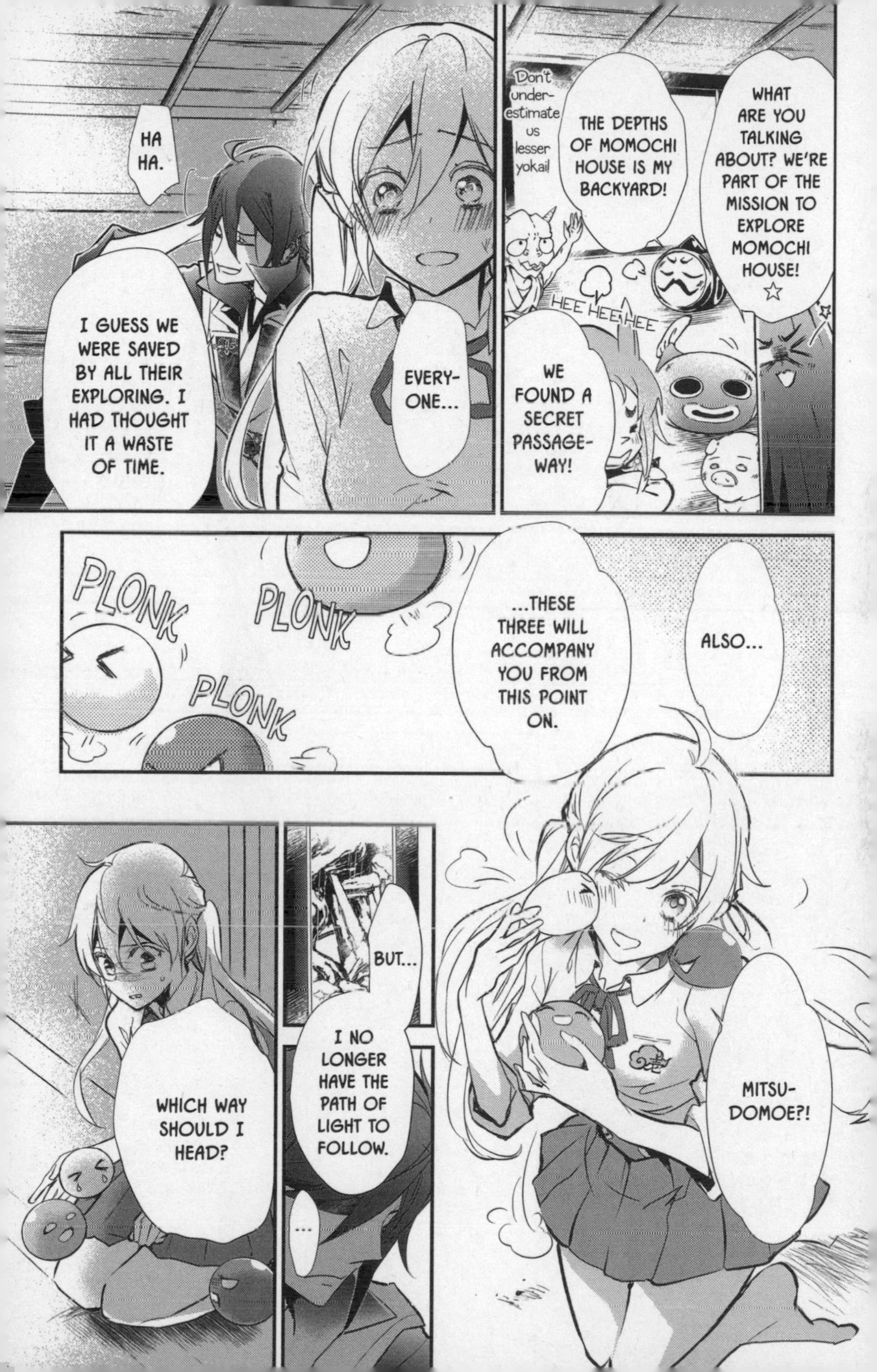

WHAT ARE YOU TALKING ABOUT? WE'RE PART OF THE MISSION TO EXPLORE MOMOCHI HOUSE! ☆
THE DEPTHS OF MOMOCHI HOUSE IS MY BACKYARD!
Don't under-estimate us lesser yokai!
HEE HEE HEE
WE FOUND A SECRET PASSAGE-WAY!
EVERY-ONE...
HA HA.
I GUESS WE WERE SAVED BY ALL THEIR EXPLORING. I HAD THOUGHT IT A WASTE OF TIME.
ALSO...
...THESE THREE WILL ACCOMPANY YOU FROM THIS POINT ON.
PLONK
PLONK
PLONK
MITSU-DOMOE?!
BUT...
I NO LONGER HAVE THE PATH OF LIGHT TO FOLLOW.
...
WHICH WAY SHOULD I HEAD?

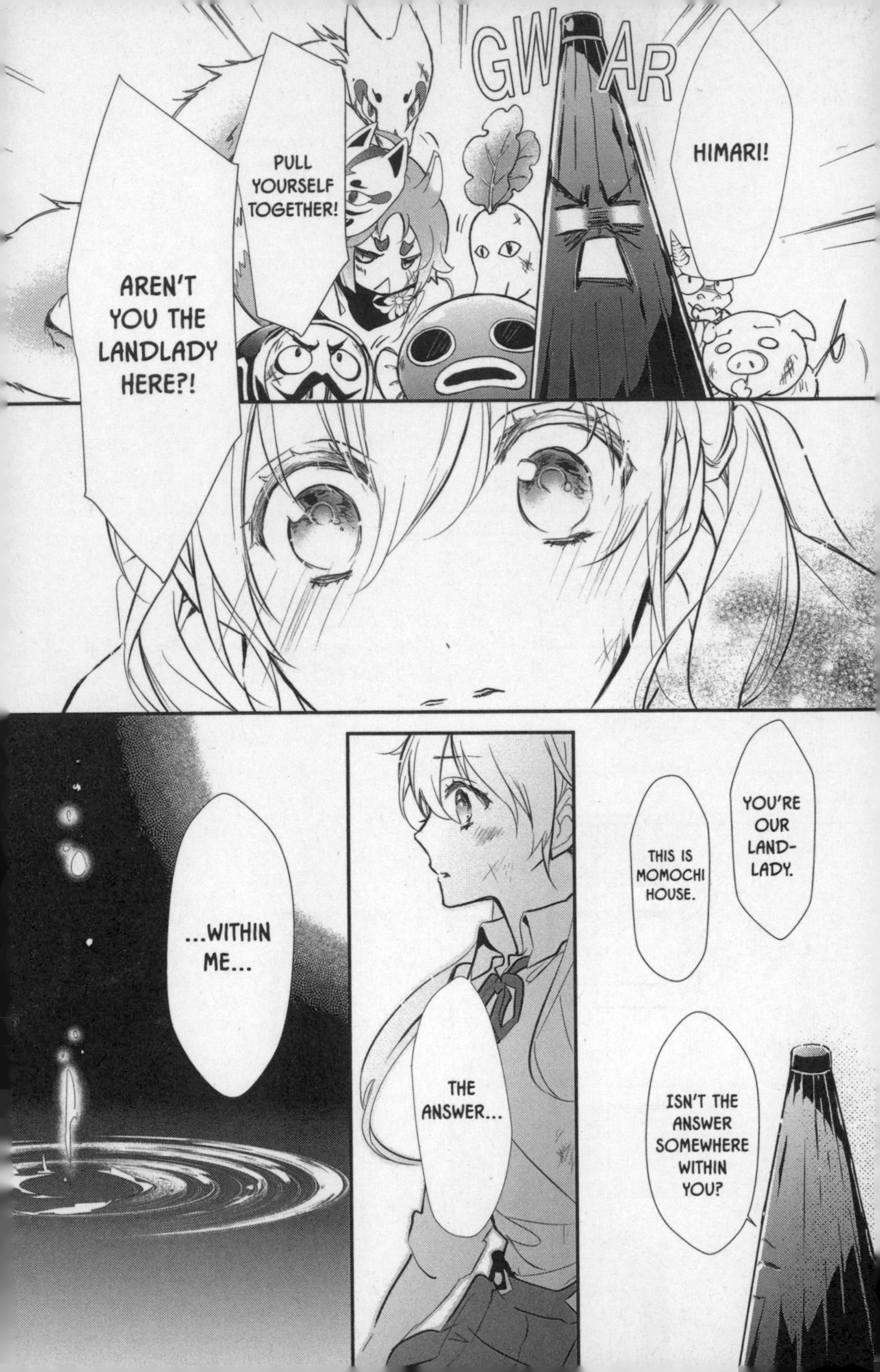
HIMARI!
GWAR
PULL YOURSELF TOGETHER!
AREN'T YOU THE LANDLADY HERE?!
YOU'RE OUR LANDLADY.
THIS IS MOMOCHI HOUSE.
ISN'T THE ANSWER SOMEWHERE WITHIN YOU?
THE ANSWER...
...WITHIN ME...

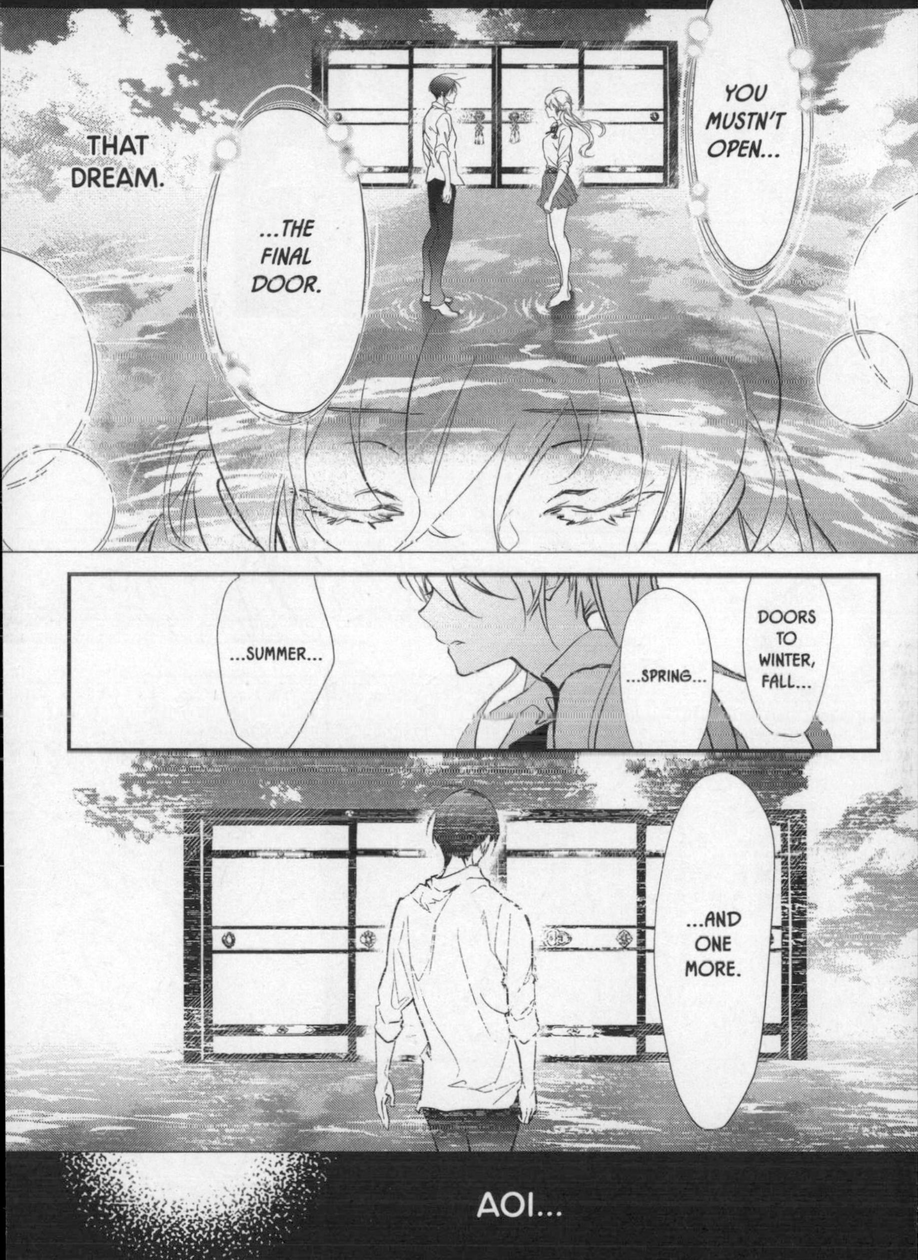
YOU MUSTN'T OPEN...
...THE FINAL DOOR.
THAT DREAM.
DOORS TO WINTER, FALL...
...SPRING...
...SUMMER...
...AND ONE MORE.
AOI...

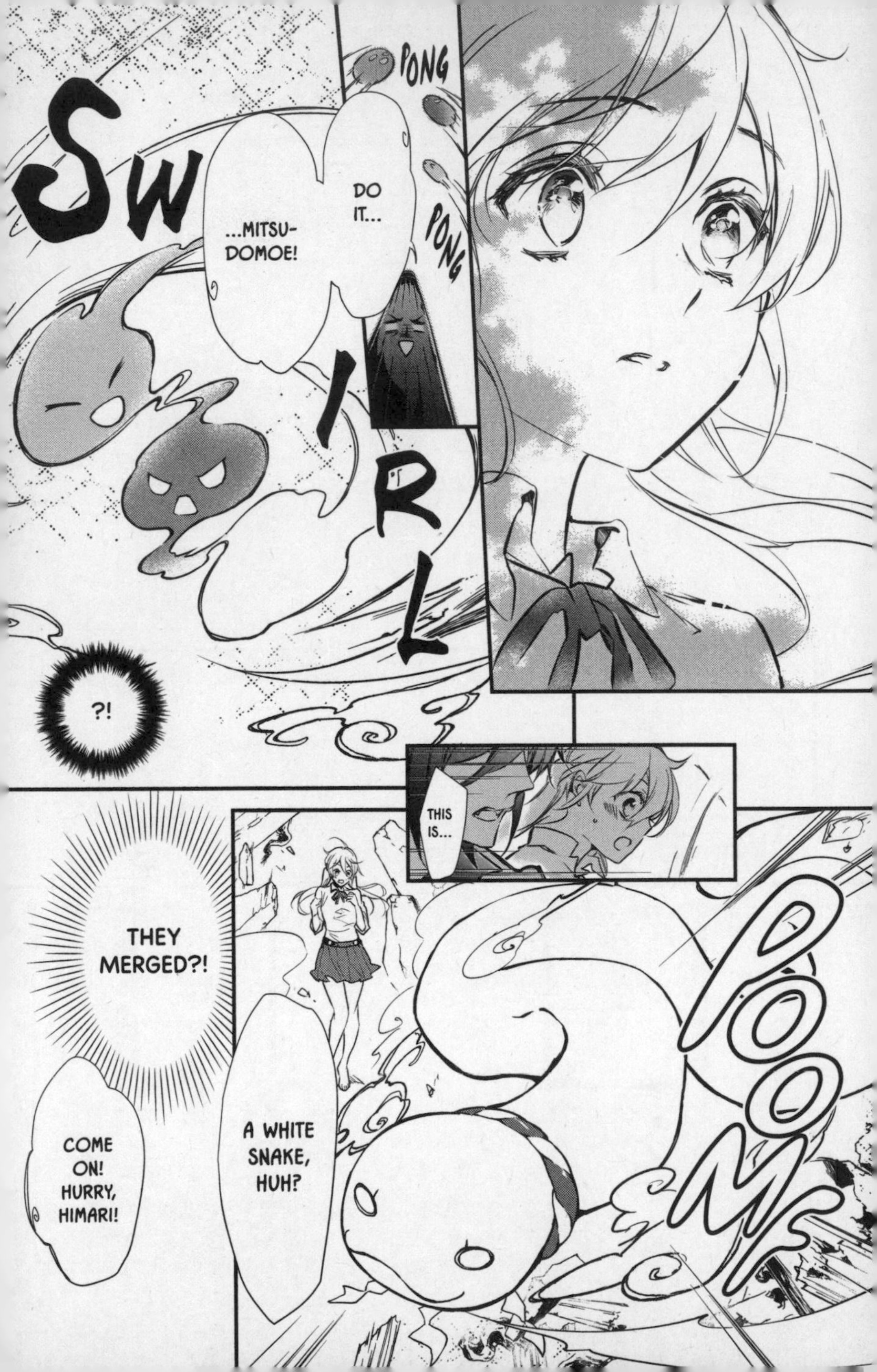
PONG
PONG
DO IT...
...MITSU-DOMOE!
SWIRL
?!
THIS IS...
POOM!
A WHITE SNAKE, HUH?
THEY MERGED?!
COME ON! HURRY, HIMARI!

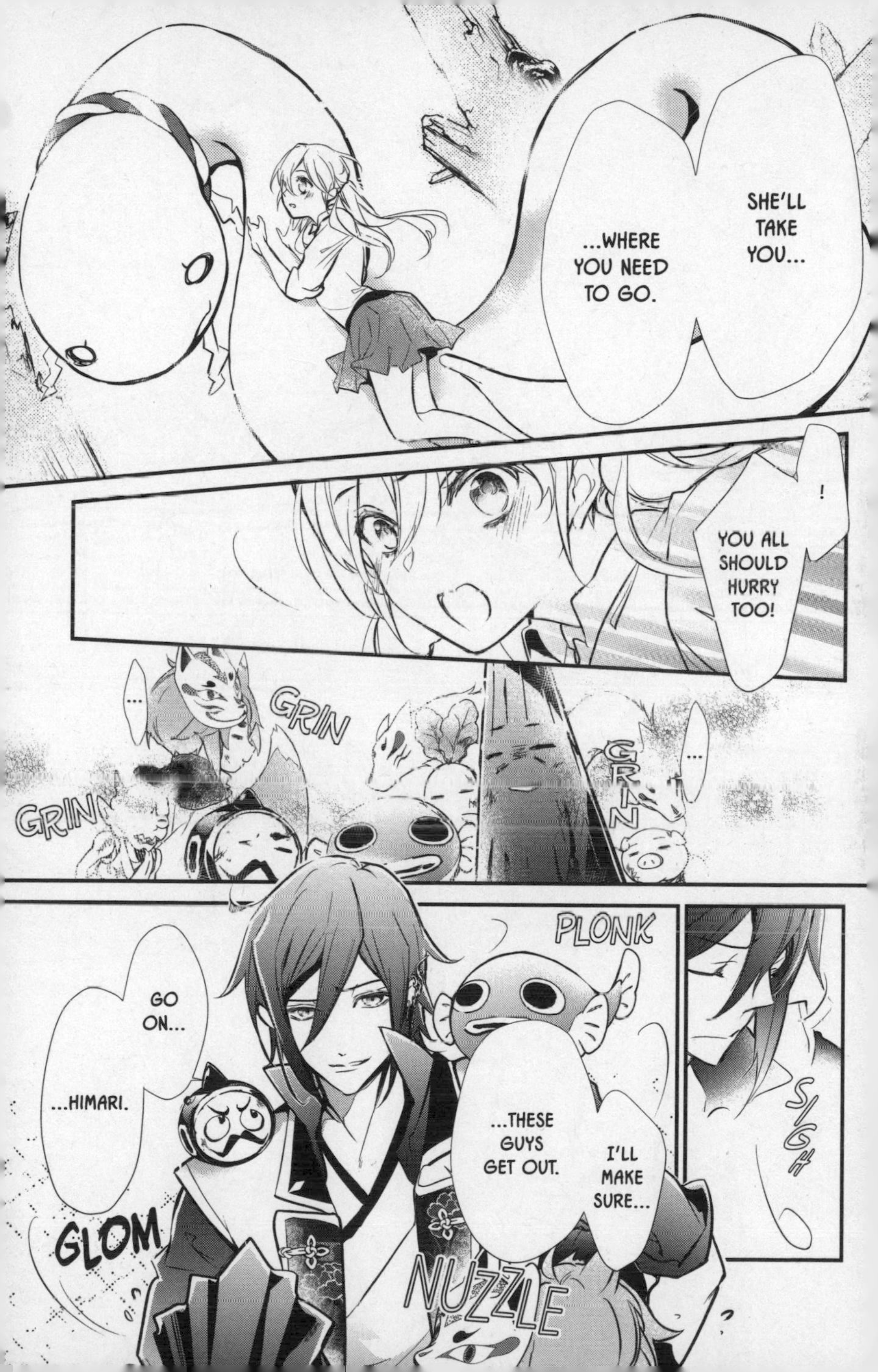
SHE'LL TAKE YOU...
...WHERE YOU NEED TO GO.
!
YOU ALL SHOULD HURRY TOO!
...
GRIN
GRIN
...
GRIN
SIGH
PLONK
I'LL MAKE SURE...
...THESE GUYS GET OUT.
GO ON...
...HIMARI.
NUZZLE
GLOM

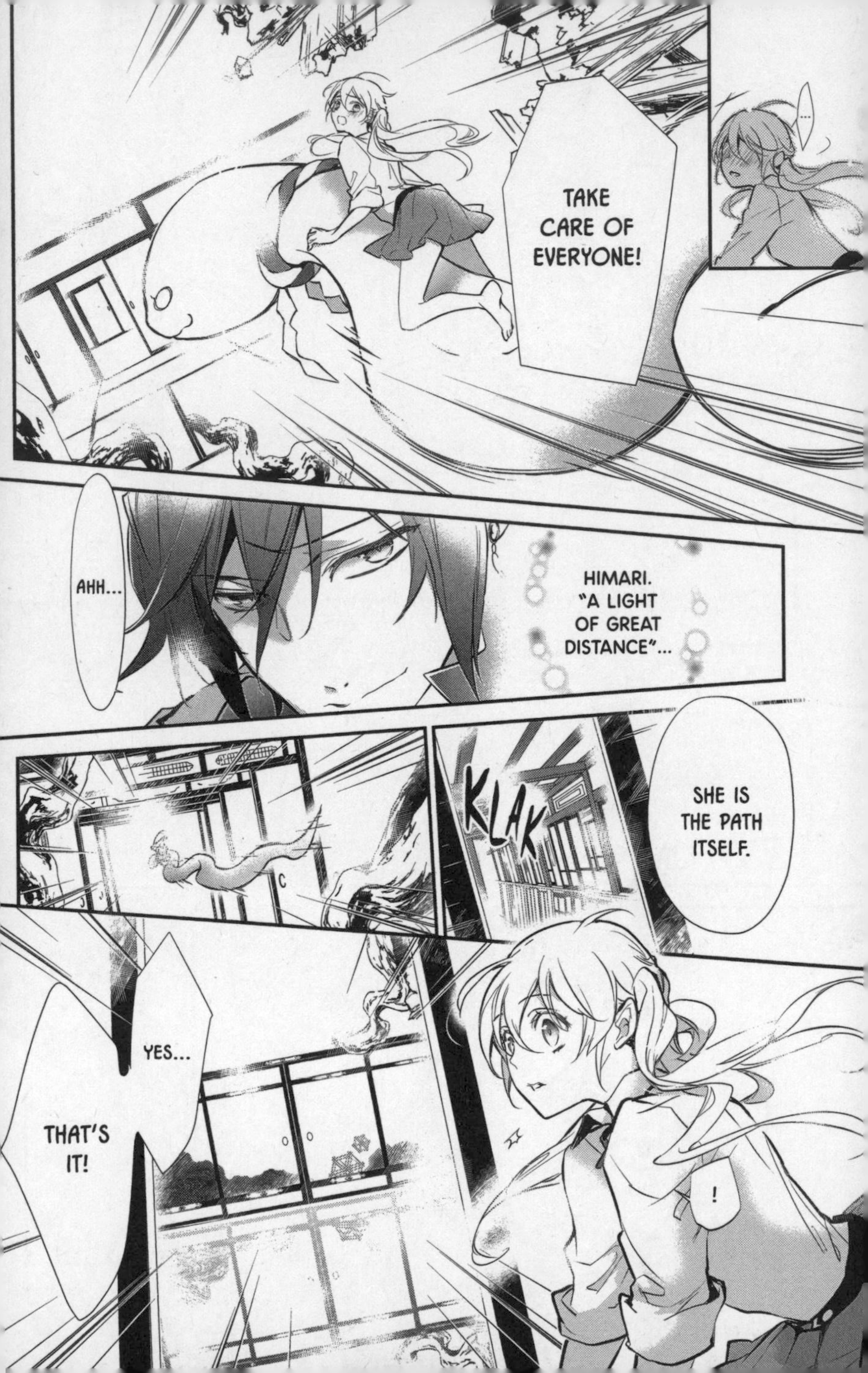
...
TAKE CARE OF EVERYONE!
HIMARI. "A LIGHT OF GREAT DISTANCE"...
AHH...
SHE IS THE PATH ITSELF.
KLAK
!
YES...
THAT'S IT!

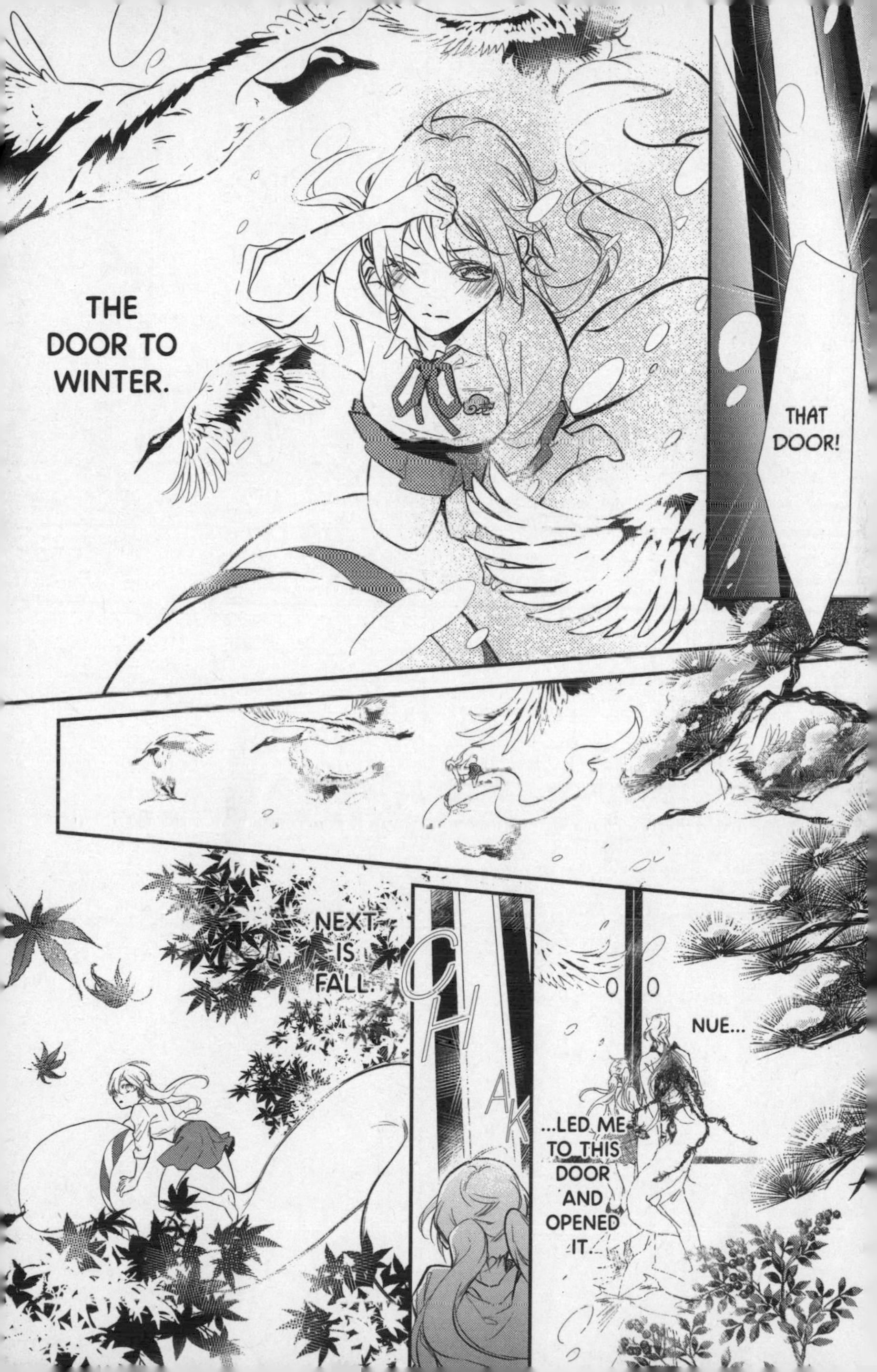
THAT DOOR!
THE DOOR TO WINTER.
NUE...
...LED ME TO THIS DOOR AND OPENED IT.
CHAK
NEXT IS FALL.

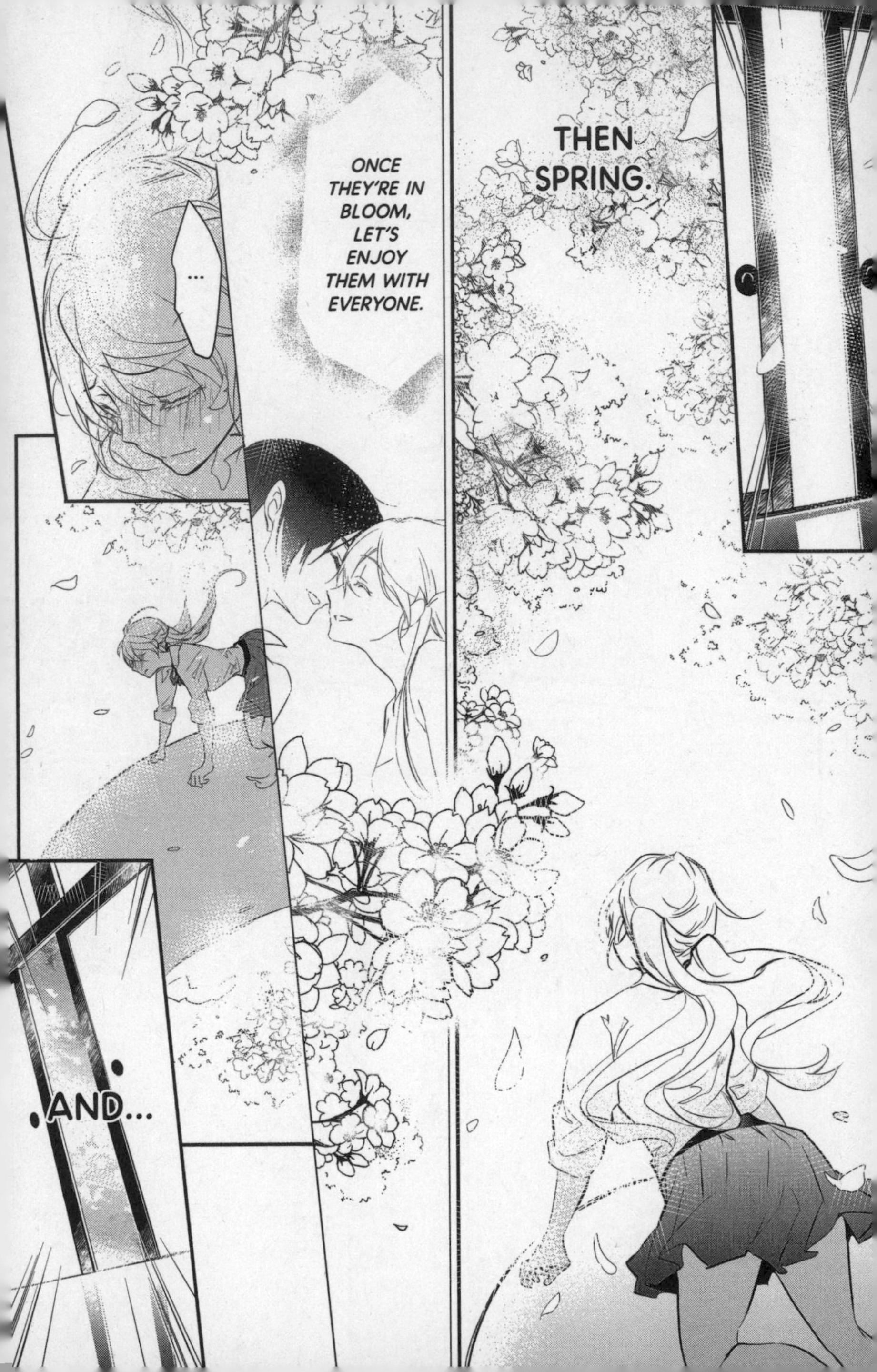
THEN SPRING.
ONCE THEY'RE IN BLOOM, LET'S ENJOY THEM WITH EVERYONE.
...
AND...

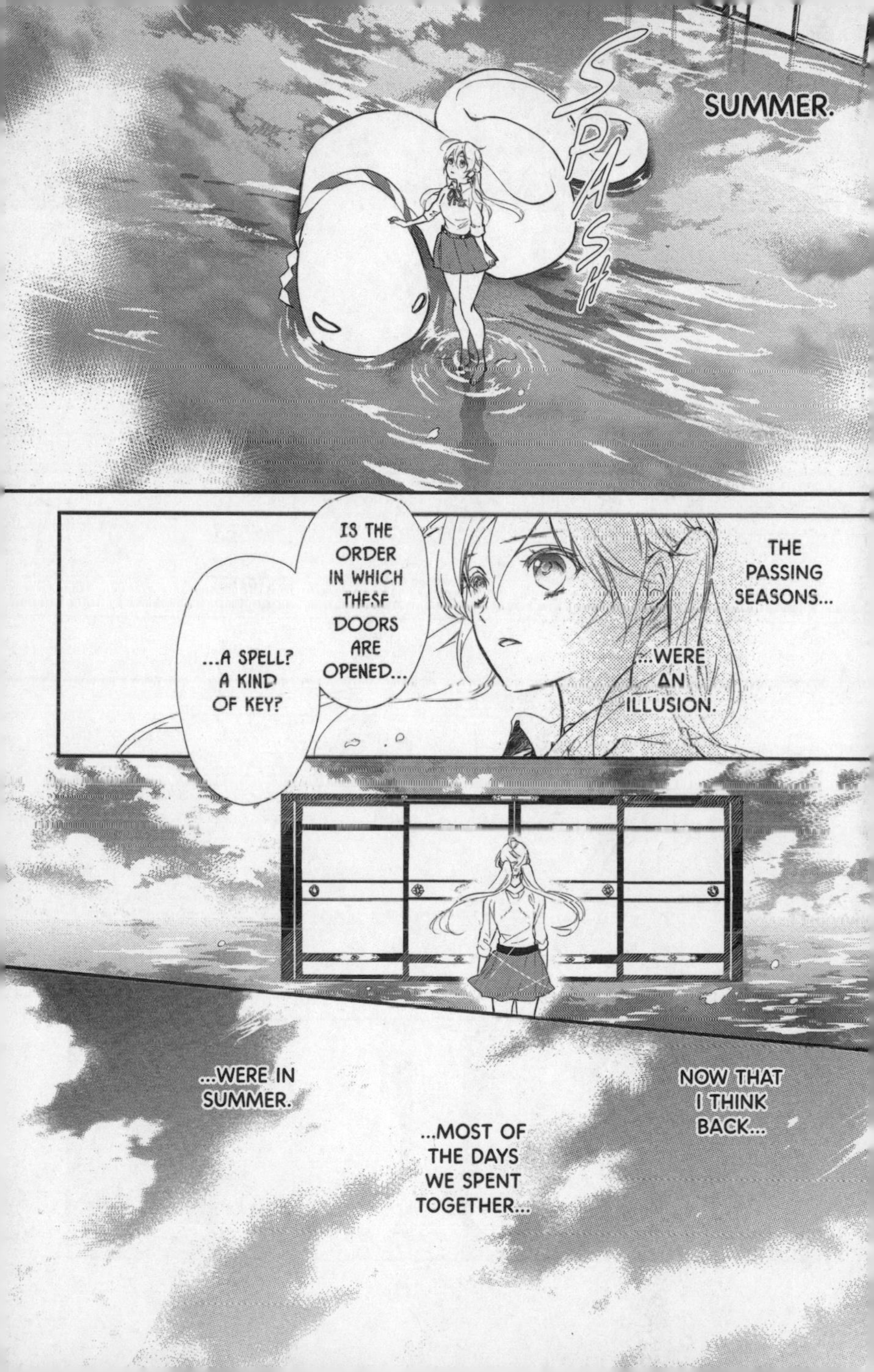
SUMMER.
SPASH
THE PASSING SEASONS...
...WERE AN ILLUSION.
IS THE ORDER IN WHICH THESE DOORS ARE OPENED...
...A SPELL? A KIND OF KEY?
NOW THAT I THINK BACK...
...MOST OF THE DAYS WE SPENT TOGETHER...
...WERE IN SUMMER.

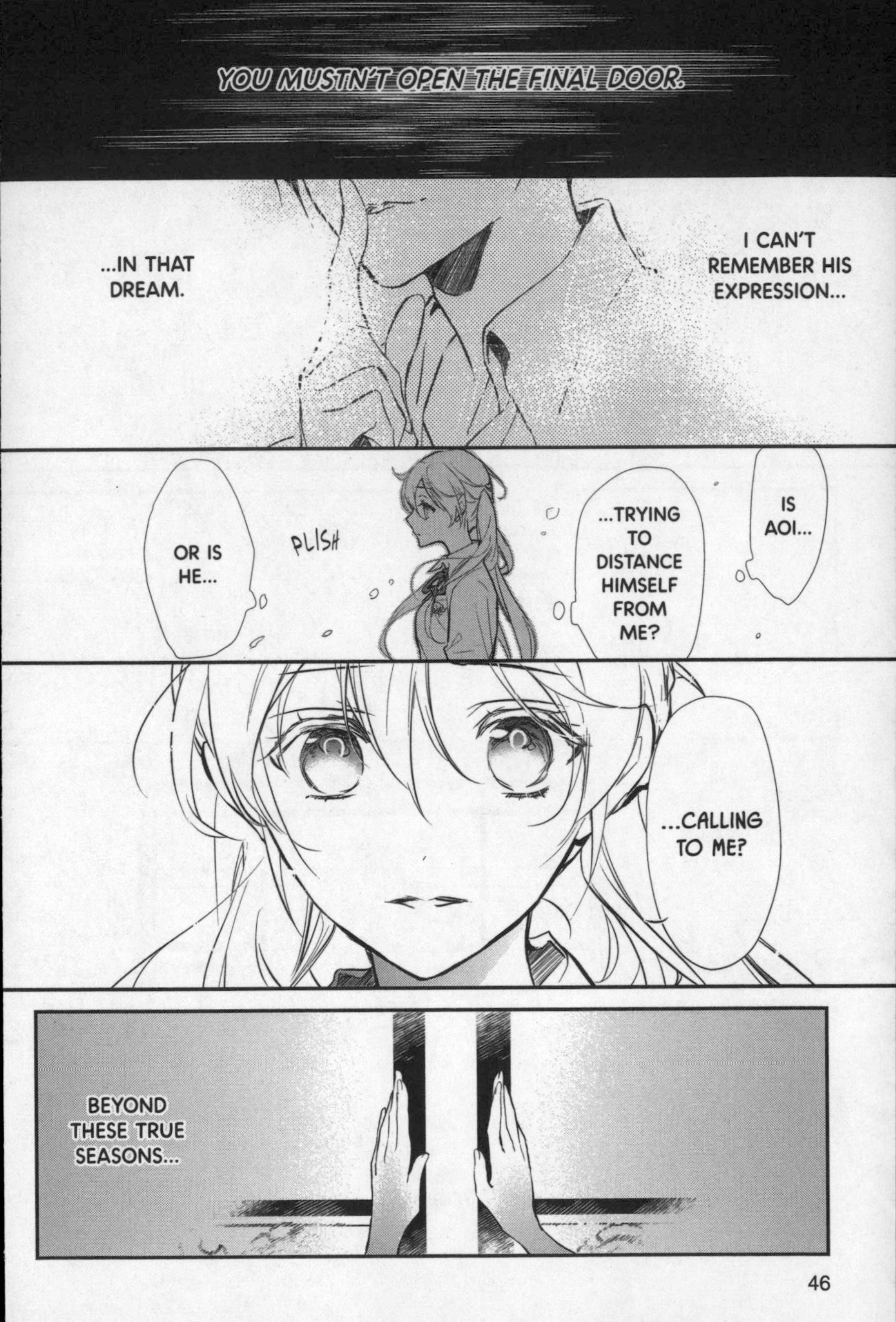
YOU MUSTN'T OPEN THE FINAL DOOR.
I CAN'T REMEMBER HIS EXPRESSION...
...IN THAT DREAM.
IS AOI...
...TRYING TO DISTANCE HIMSELF FROM ME?
PLISH
OR IS HE...
...CALLING TO ME?
BEYOND THESE TRUE SEASONS...

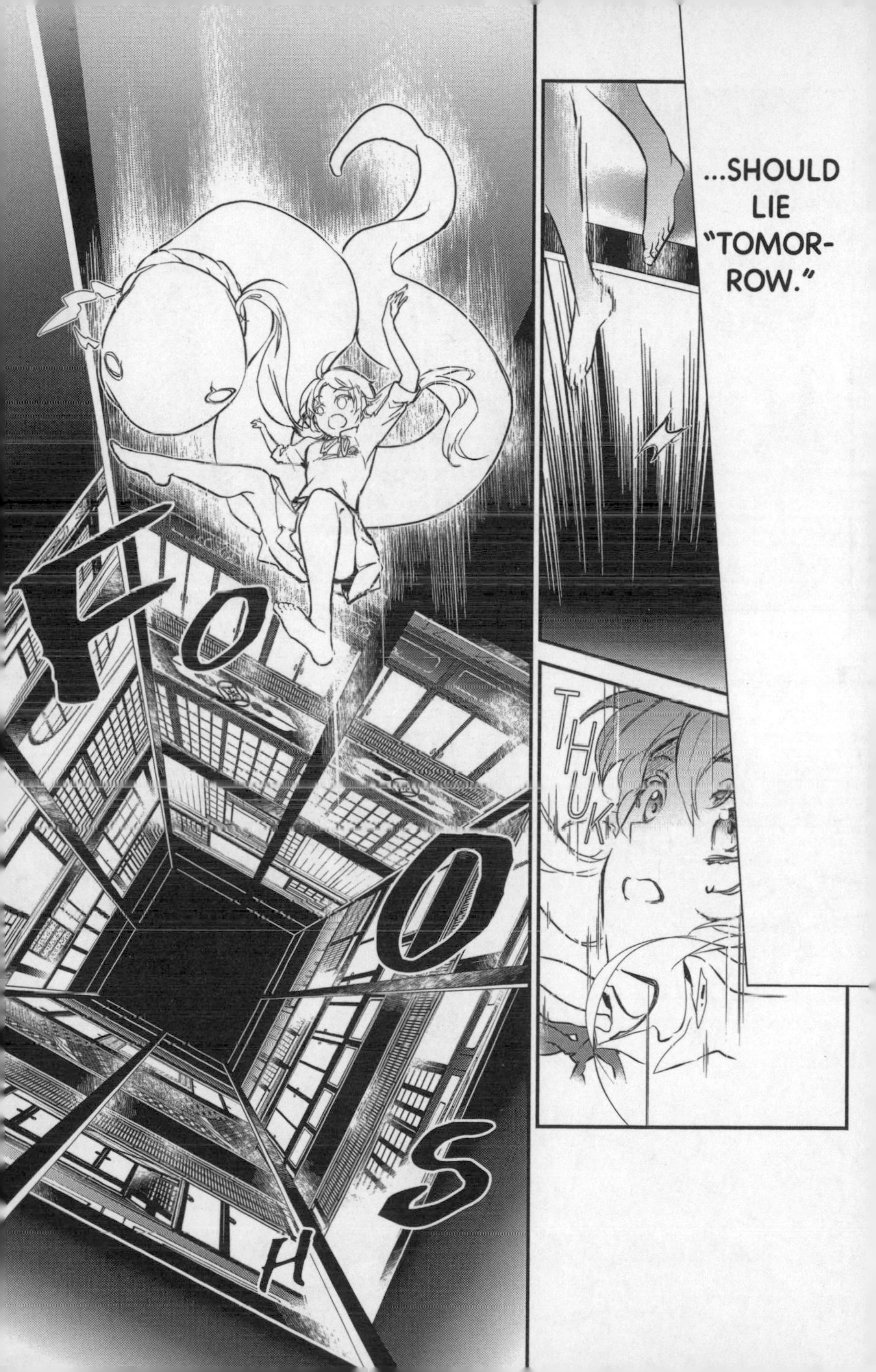
...SHOULD LIE "TOMOR-ROW."
THUK

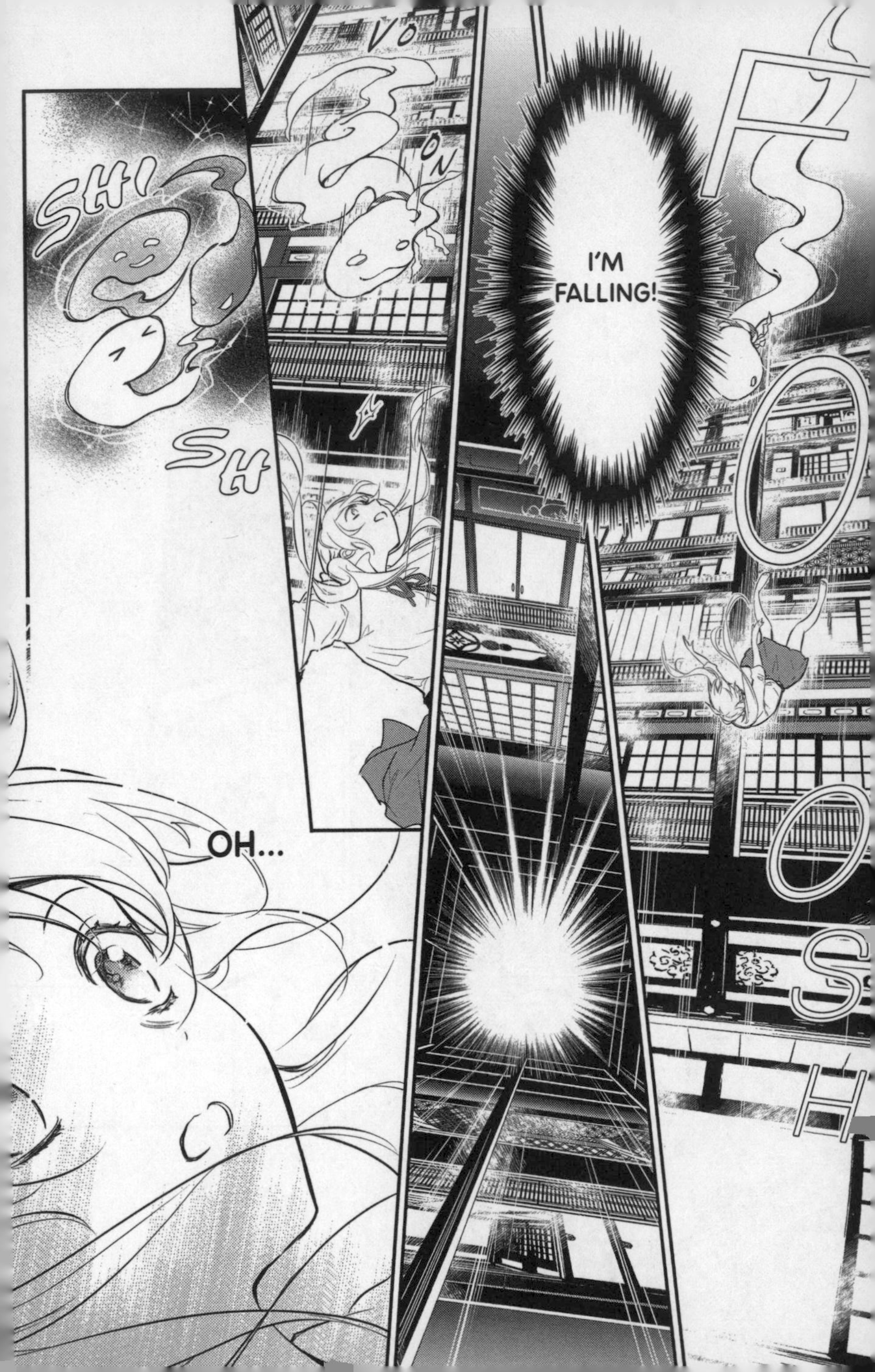
FWOOSH
I'M FALLING!
VOON
SHI
SH
OH...

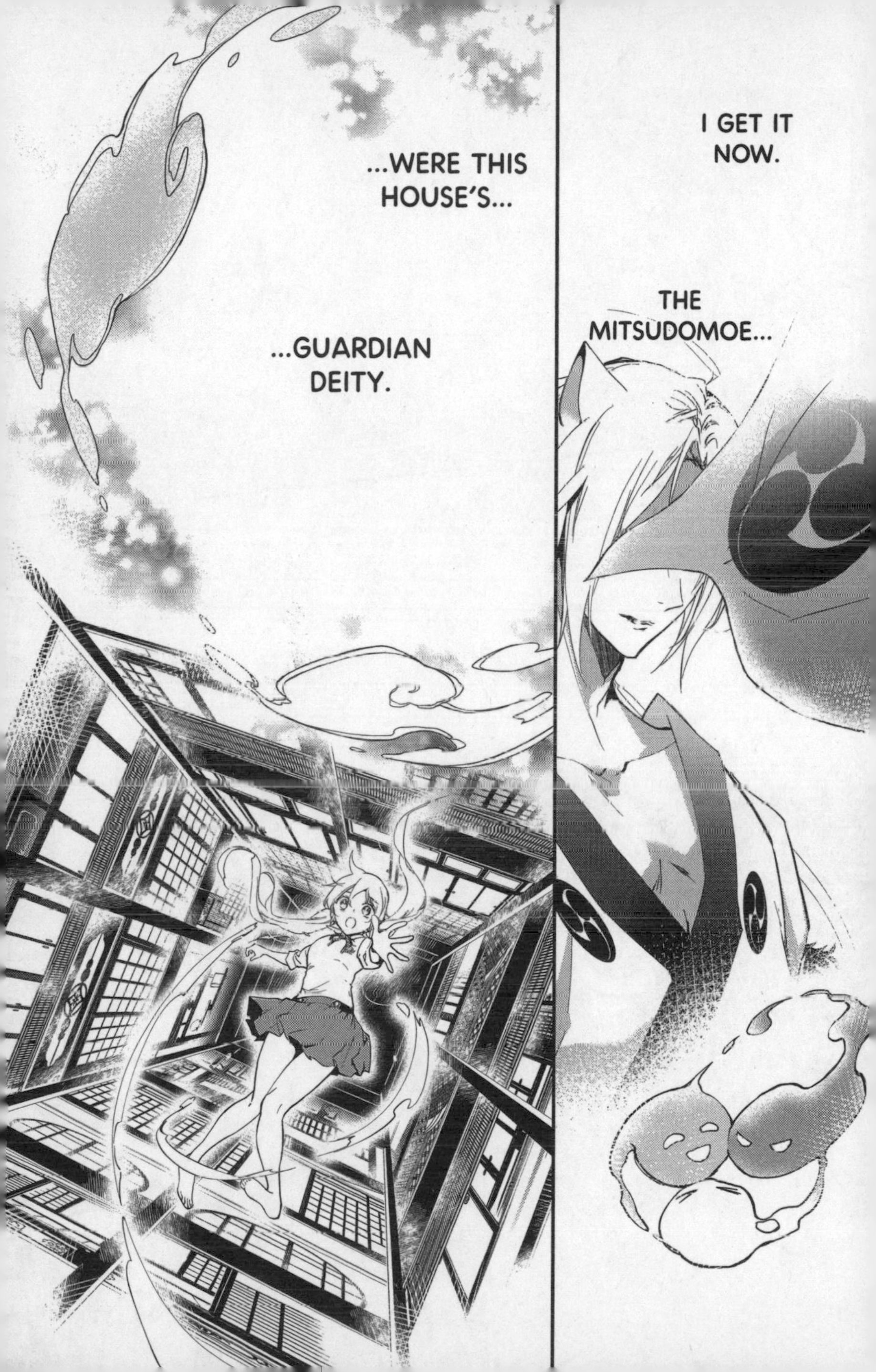
I GET IT NOW.
THE MITSUDOMOE...
...WERE THIS HOUSE'S...
...GUARDIAN DEITY.

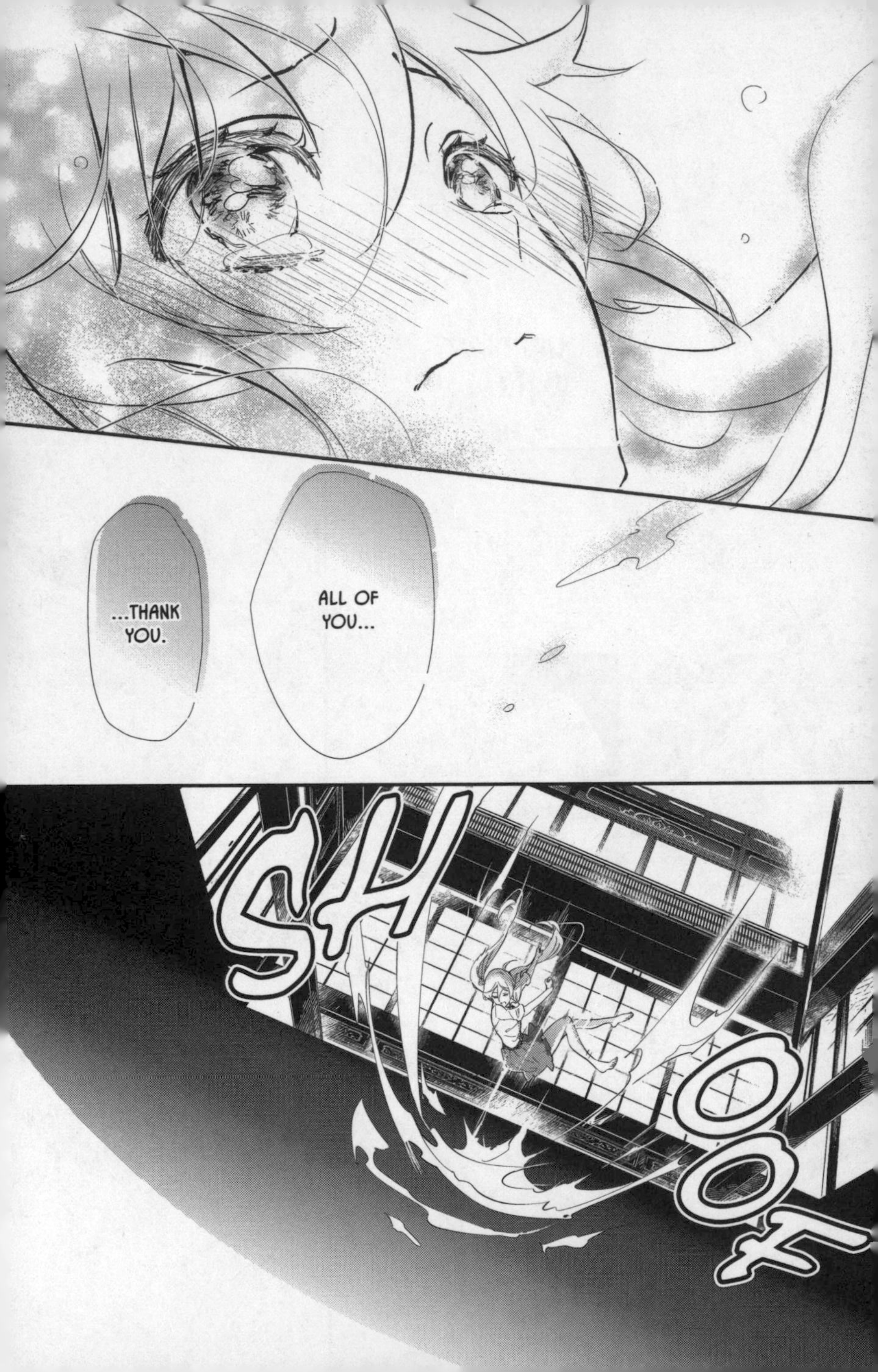
ALL OF YOU...
...THANK YOU.
SHOOF

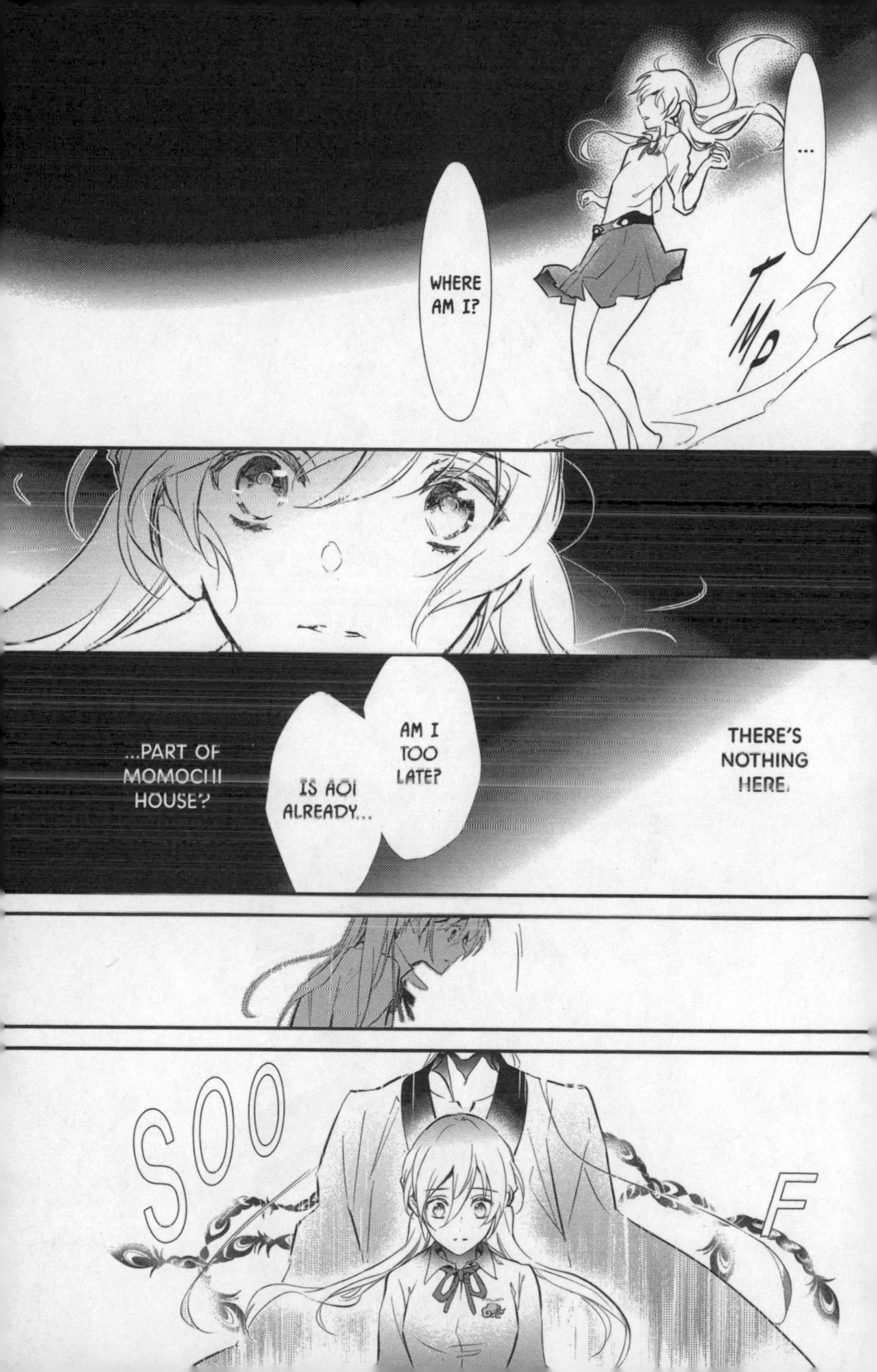
...
WHERE AM I?
TMP
THERE'S NOTHING HERE.
AM I TOO LATE?
IS AOI ALREADY...
...PART OF MOMOCHI HOUSE?
SOOF

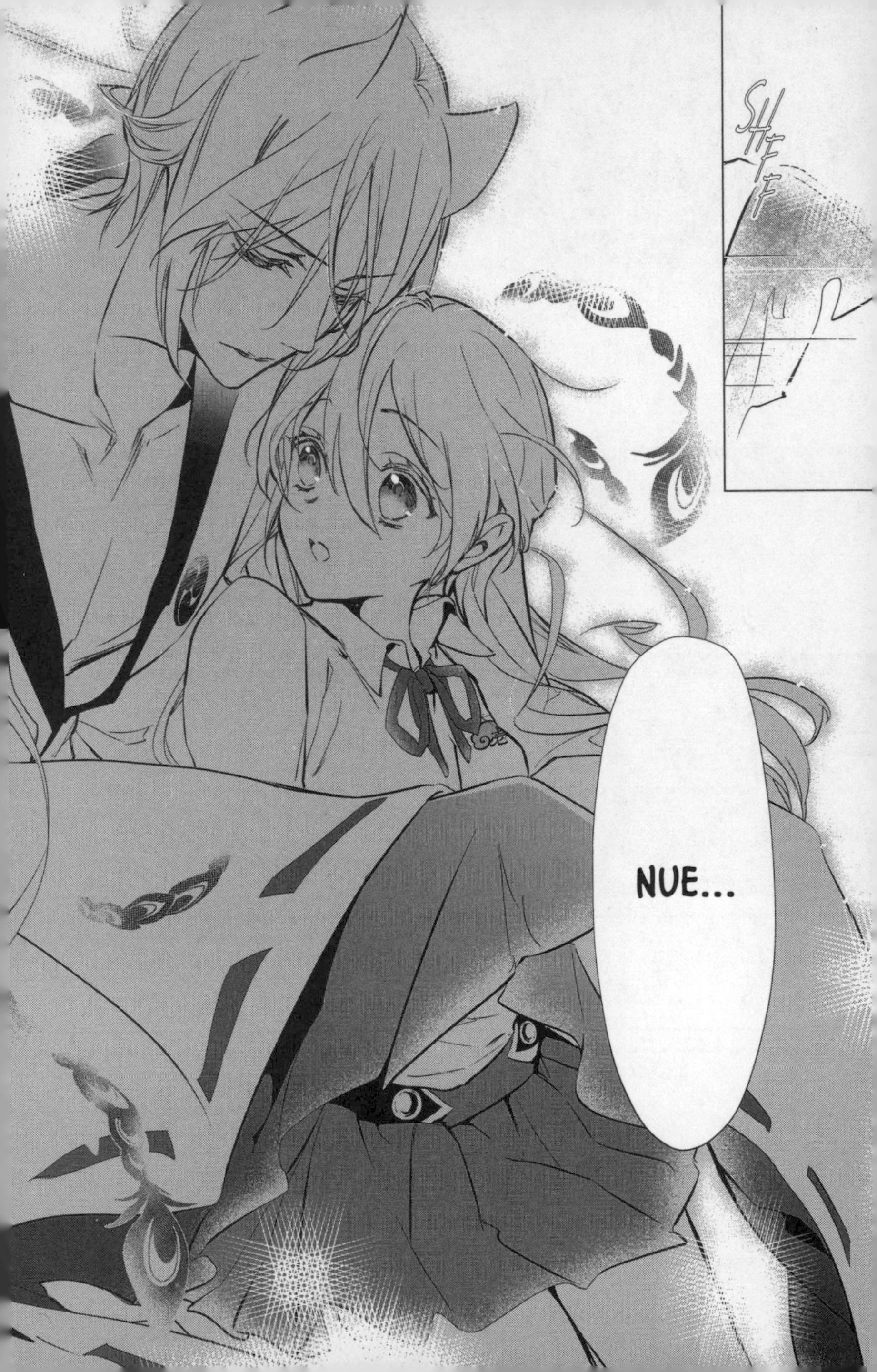
SHFF
NUE...

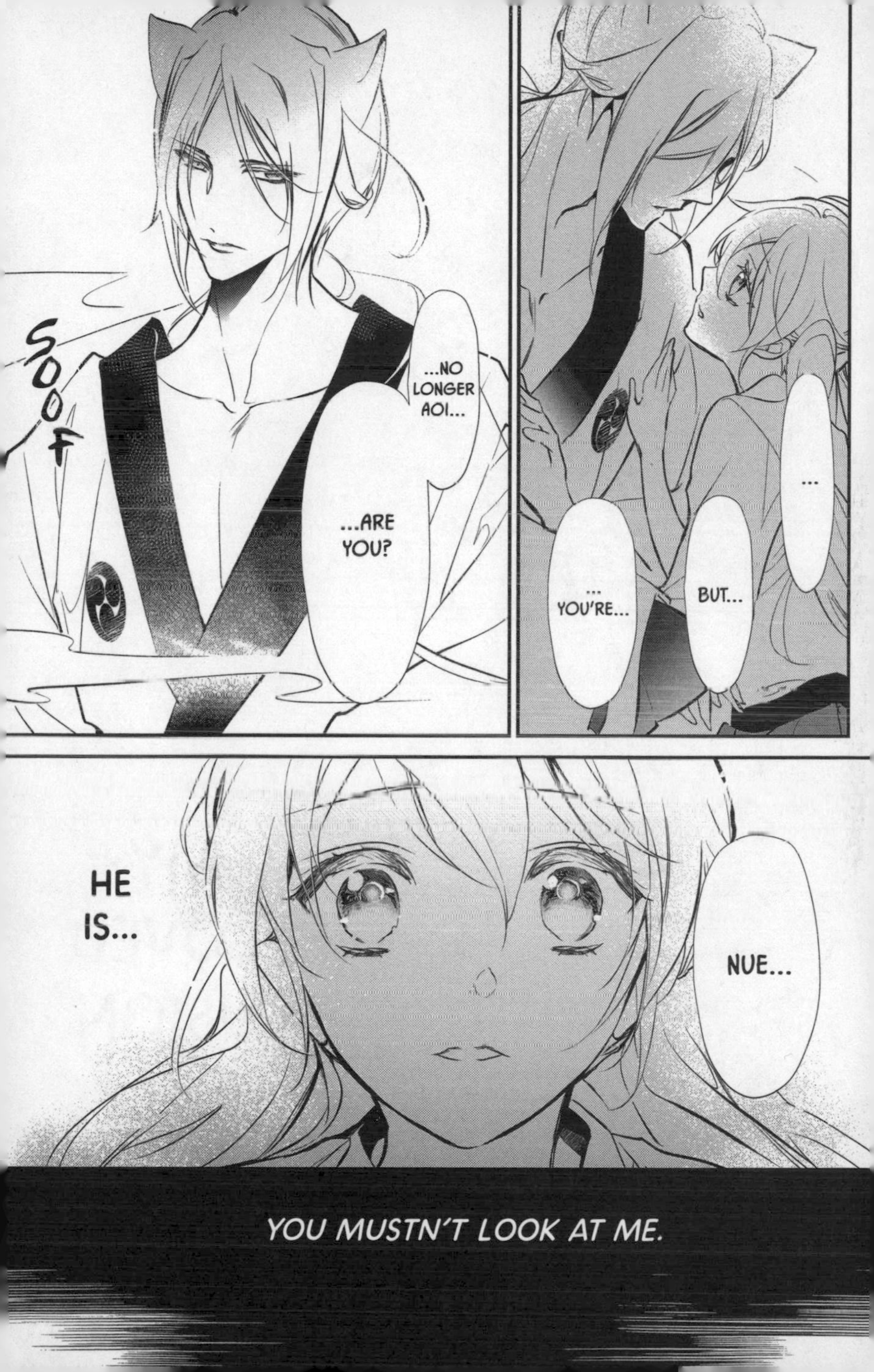
...
BUT...
...YOU'RE...
...NO LONGER AOI...
...ARE YOU?
SOOF
NUE...
HE IS...
YOU MUSTN'T LOOK AT ME.

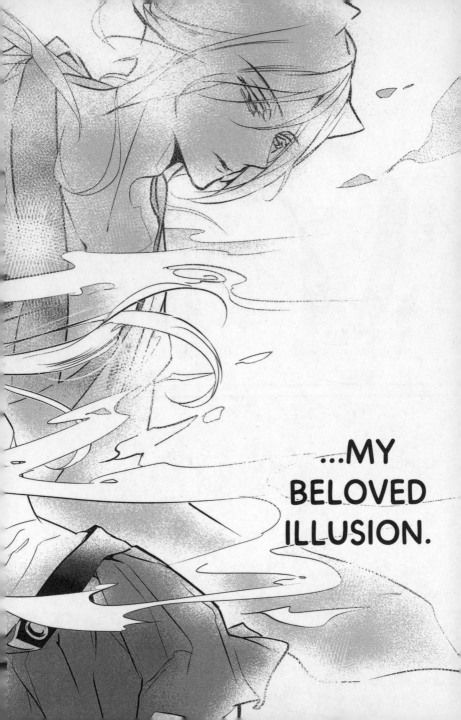

...MY
BELOVED
ILLUSION.

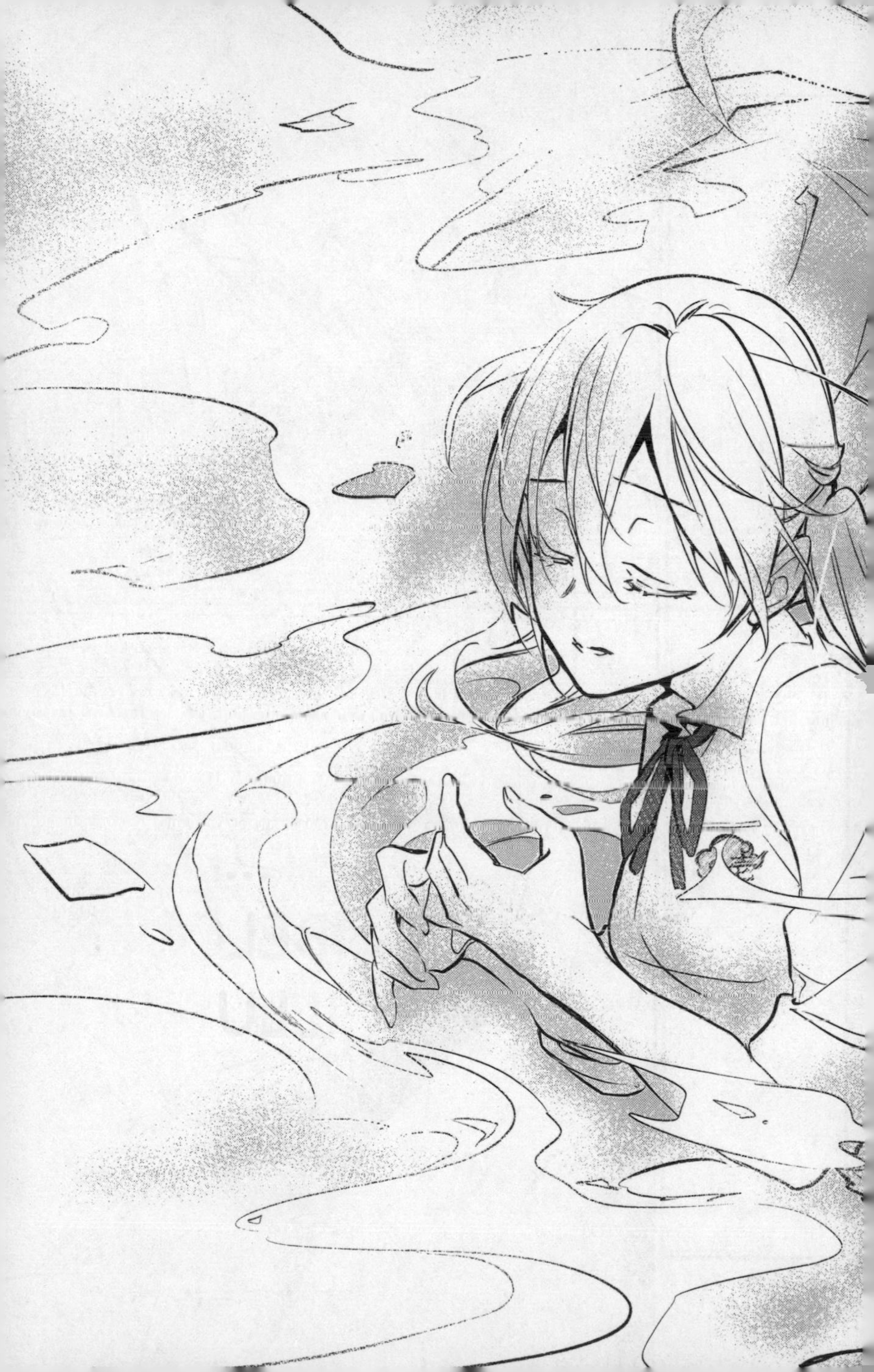

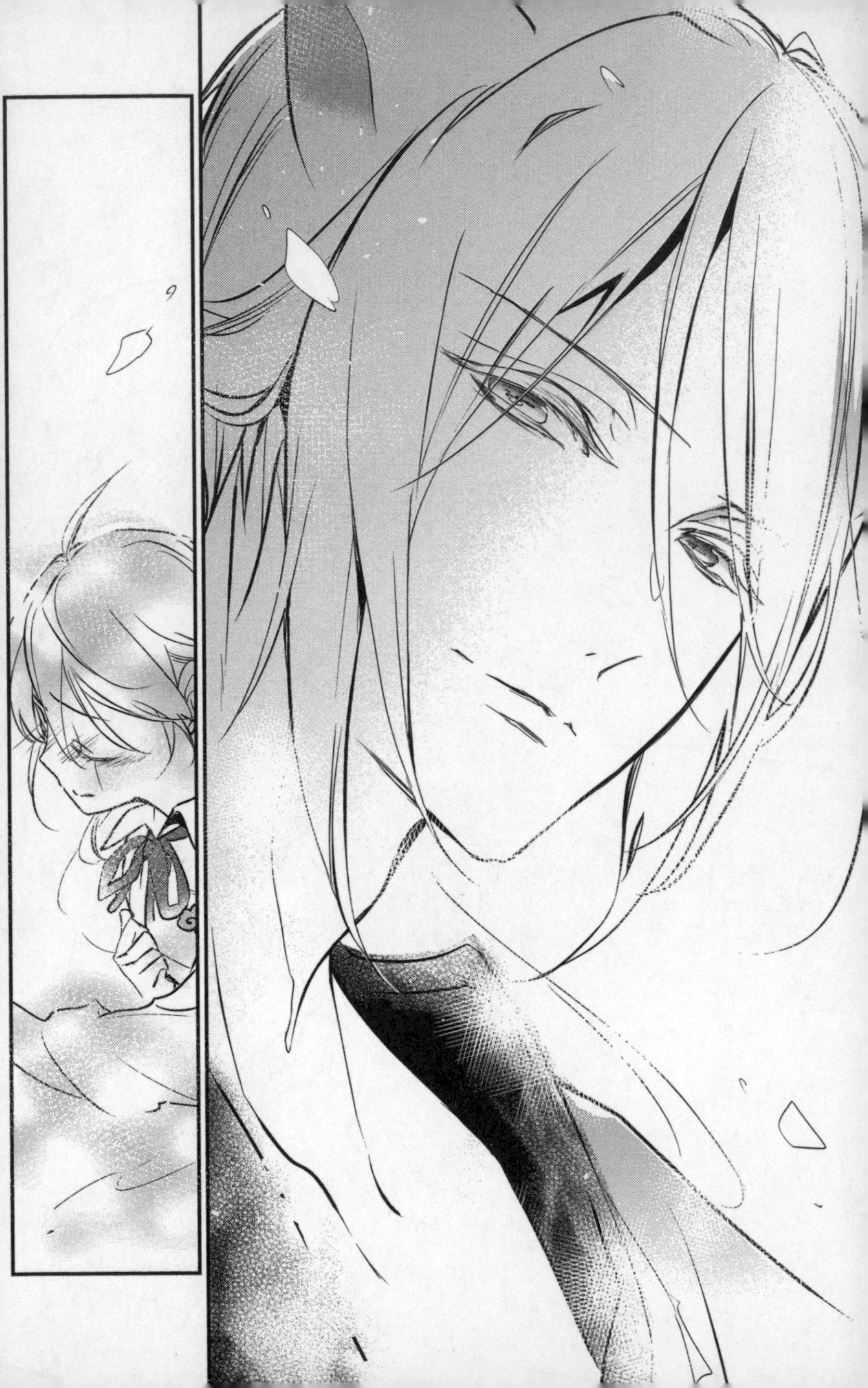

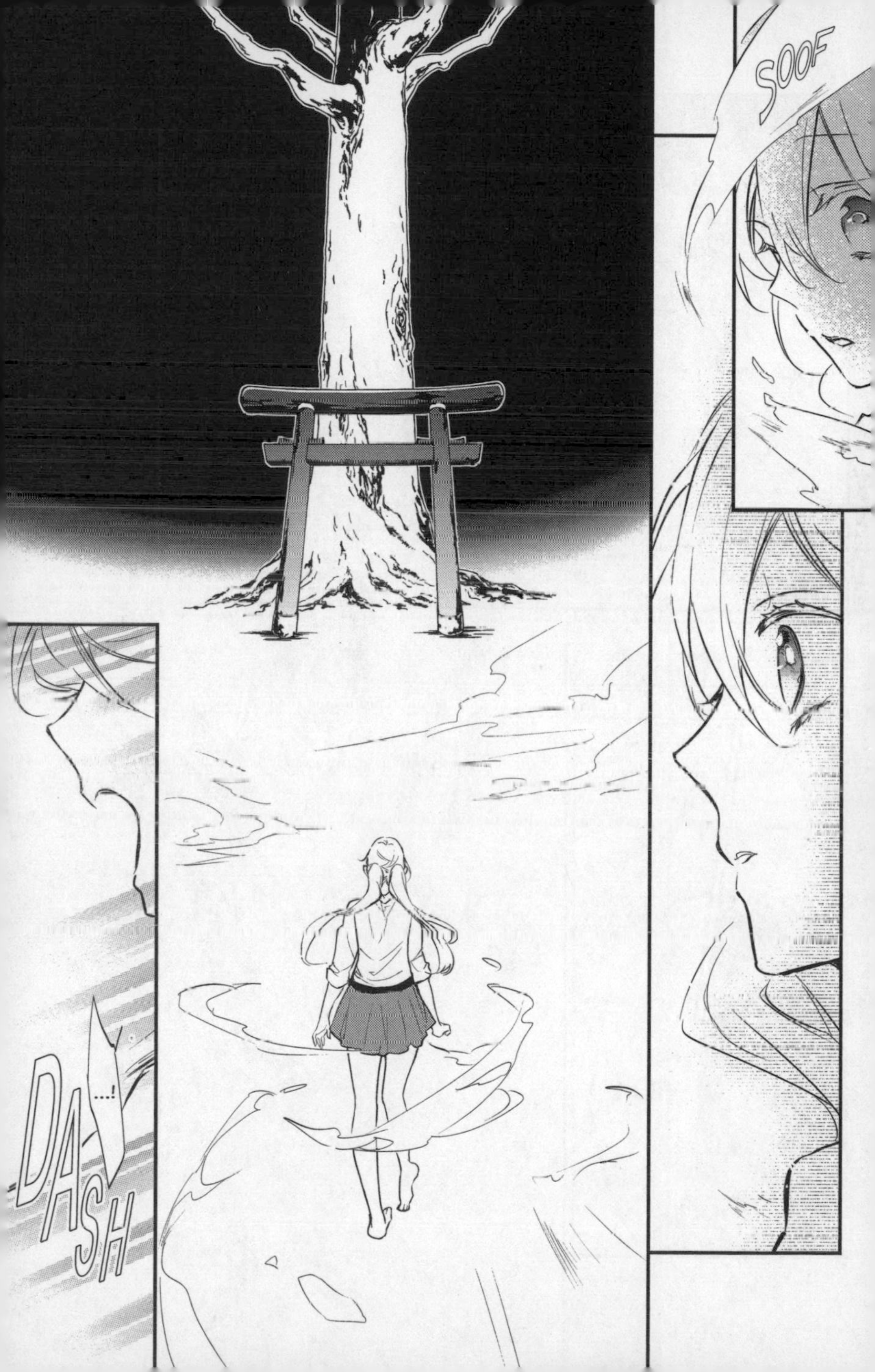
SOOF
....!
DASH

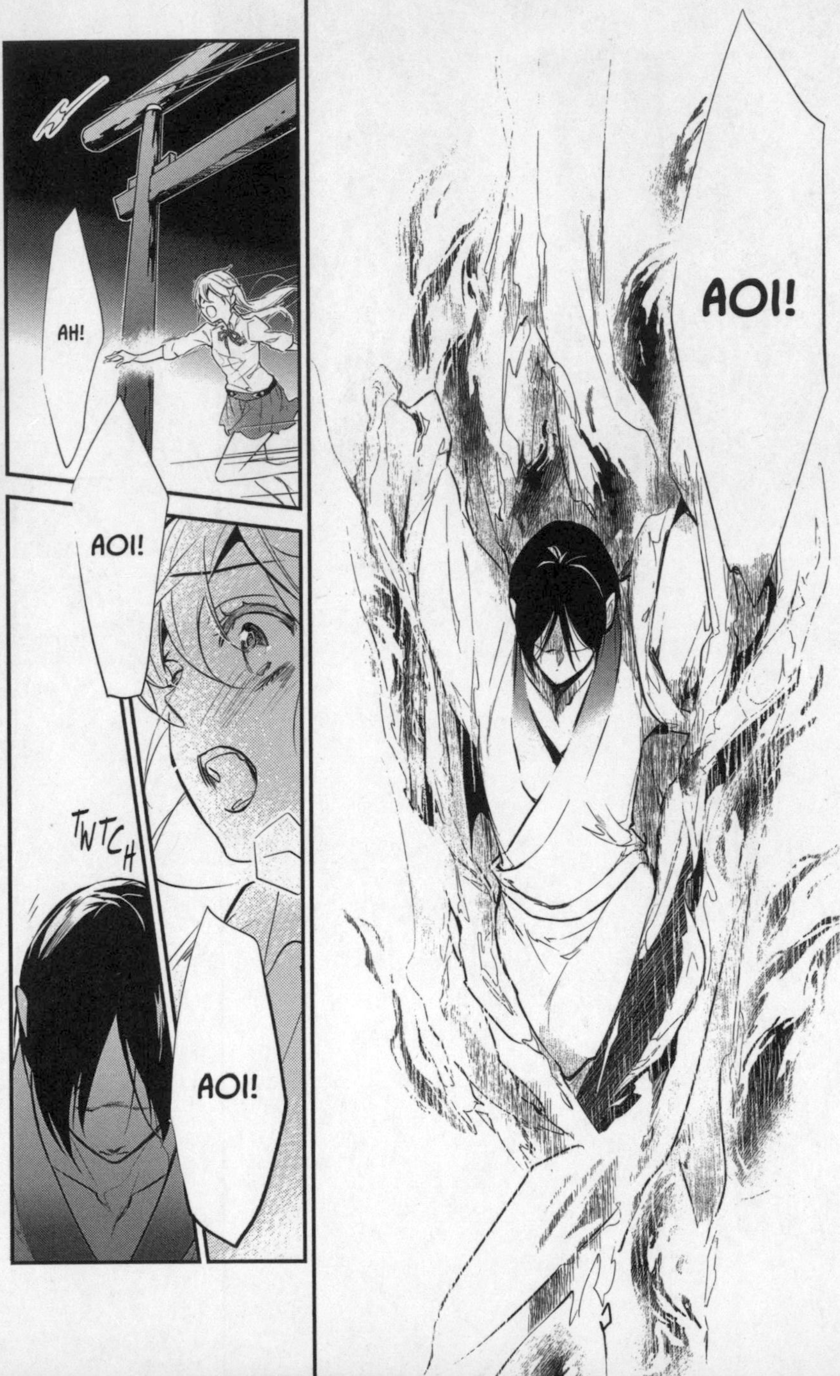
AOI!
AH!
AOI!
TWTCH
AOI!

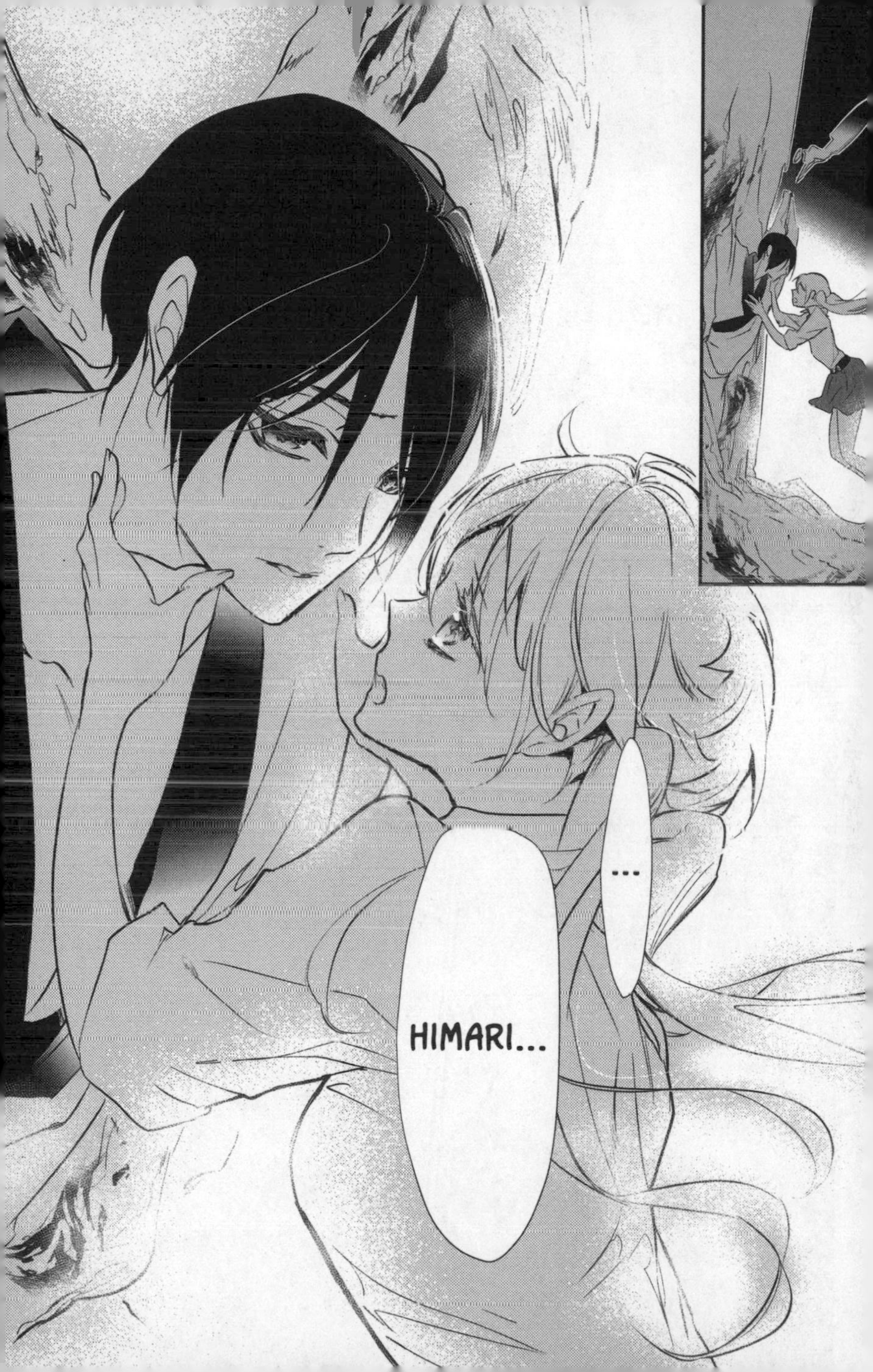
...
HIMARI...

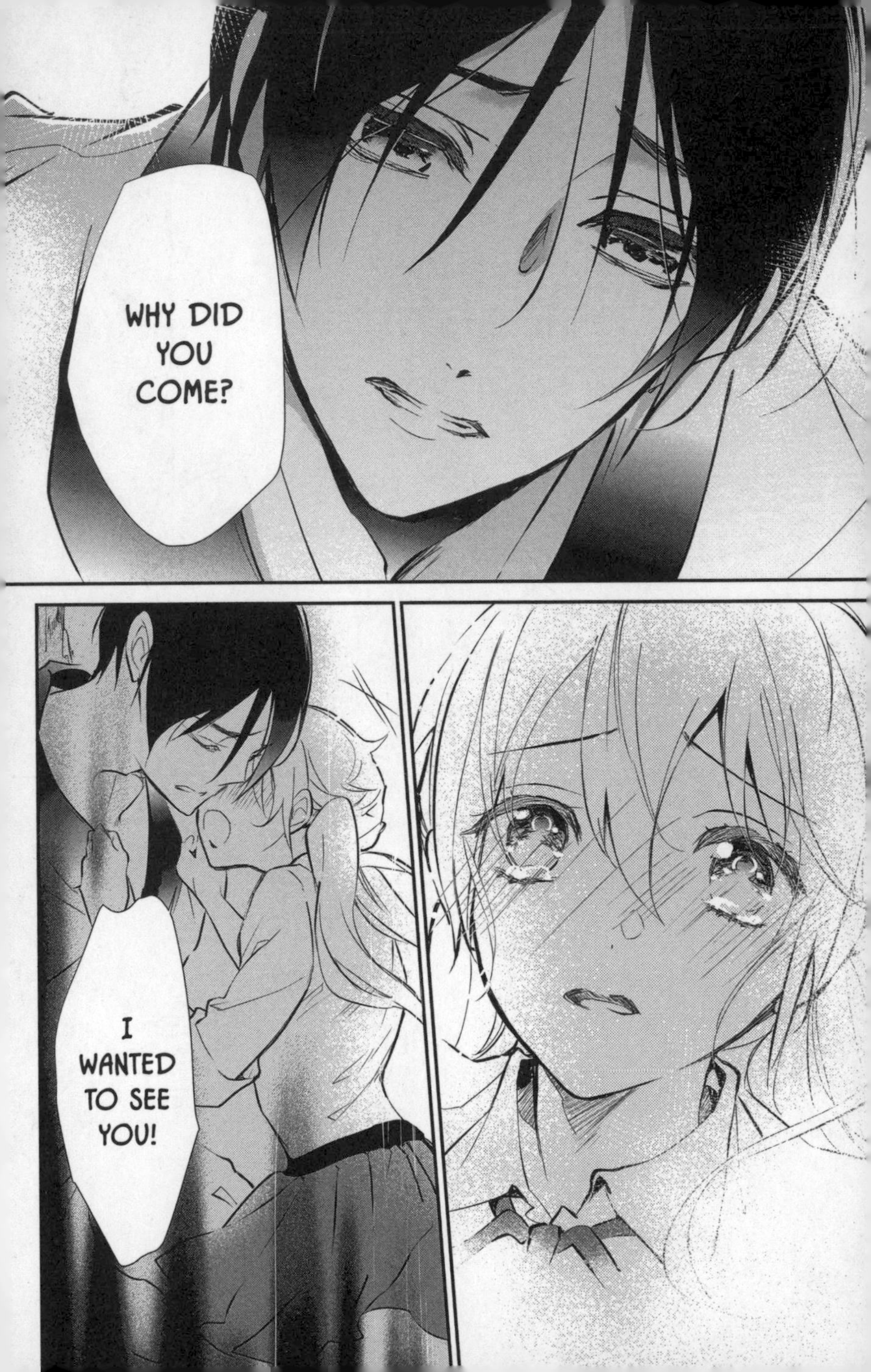
WHY DID YOU COME?
I WANTED TO SEE YOU!

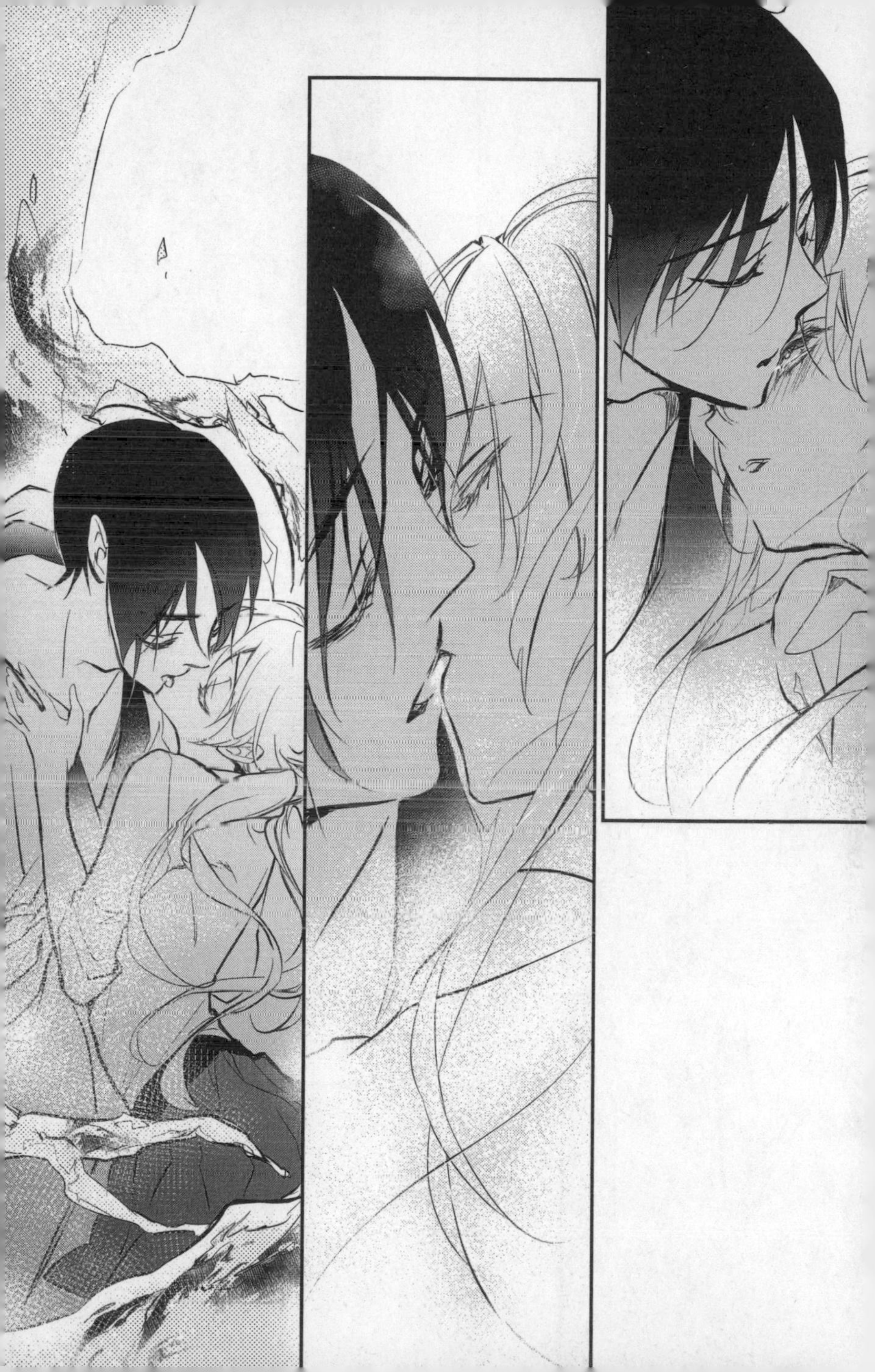

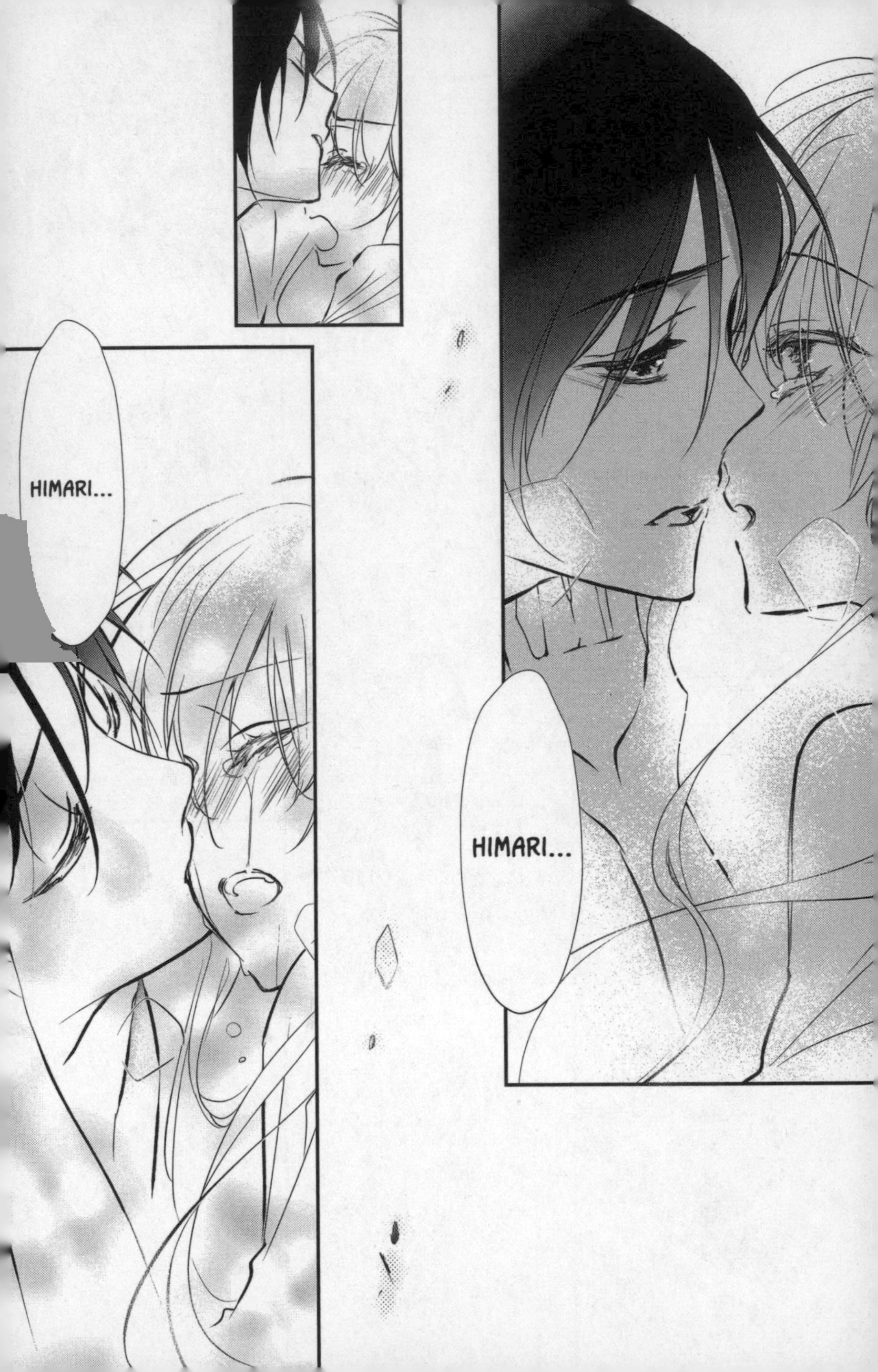
HIMARI...
HIMARI...

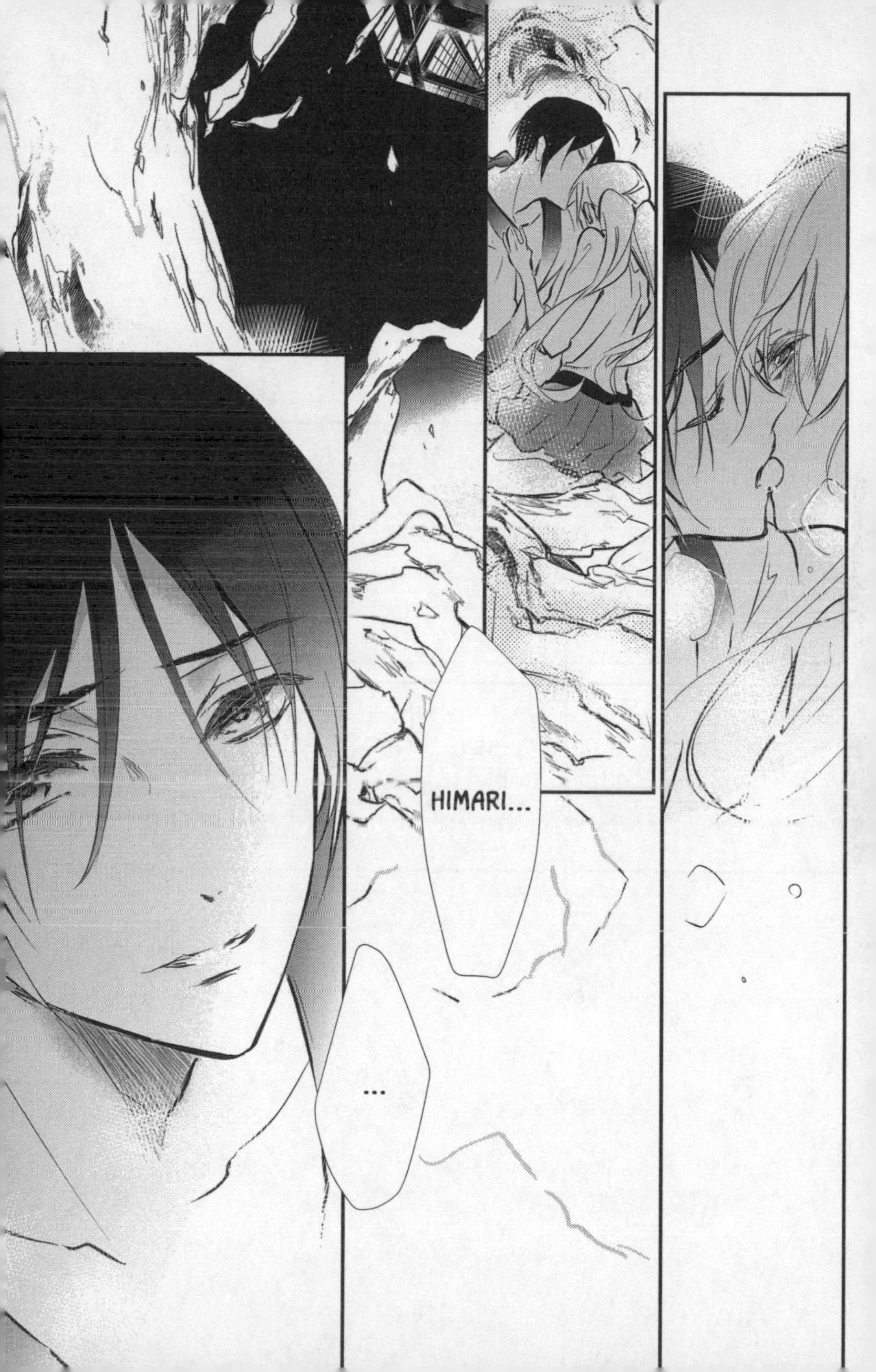
HIMARI...
...

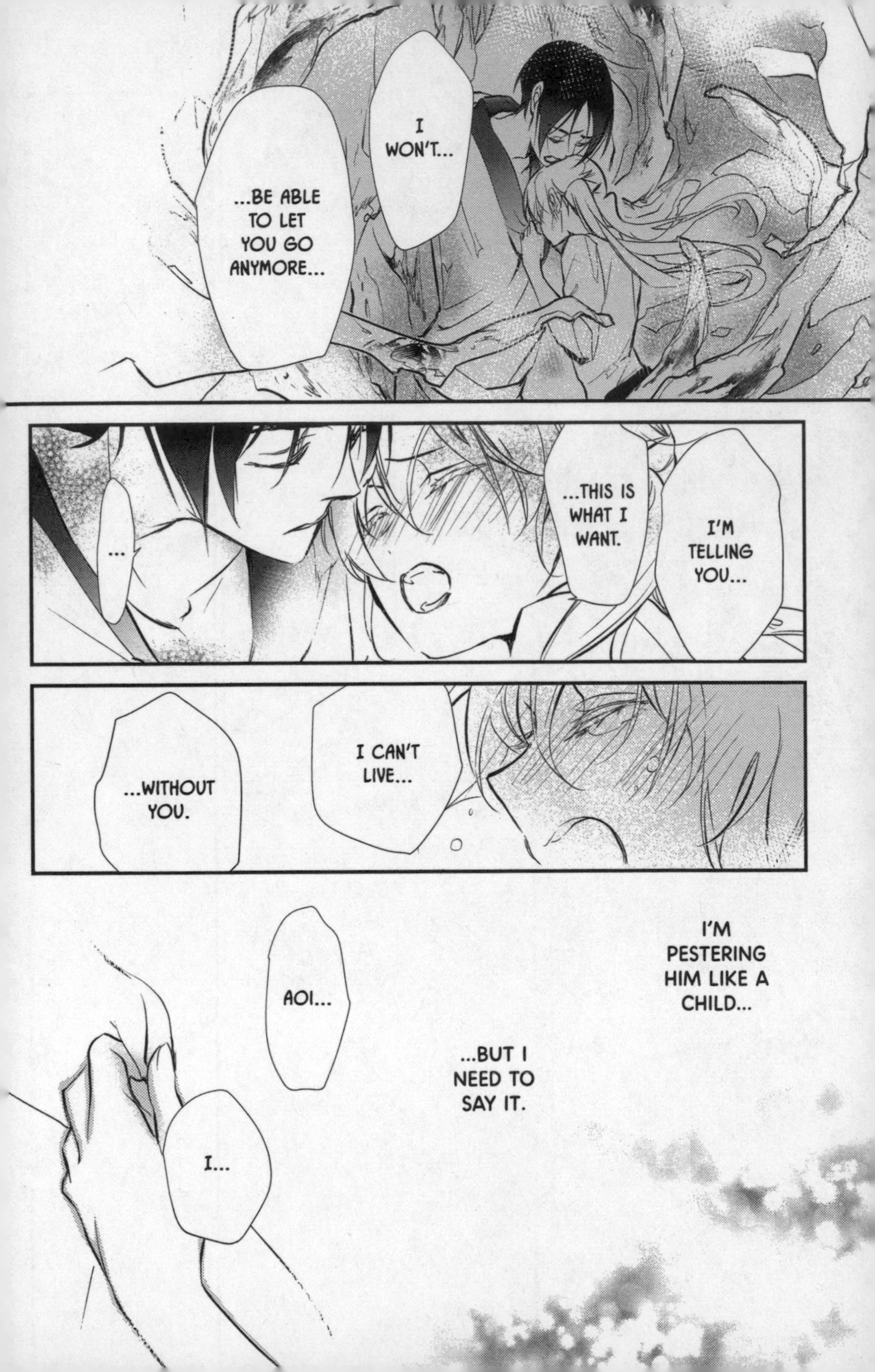
I WON'T...
...BE ABLE TO LET YOU GO ANYMORE...
I'M TELLING YOU...
...THIS IS WHAT I WANT.
...
I CAN'T LIVE...
...WITHOUT YOU.
I'M PESTERING HIM LIKE A CHILD...
...BUT I NEED TO SAY IT.
AOI...
I...

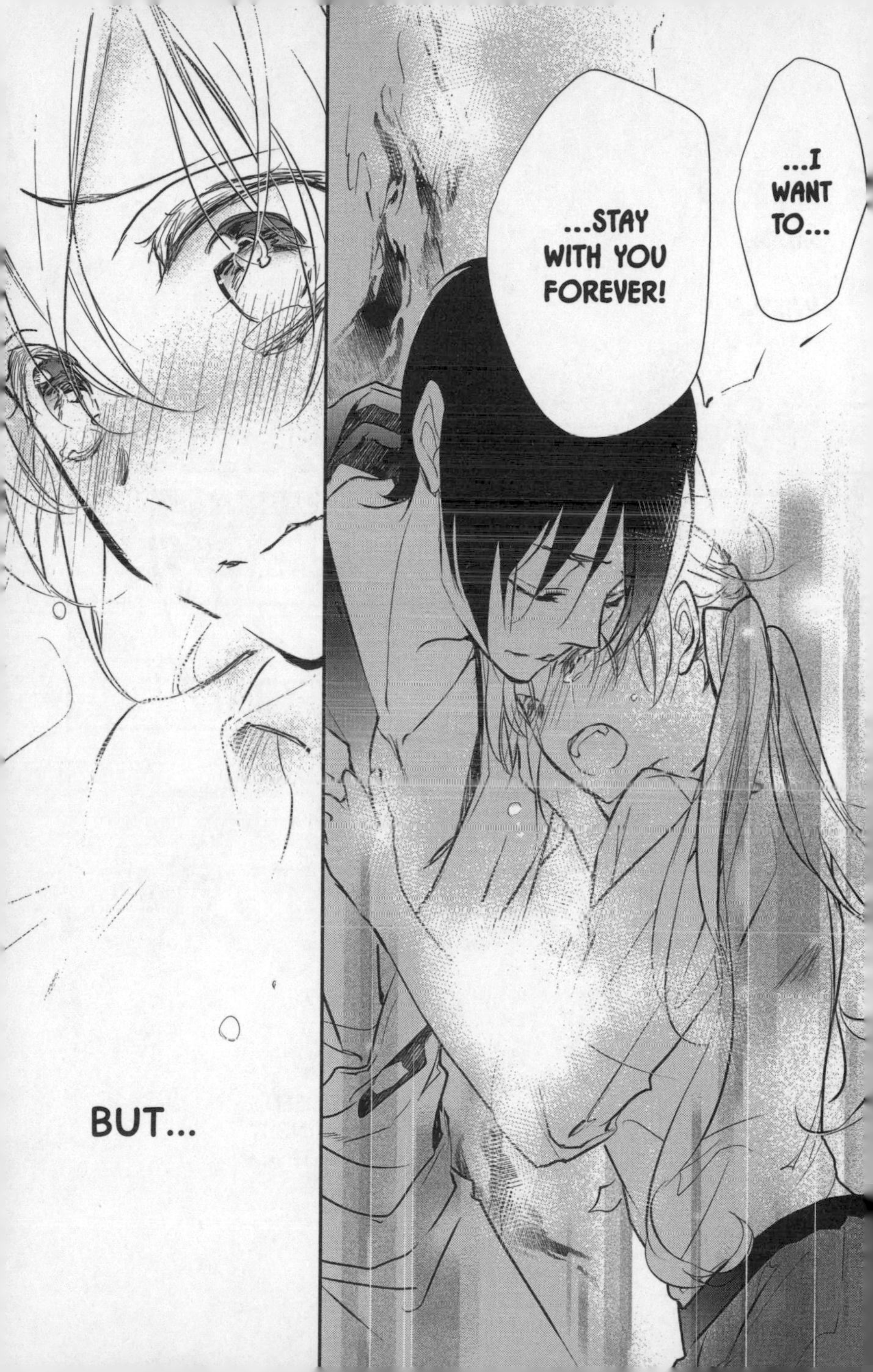
...I WANT TO...
...STAY WITH YOU FOREVER!
BUT...

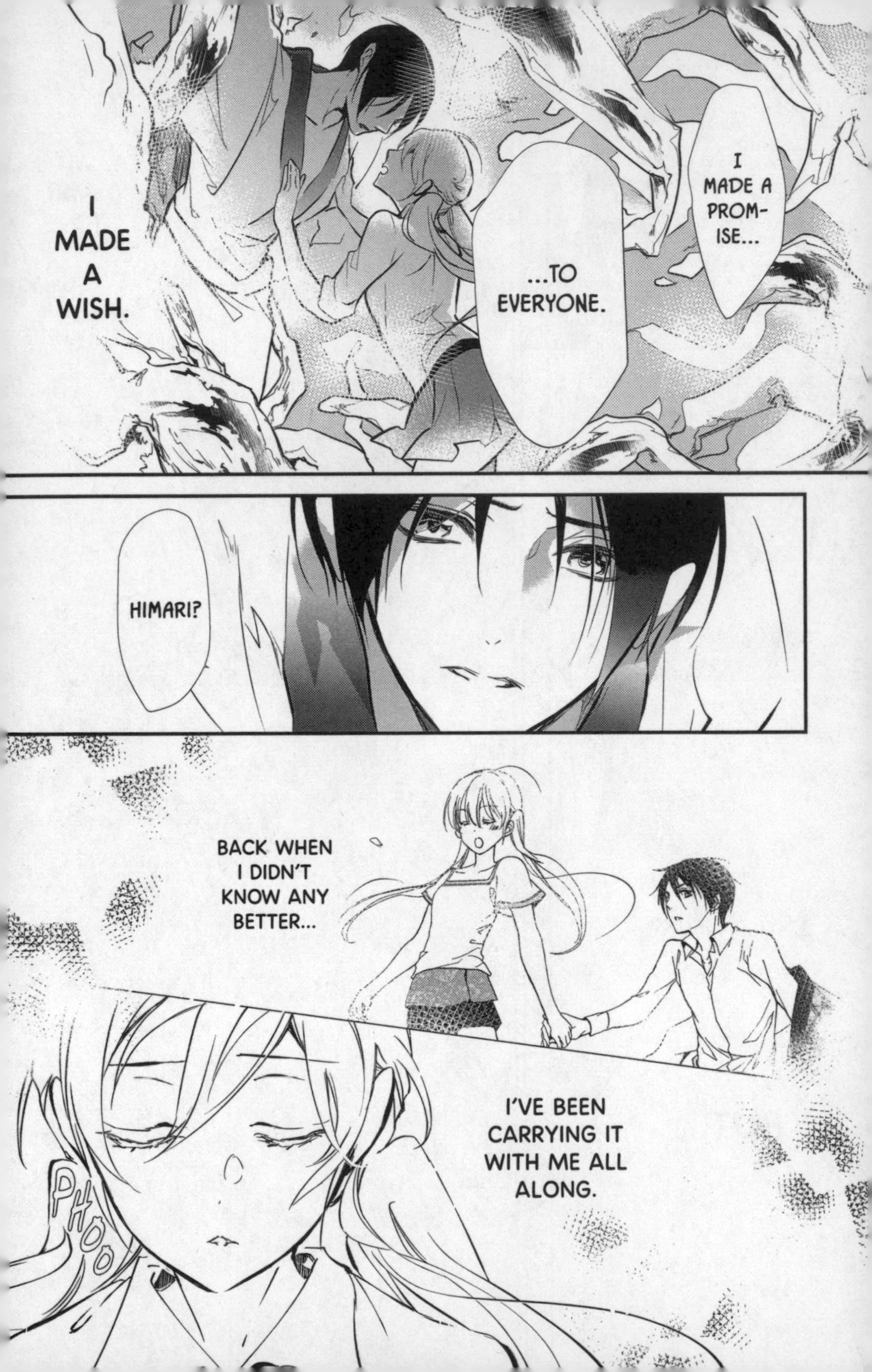
I MADE A PROMISE...
...TO EVERYONE.
I MADE A WISH.
HIMARI?
BACK WHEN I DIDN'T KNOW ANY BETTER...
I'VE BEEN CARRYING IT WITH ME ALL ALONG.
PHOO

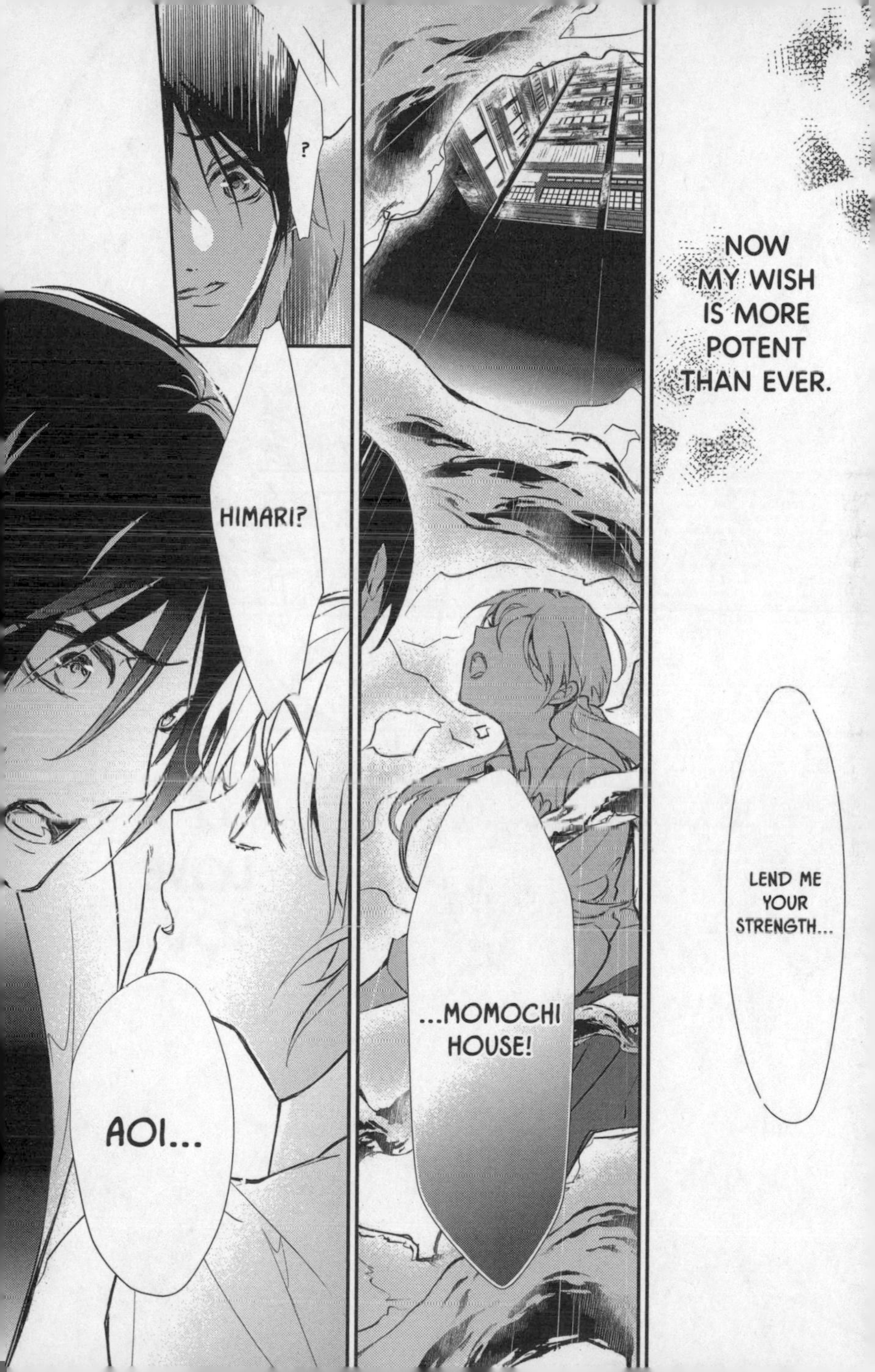
NOW MY WISH IS MORE POTENT THAN EVER.
LEND ME YOUR STRENGTH...
...MOMOCHI HOUSE!
?
HIMARI?
AOI...

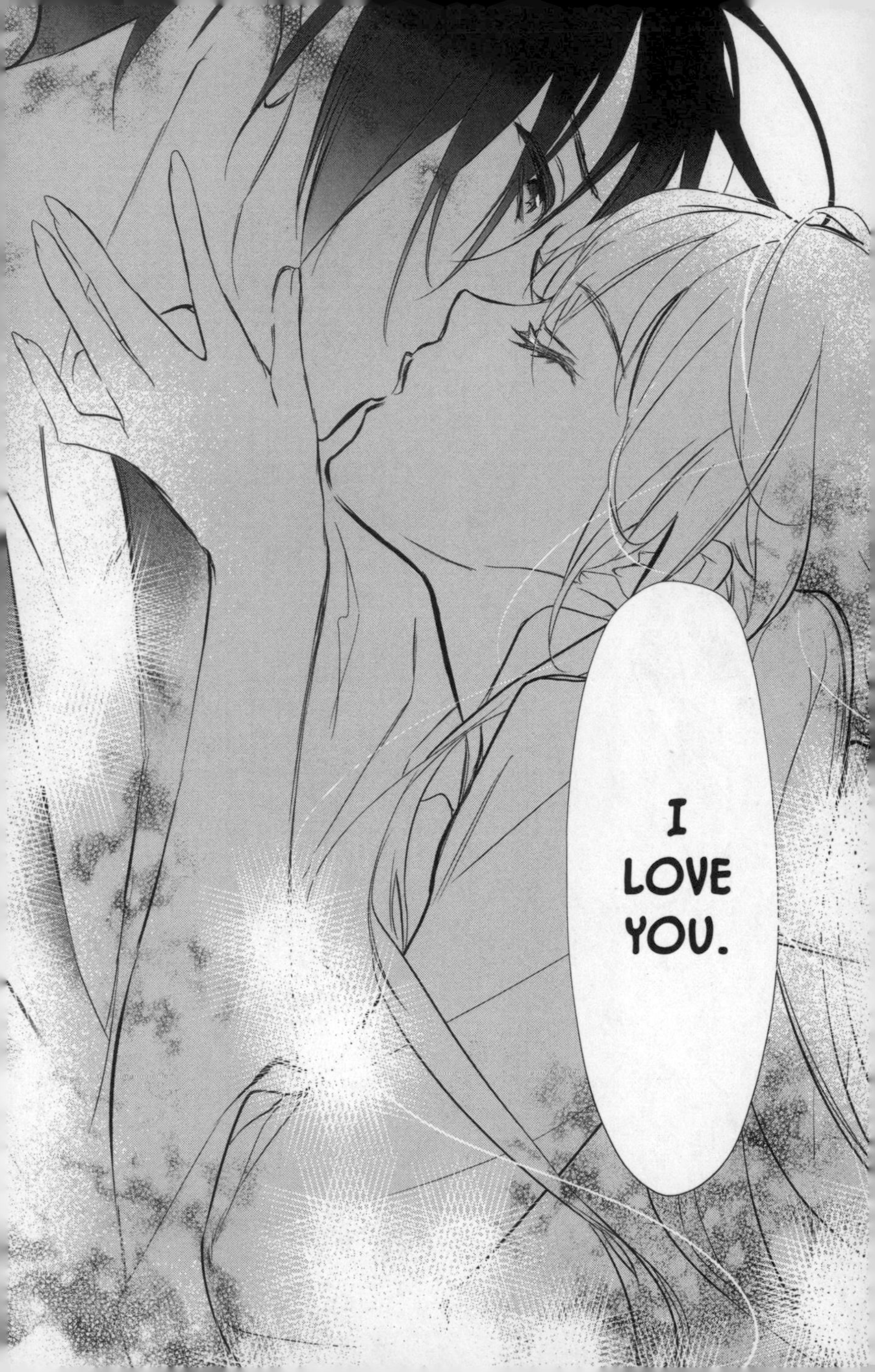
I LOVE YOU.

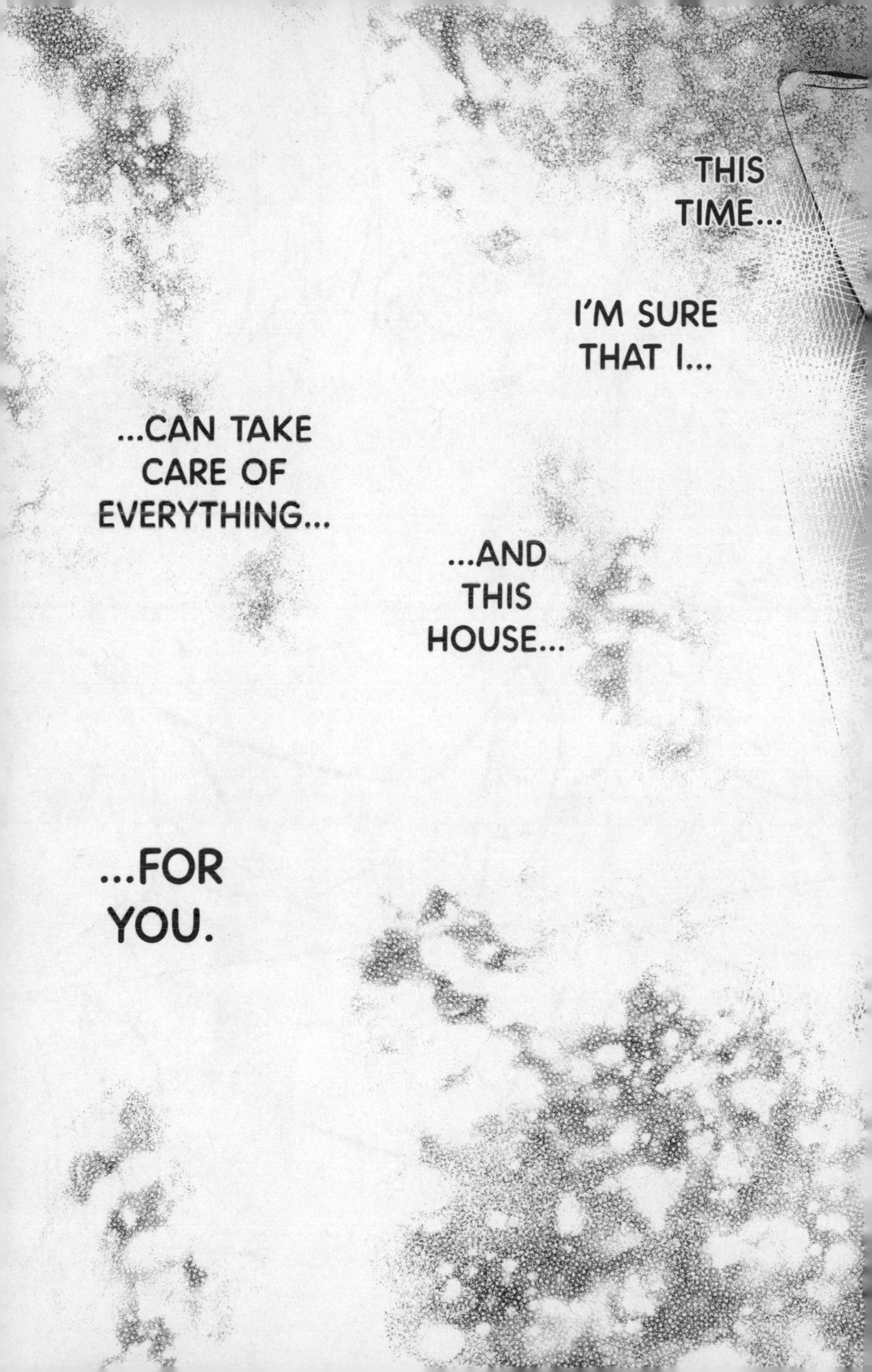
THIS TIME...
I'M SURE THAT I...
...CAN TAKE CARE OF EVERYTHING...
...AND THIS HOUSE...
...FOR YOU.

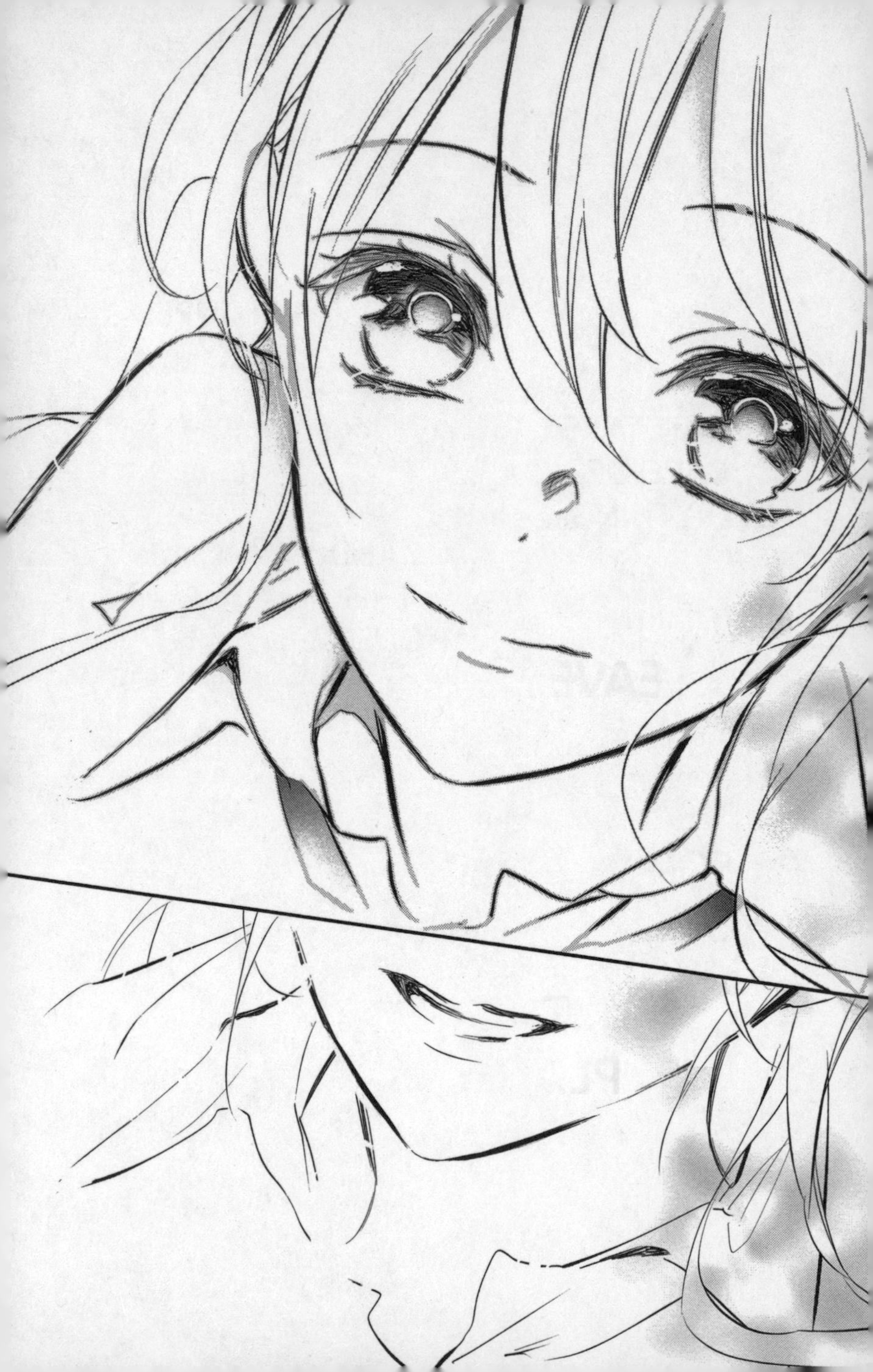

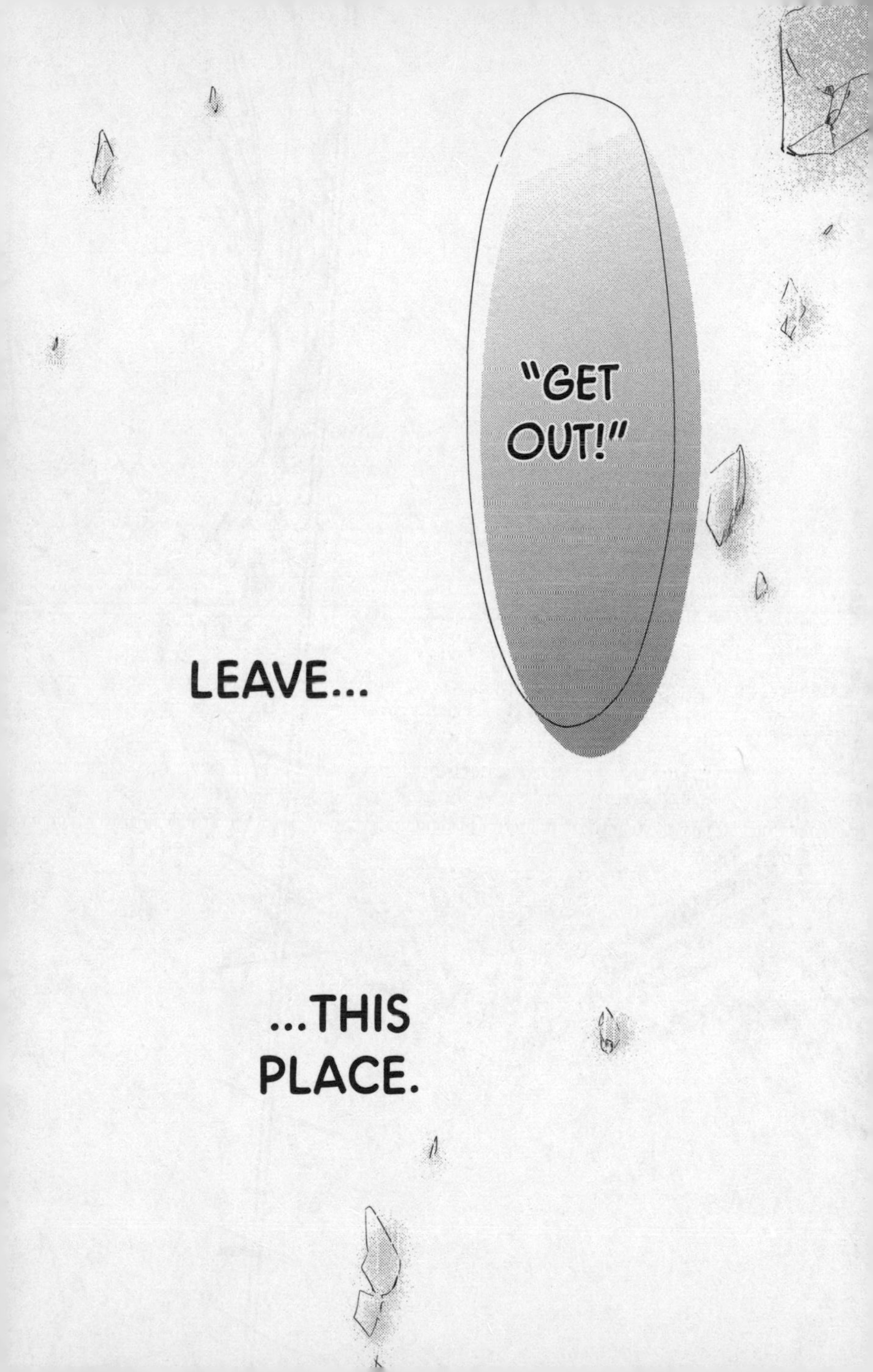
"GET OUT!"
LEAVE...
...THIS PLACE.

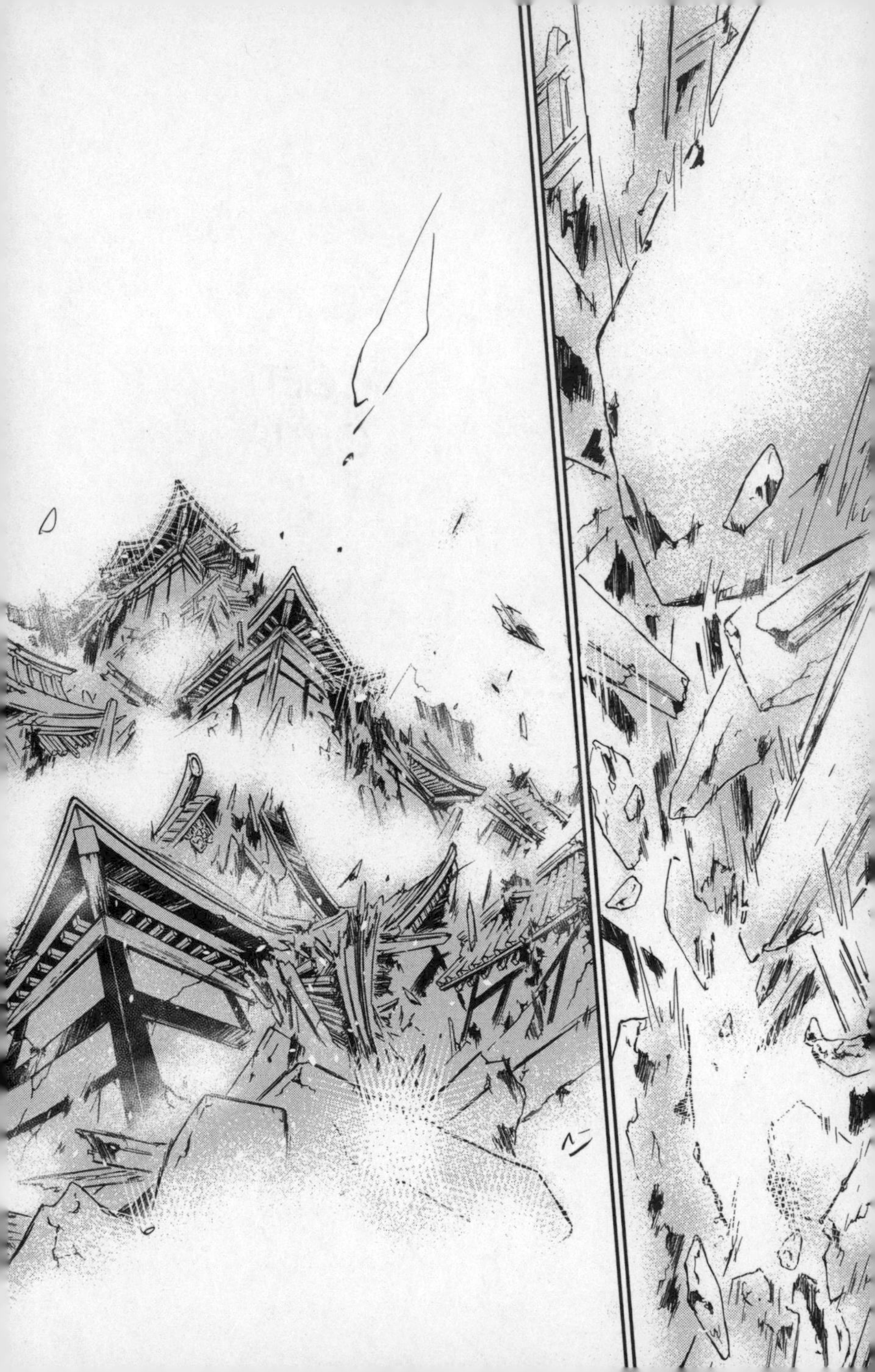

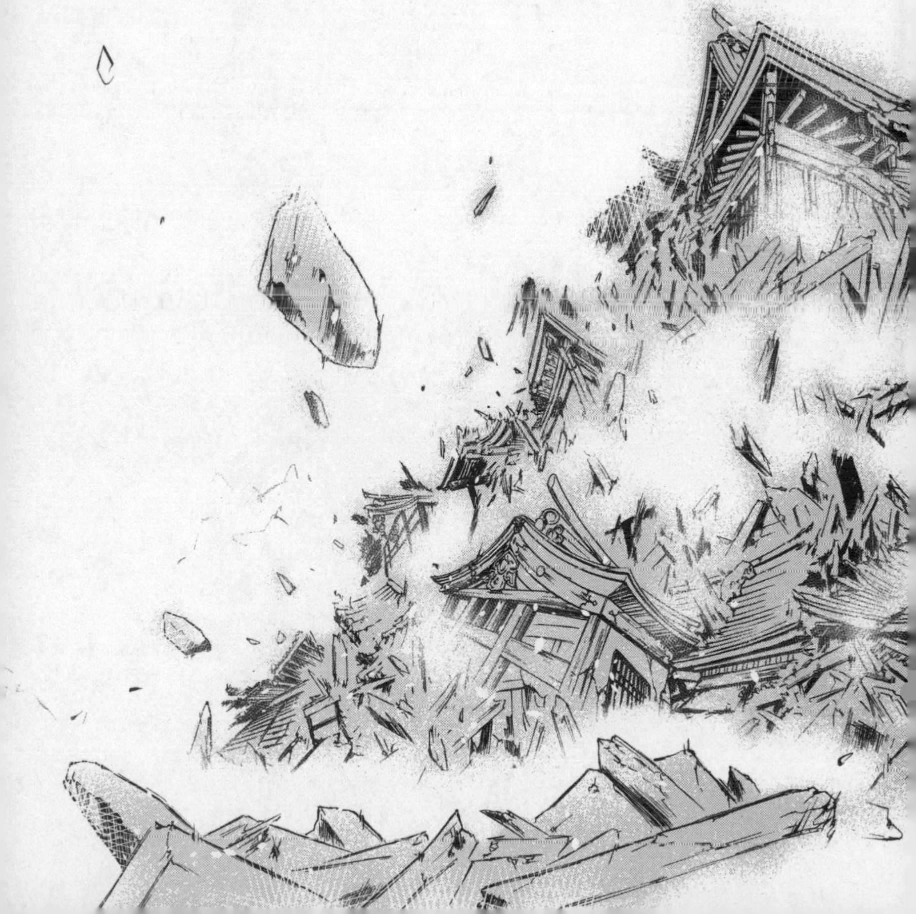

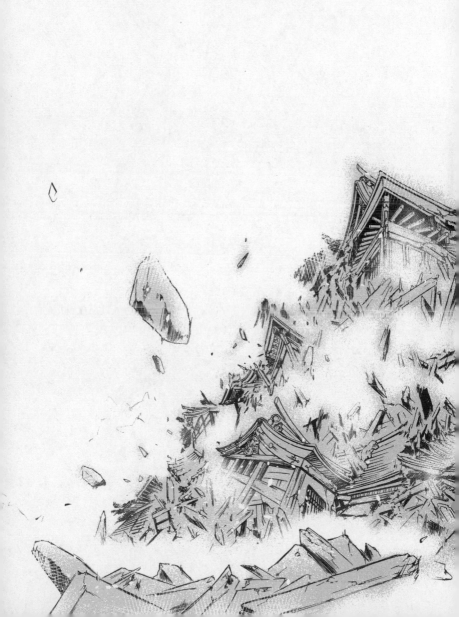

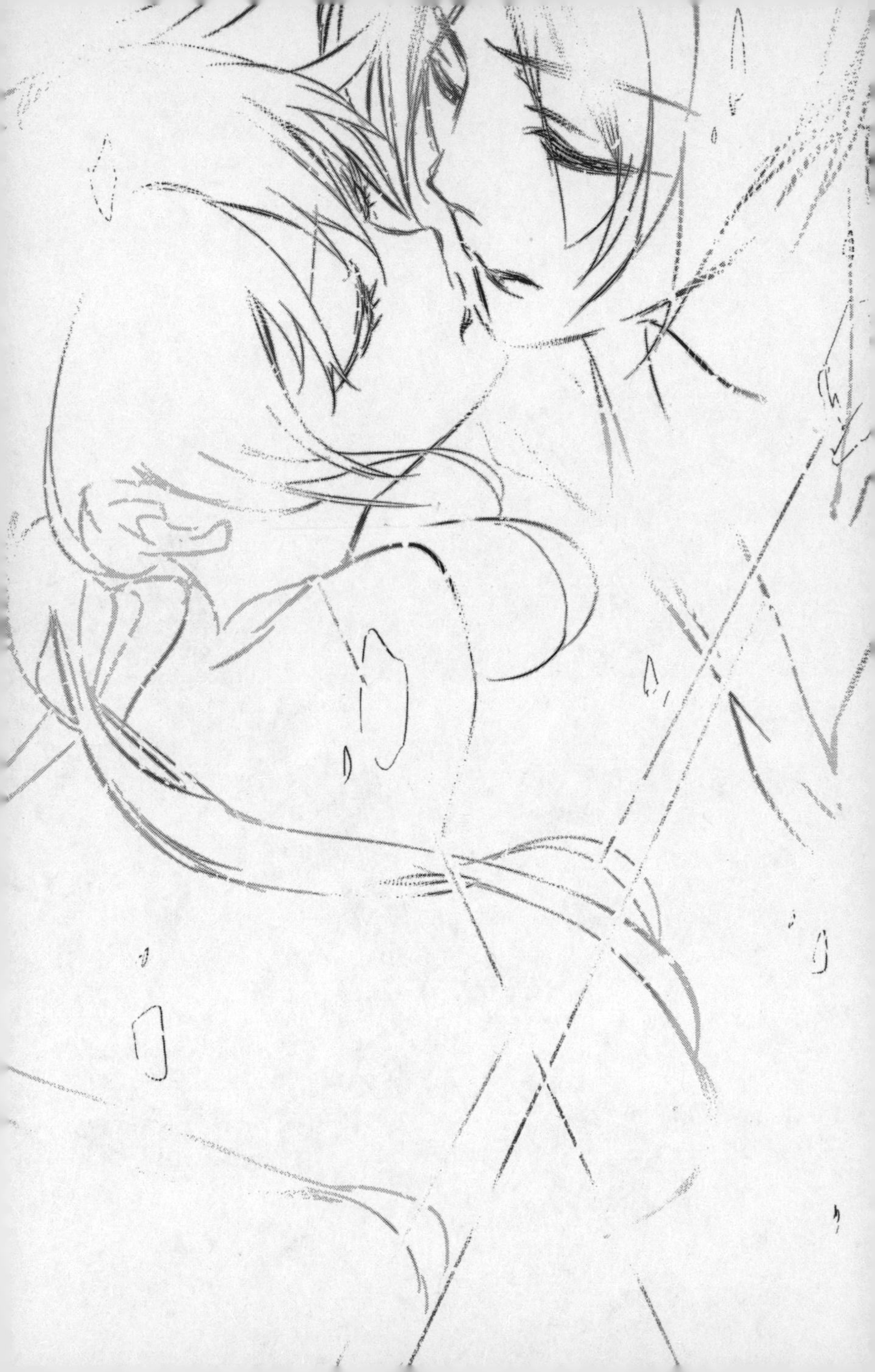

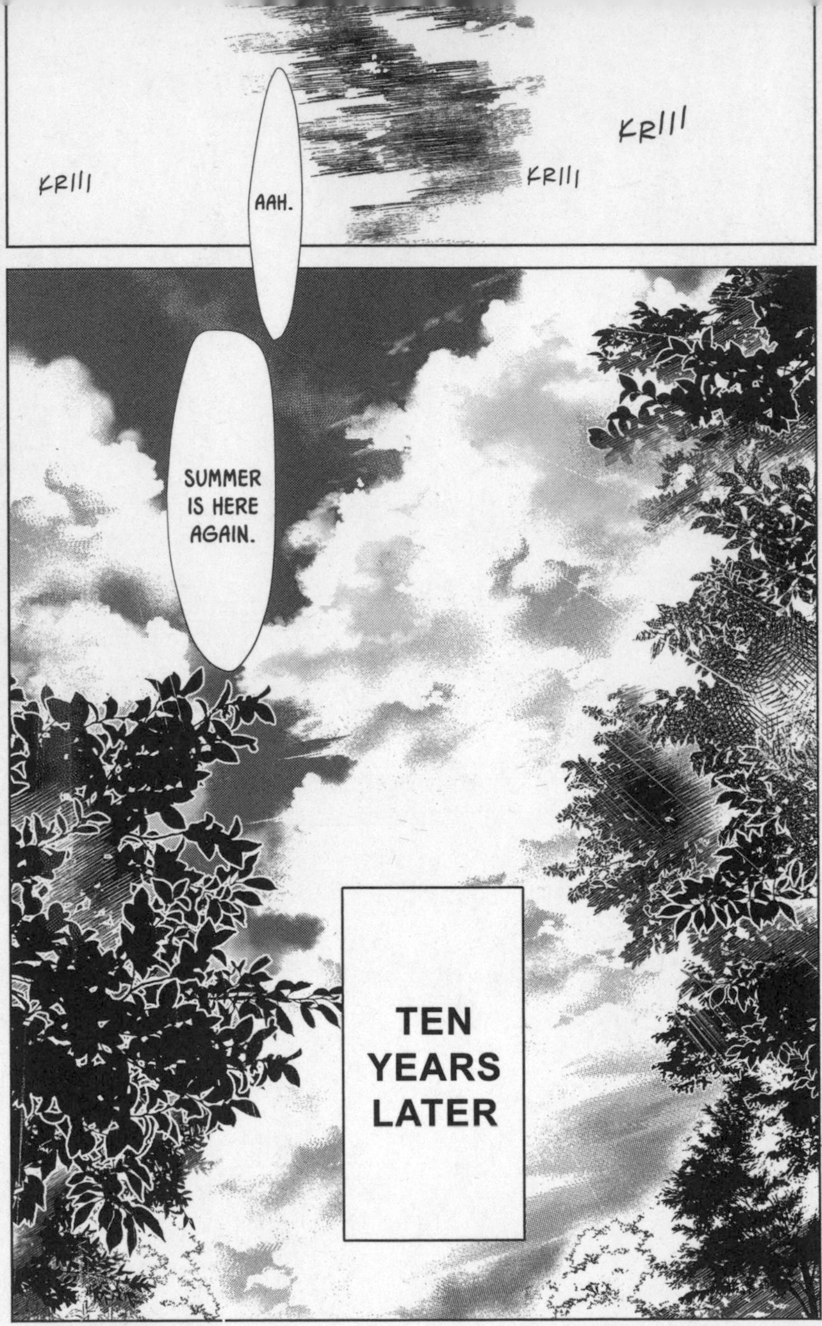
KRIII
KRIII
KRIII
AAH.
SUMMER IS HERE AGAIN.
TEN YEARS LATER

The DEMON PRINCE of MOMOCHI HOUSE

The
DEMON
PRINCE
of MOMOCHI
HOUSE

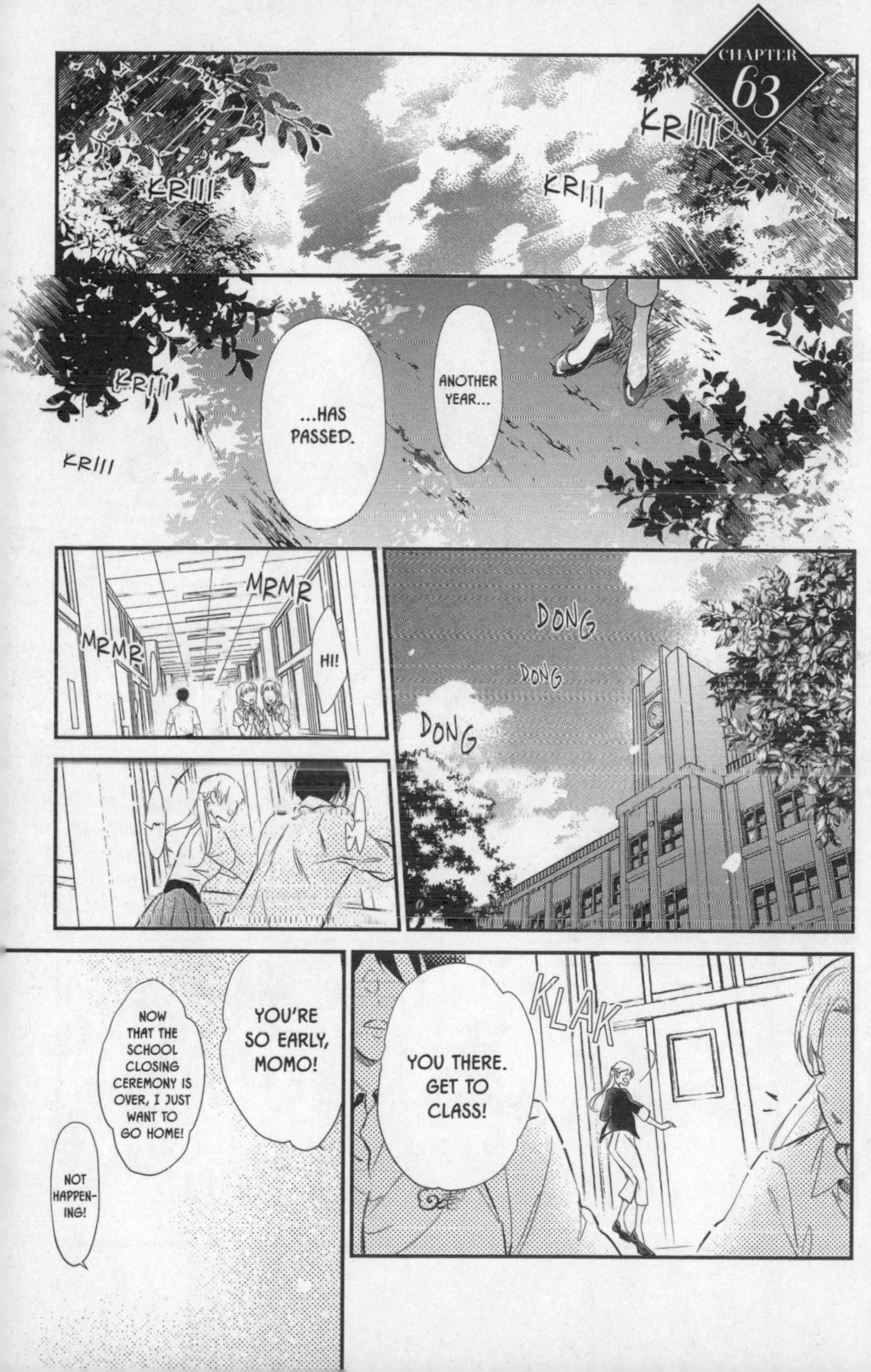
CHAPTER 63
KRIII
KRIII
KRIII
ANOTHER YEAR...
...HAS PASSED.
KRIII
KRIII
DONG
DONG
DONG
MRMR
HI!
MRMR
KLAK
YOU THERE. GET TO CLASS!
YOU'RE SO EARLY, MOMO!
NOW THAT THE SCHOOL CLOSING CEREMONY IS OVER, I JUST WANT TO GO HOME!
NOT HAPPEN-ING!

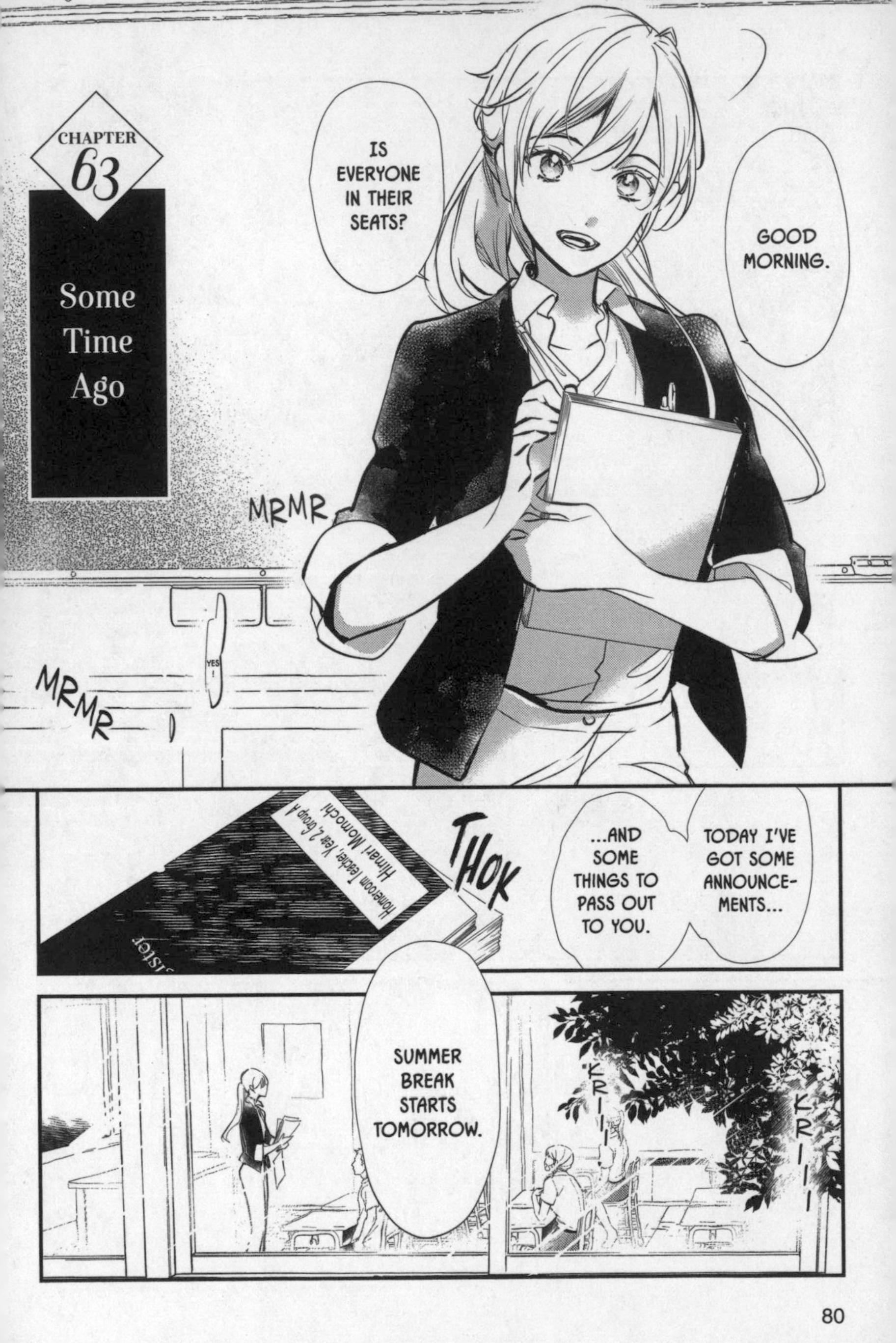

CHAPTER 63
Some Time Ago
GOOD MORNING.
IS EVERYONE IN THEIR SEATS?
MRMR
YES!
MRMR
TODAY I'VE GOT SOME ANNOUNCE-MENTS...
...AND SOME THINGS TO PASS OUT TO YOU.
THOK
Homeroom Teacher, Year 2, Group 4
Himari Momochi
SUMMER BREAK STARTS TOMORROW.
KRI-I-I
KRI-I-I

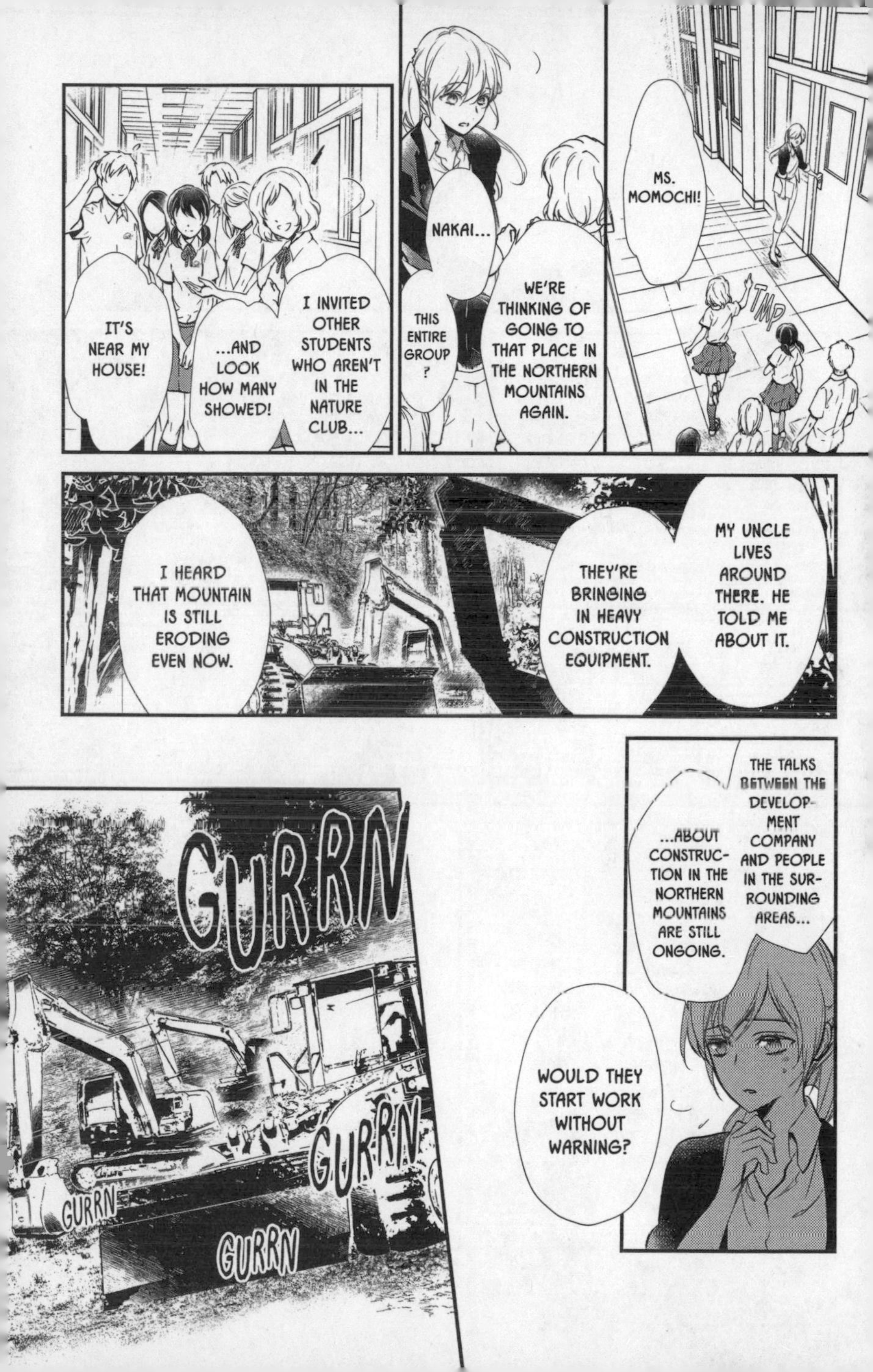
MS. MOMOCHI!
TMP
NAKAI...
WE'RE THINKING OF GOING TO THAT PLACE IN THE NORTHERN MOUNTAINS AGAIN.
THIS ENTIRE GROUP?
I INVITED OTHER STUDENTS WHO AREN'T IN THE NATURE CLUB...
...AND LOOK HOW MANY SHOWED!
IT'S NEAR MY HOUSE!
MY UNCLE LIVES AROUND THERE. HE TOLD ME ABOUT IT.
THEY'RE BRINGING IN HEAVY CONSTRUCTION EQUIPMENT.
I HEARD THAT MOUNTAIN IS STILL ERODING EVEN NOW.
THE TALKS BETWEEN THE DEVELOPMENT COMPANY AND PEOPLE IN THE SURROUNDING AREAS...
...ABOUT CONSTRUCTION IN THE NORTHERN MOUNTAINS ARE STILL ONGOING.
WOULD THEY START WORK WITHOUT WARNING?
GURRN
GURRN
GURRN
GURRN

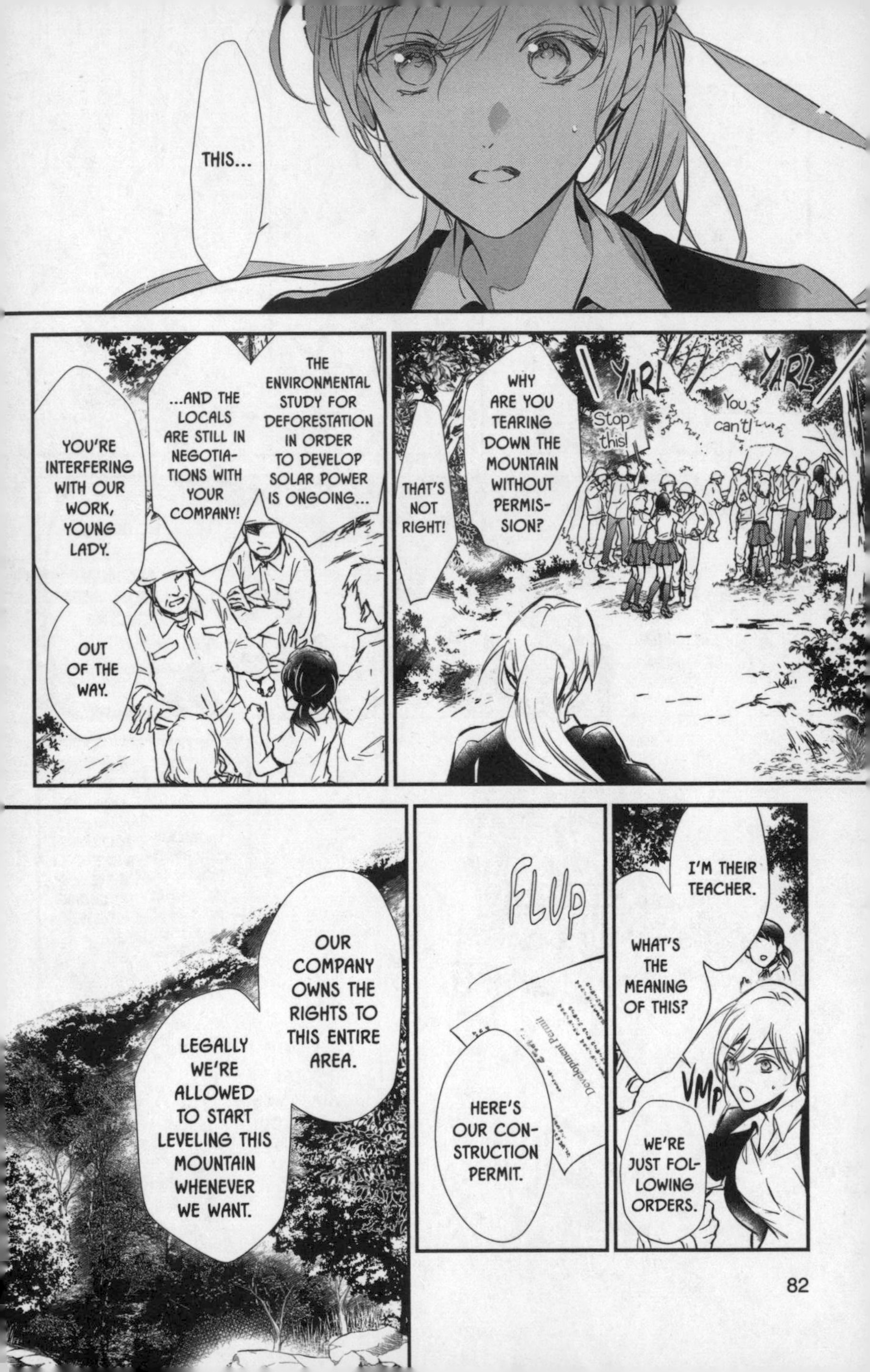
THIS...
YARL
You can't!
YARL
Stop this!
WHY ARE YOU TEARING DOWN THE MOUNTAIN WITHOUT PERMISSION?
THAT'S NOT RIGHT!
THE ENVIRONMENTAL STUDY FOR DEFORESTATION IN ORDER TO DEVELOP SOLAR POWER IS ONGOING...
...AND THE LOCALS ARE STILL IN NEGOTIATIONS WITH YOUR COMPANY!
YOU'RE INTERFERING WITH OUR WORK, YOUNG LADY.
OUT OF THE WAY.
I'M THEIR TEACHER.
WHAT'S THE MEANING OF THIS?
VMP
WE'RE JUST FOLLOWING ORDERS.
FLUP
Development Permit
HERE'S OUR CONSTRUCTION PERMIT.
OUR COMPANY OWNS THE RIGHTS TO THIS ENTIRE AREA.
LEGALLY WE'RE ALLOWED TO START LEVELING THIS MOUNTAIN WHENEVER WE WANT.

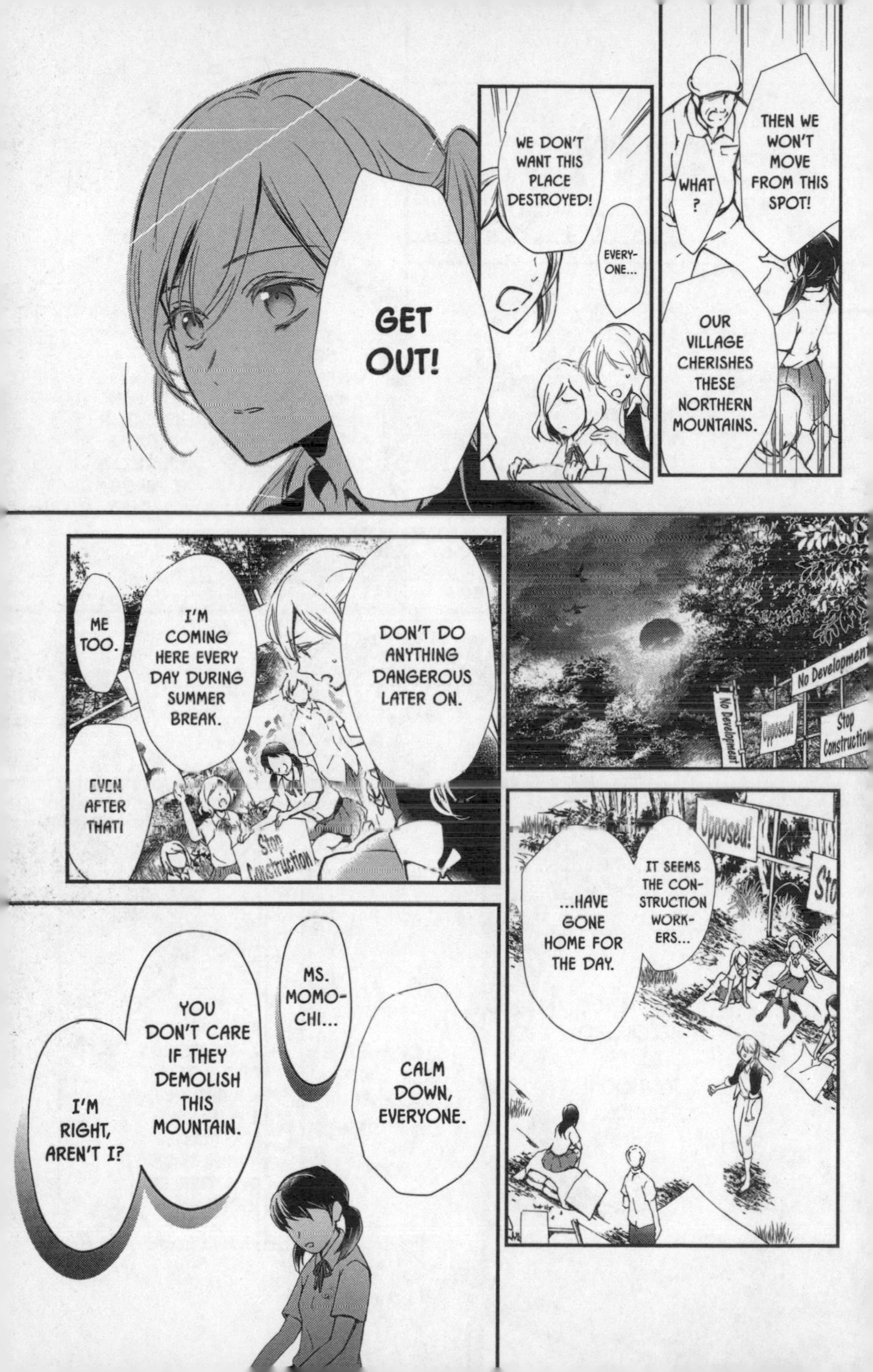
THEN WE WON'T MOVE FROM THIS SPOT!
WHAT?
OUR VILLAGE CHERISHES THESE NORTHERN MOUNTAINS.
WE DON'T WANT THIS PLACE DESTROYED!
EVERY-ONE...
GET OUT!
No Development
Stop Construction
Opposed!
No Development
IT SEEMS THE CON-STRUCTION WORK-ERS...
...HAVE GONE HOME FOR THE DAY.
Opposed!
DON'T DO ANYTHING DANGEROUS LATER ON.
I'M COMING HERE EVERY DAY DURING SUMMER BREAK.
ME TOO.
EVEN AFTER THAT!
Stop Construction
CALM DOWN, EVERYONE.
MS. MOMO-CHI...
YOU DON'T CARE IF THEY DEMOLISH THIS MOUNTAIN.
I'M RIGHT, AREN'T I?

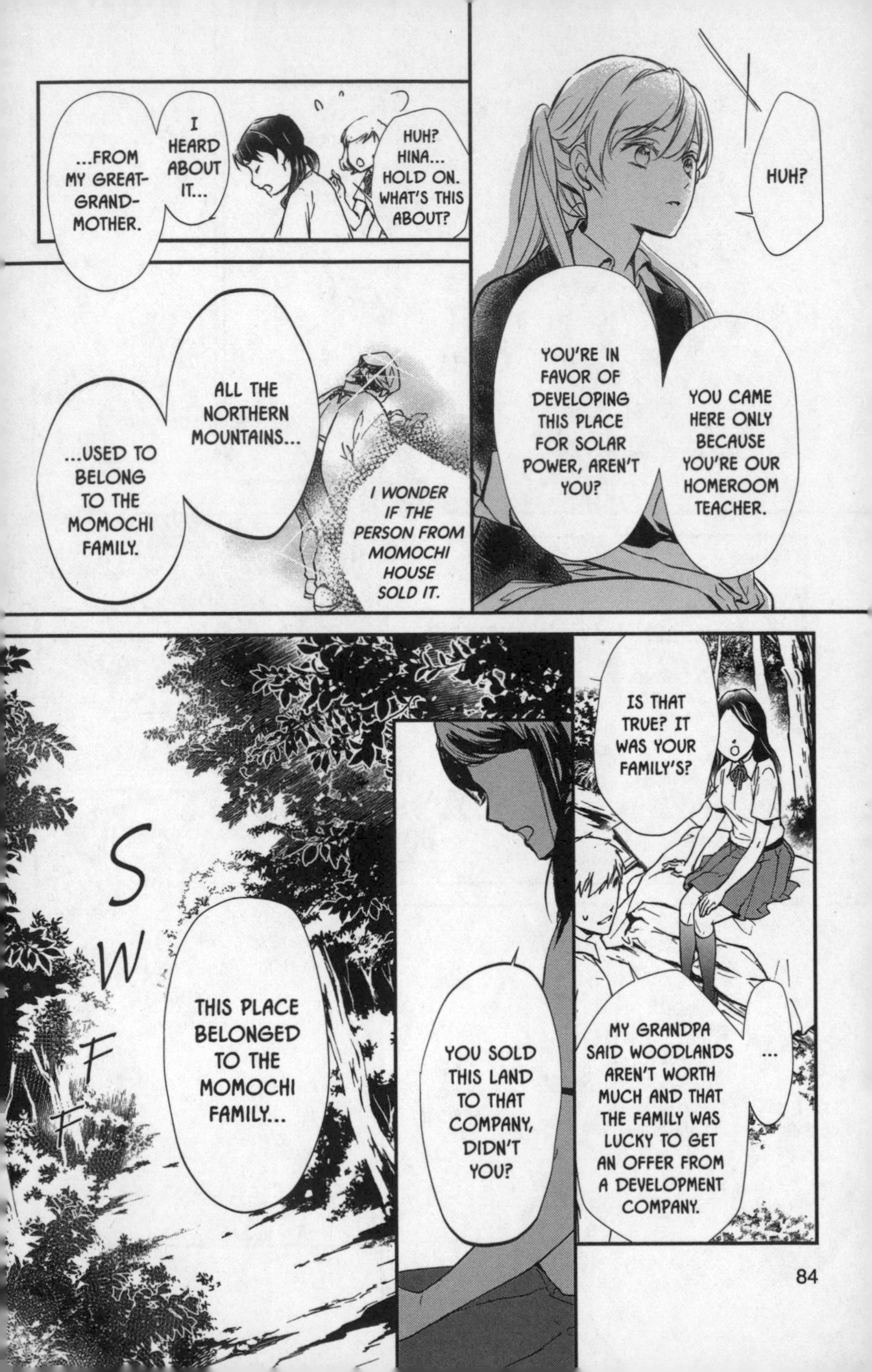
HUH?
YOU CAME HERE ONLY BECAUSE YOU'RE OUR HOMEROOM TEACHER.
YOU'RE IN FAVOR OF DEVELOPING THIS PLACE FOR SOLAR POWER, AREN'T YOU?
HUH? HINA... HOLD ON. WHAT'S THIS ABOUT?
I HEARD ABOUT IT...
...FROM MY GREAT-GRANDMOTHER.
ALL THE NORTHERN MOUNTAINS...
...USED TO BELONG TO THE MOMOCHI FAMILY.
I WONDER IF THE PERSON FROM MOMOCHI HOUSE SOLD IT.
IS THAT TRUE? IT WAS YOUR FAMILY'S?
...
MY GRANDPA SAID WOODLANDS AREN'T WORTH MUCH AND THAT THE FAMILY WAS LUCKY TO GET AN OFFER FROM A DEVELOPMENT COMPANY.
YOU SOLD THIS LAND TO THAT COMPANY, DIDN'T YOU?
SWFF
THIS PLACE BELONGED TO THE MOMOCHI FAMILY...

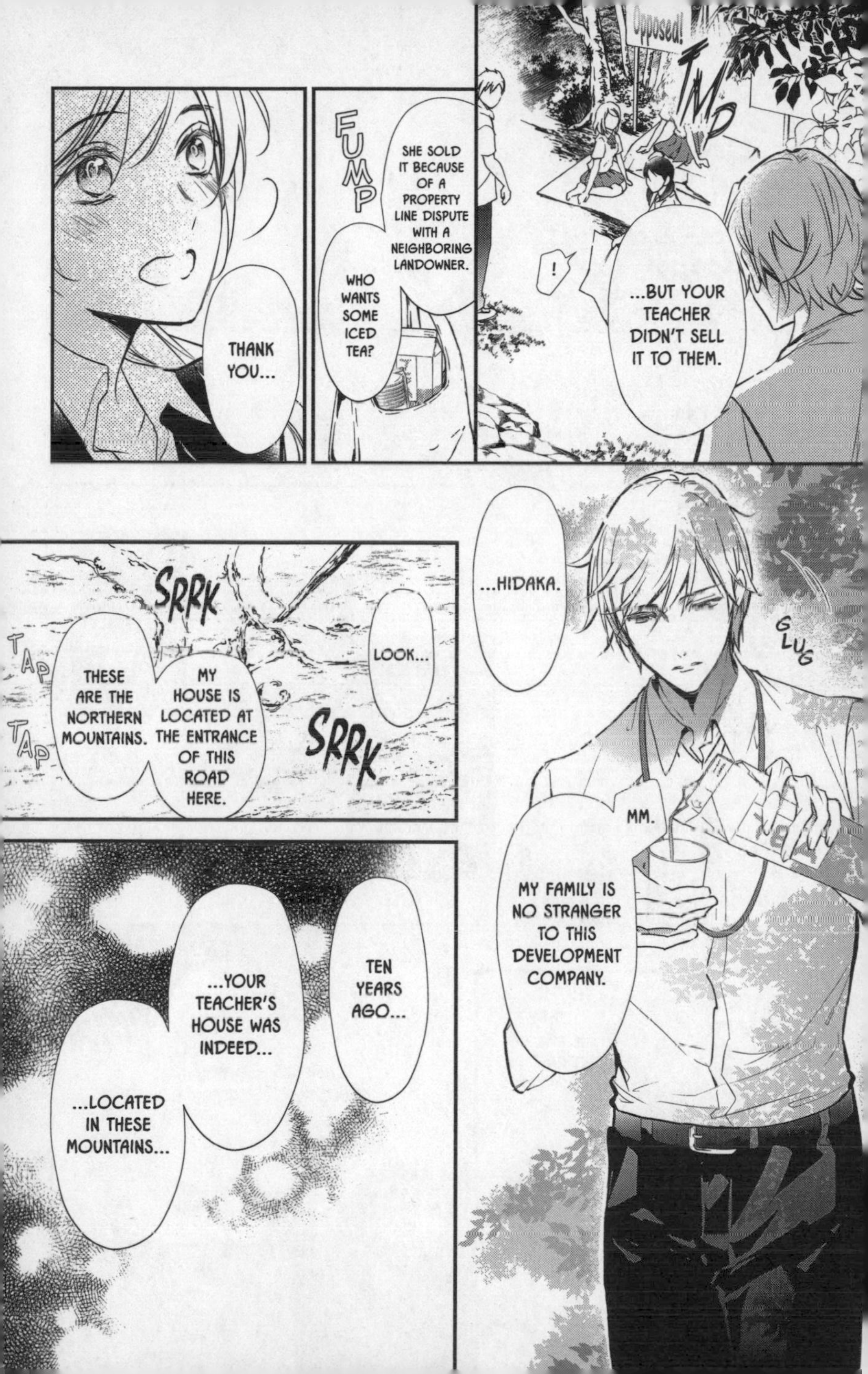
Opposed!
TMP
!
...BUT YOUR TEACHER DIDN'T SELL IT TO THEM.
FUMP
SHE SOLD IT BECAUSE OF A PROPERTY LINE DISPUTE WITH A NEIGHBORING LANDOWNER.
WHO WANTS SOME ICED TEA?
THANK YOU...
...HIDAKA.
GLUG
MM.
MY FAMILY IS NO STRANGER TO THIS DEVELOPMENT COMPANY.
LOOK...
SRRK
SRRK
MY HOUSE IS LOCATED AT THE ENTRANCE OF THIS ROAD HERE.
THESE ARE THE NORTHERN MOUNTAINS.
TAP
TAP
TEN YEARS AGO...
...YOUR TEACHER'S HOUSE WAS INDEED...
...LOCATED IN THESE MOUNTAINS...

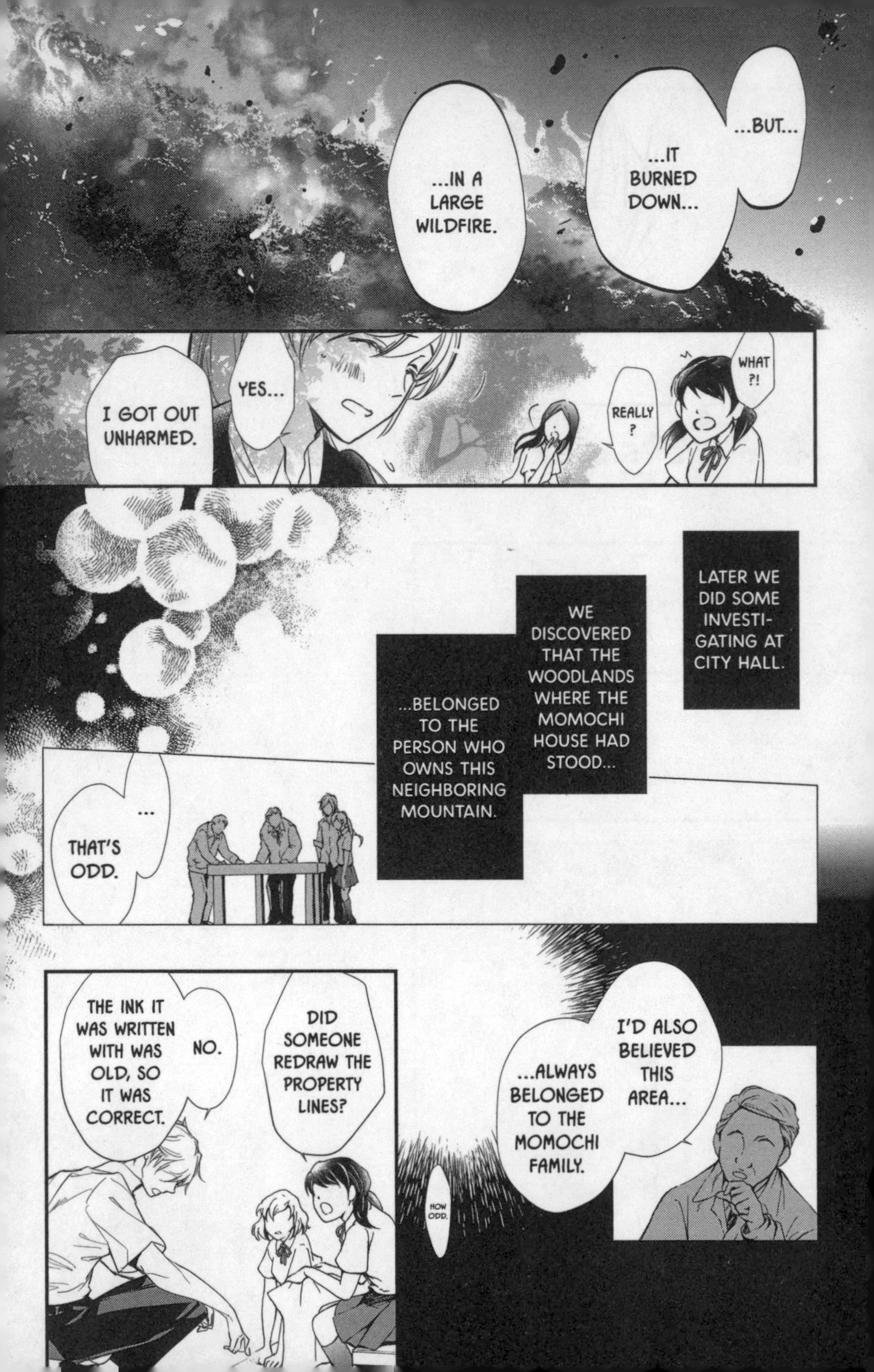
...BUT...
...IT BURNED DOWN...
...IN A LARGE WILDFIRE.
WHAT ?!
REALLY ?
YES...
I GOT OUT UNHARMED.
LATER WE DID SOME INVESTIGATING AT CITY HALL.
WE DISCOVERED THAT THE WOODLANDS WHERE THE MOMOCHI HOUSE HAD STOOD...
...BELONGED TO THE PERSON WHO OWNS THIS NEIGHBORING MOUNTAIN.
... THAT'S ODD.
I'D ALSO BELIEVED THIS AREA...
...ALWAYS BELONGED TO THE MOMOCHI FAMILY.
HOW ODD.
DID SOMEONE REDRAW THE PROPERTY LINES?
NO.
THE INK IT WAS WRITTEN WITH WAS OLD, SO IT WAS CORRECT.

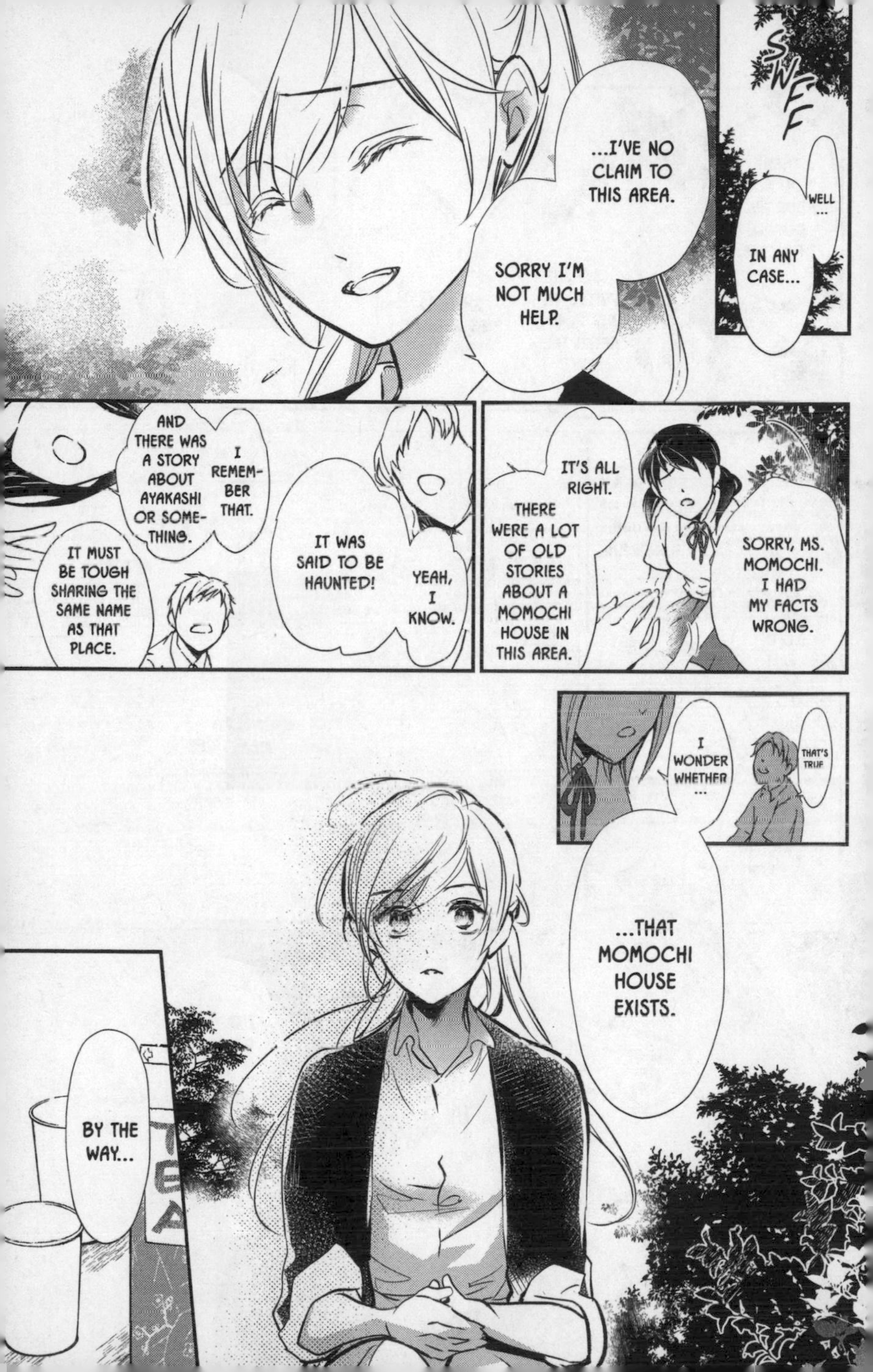
SNFF
WELL ...
IN ANY CASE...
...I'VE NO CLAIM TO THIS AREA.
SORRY I'M NOT MUCH HELP.
SORRY, MS. MOMOCHI. I HAD MY FACTS WRONG.
IT'S ALL RIGHT.
THERE WERE A LOT OF OLD STORIES ABOUT A MOMOCHI HOUSE IN THIS AREA.
YEAH, I KNOW.
IT WAS SAID TO BE HAUNTED!
I REMEMBER THAT.
AND THERE WAS A STORY ABOUT AYAKASHI OR SOMETHING.
IT MUST BE TOUGH SHARING THE SAME NAME AS THAT PLACE.
THAT'S TRUE
I WONDER WHETHER ...
...THAT MOMOCHI HOUSE EXISTS.
BY THE WAY...
TEA

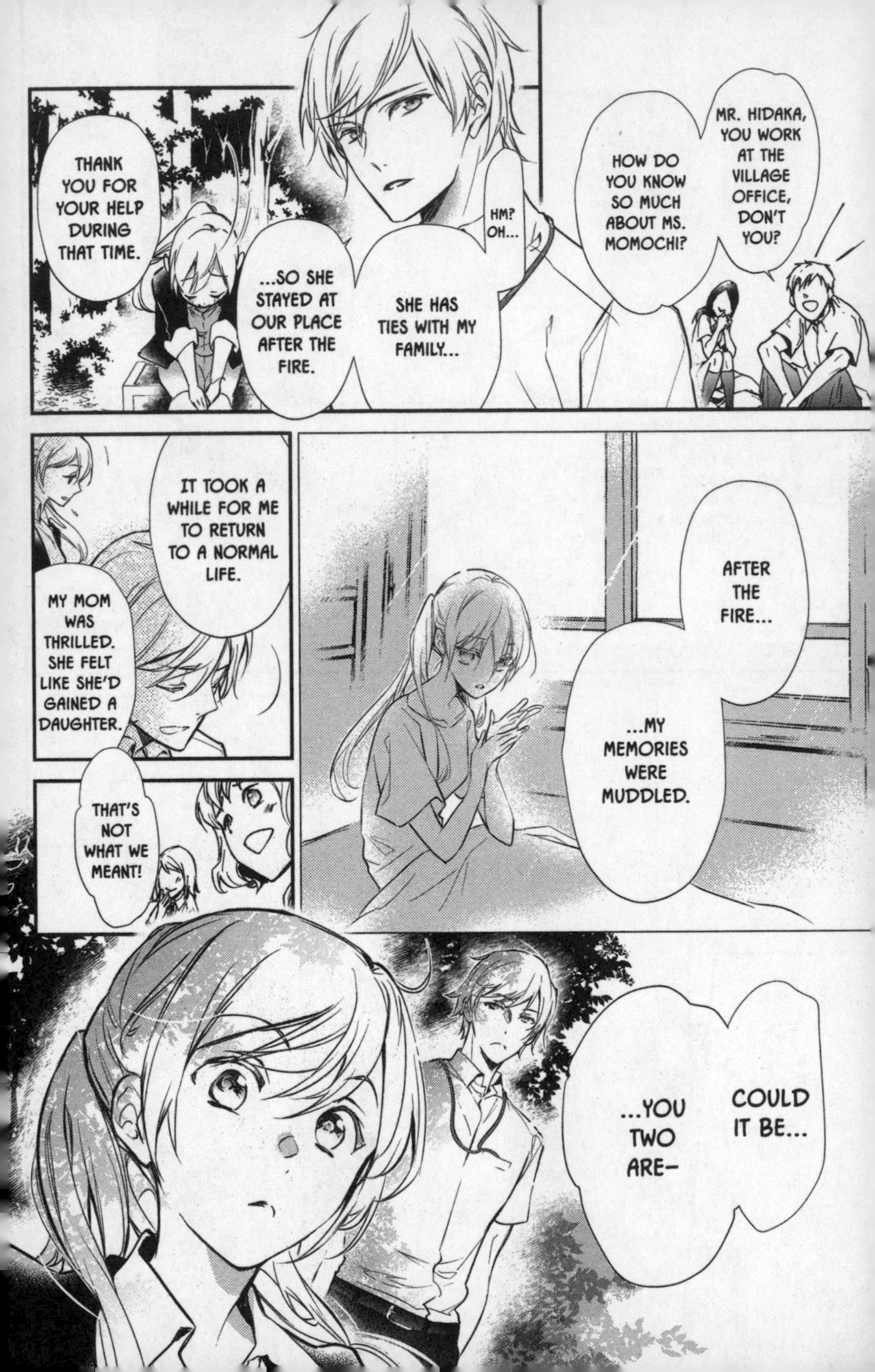
MR. HIDAKA, YOU WORK AT THE VILLAGE OFFICE, DON'T YOU?
HOW DO YOU KNOW SO MUCH ABOUT MS. MOMOCHI?
HM? OH...
SHE HAS TIES WITH MY FAMILY...
...SO SHE STAYED AT OUR PLACE AFTER THE FIRE.
THANK YOU FOR YOUR HELP DURING THAT TIME.
AFTER THE FIRE...
...MY MEMORIES WERE MUDDLED.
IT TOOK A WHILE FOR ME TO RETURN TO A NORMAL LIFE.
MY MOM WAS THRILLED. SHE FELT LIKE SHE'D GAINED A DAUGHTER.
THAT'S NOT WHAT WE MEANT!
COULD IT BE...
...YOU TWO ARE–

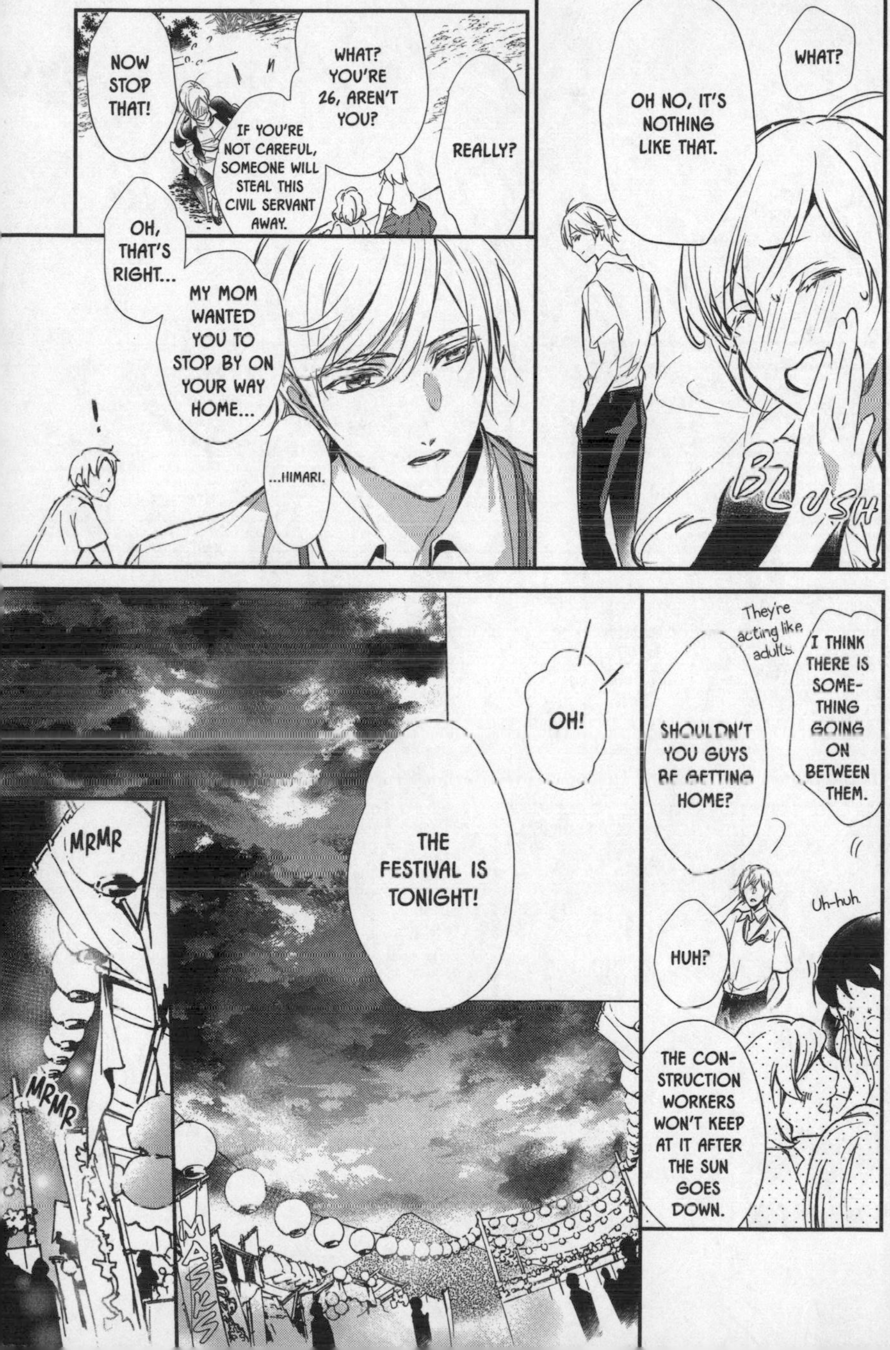
WHAT?
OH NO, IT'S NOTHING LIKE THAT.
BLUSH
REALLY?
WHAT? YOU'RE 26, AREN'T YOU?
IF YOU'RE NOT CAREFUL, SOMEONE WILL STEAL THIS CIVIL SERVANT AWAY.
NOW STOP THAT!
OH, THAT'S RIGHT...
MY MOM WANTED YOU TO STOP BY ON YOUR WAY HOME...
...HIMARI.
!
They're acting like adults.
I THINK THERE IS SOME-THING GOING ON BETWEEN THEM.
SHOULDN'T YOU GUYS BE GETTING HOME?
Uh-huh.
HUH?
THE CON-STRUCTION WORKERS WON'T KEEP AT IT AFTER THE SUN GOES DOWN.
OH!
THE FESTIVAL IS TONIGHT!
MRMR
MRMR
MASKS

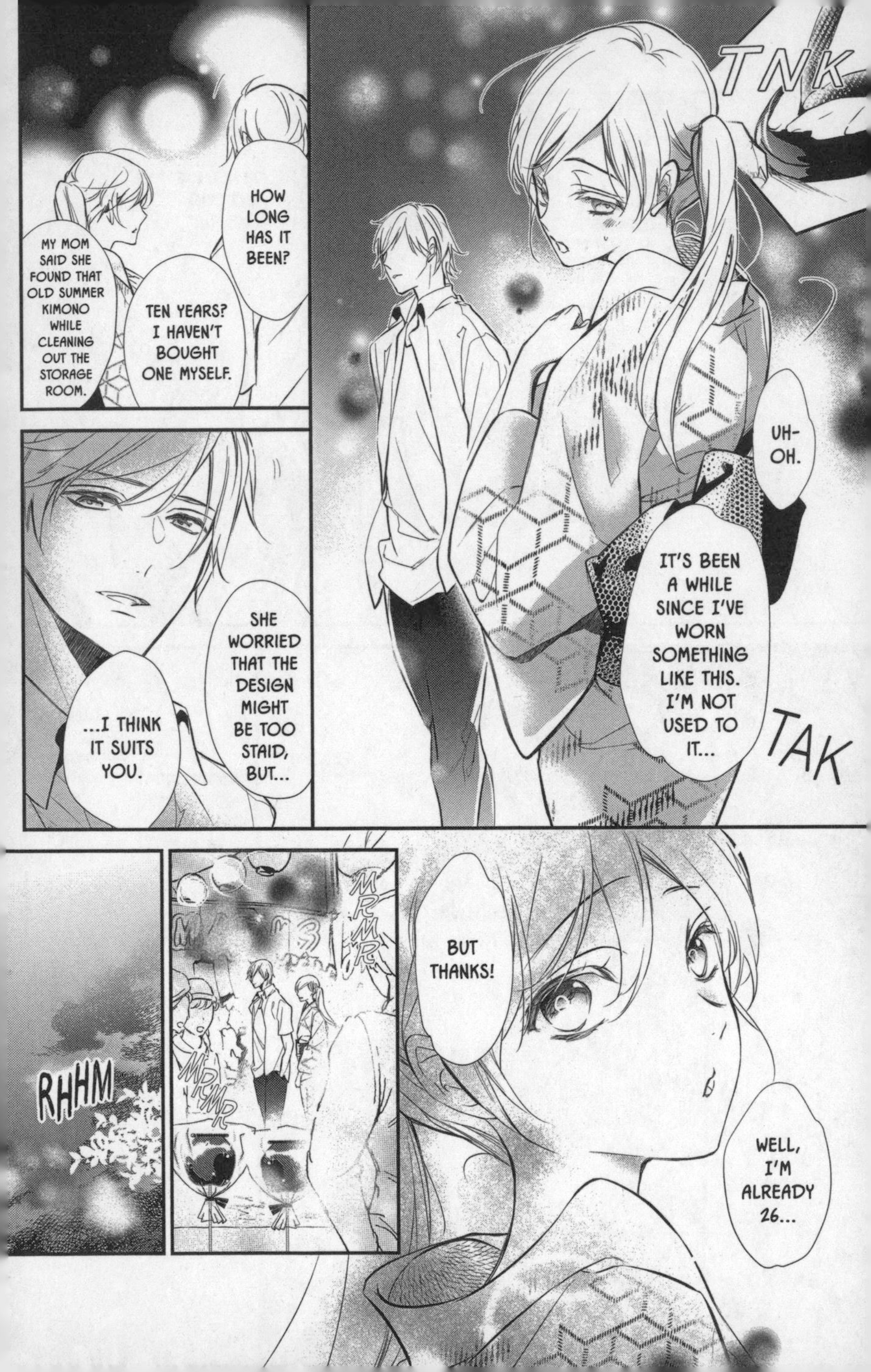
TNK
UH-OH.
IT'S BEEN A WHILE SINCE I'VE WORN SOMETHING LIKE THIS. I'M NOT USED TO IT...
TAK
HOW LONG HAS IT BEEN?
TEN YEARS? I HAVEN'T BOUGHT ONE MYSELF.
MY MOM SAID SHE FOUND THAT OLD SUMMER KIMONO WHILE CLEANING OUT THE STORAGE ROOM.
SHE WORRIED THAT THE DESIGN MIGHT BE TOO STAID, BUT...
...I THINK IT SUITS YOU.
WELL, I'M ALREADY 26...
BUT THANKS!
MRMR
MRMR
RHHM

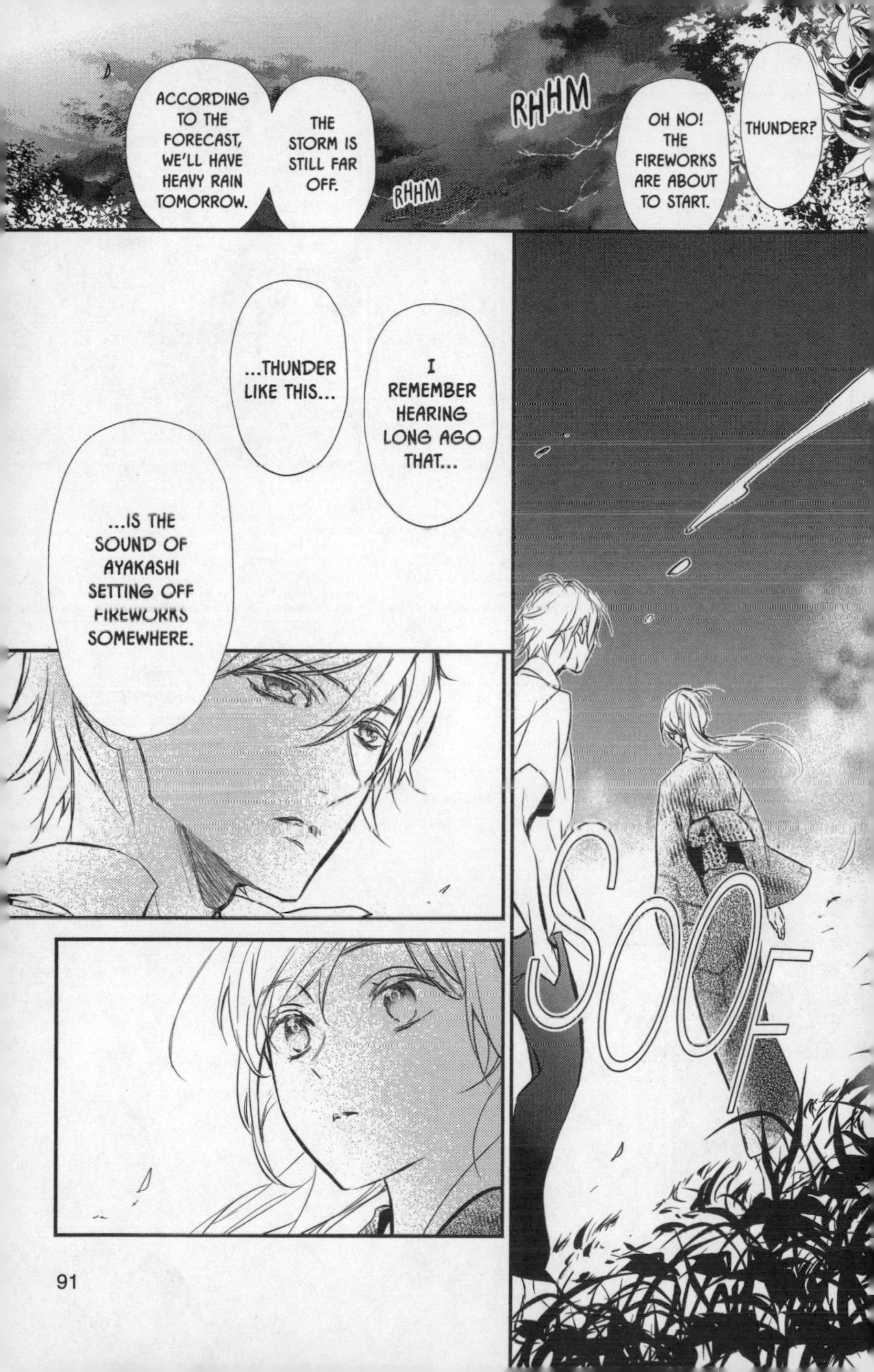
THUNDER?
OH NO! THE FIREWORKS ARE ABOUT TO START.
RHHM
RHHM
THE STORM IS STILL FAR OFF.
ACCORDING TO THE FORECAST, WE'LL HAVE HEAVY RAIN TOMORROW.
SOOF
I REMEMBER HEARING LONG AGO THAT...
...THUNDER LIKE THIS...
...IS THE SOUND OF AYAKASHI SETTING OFF FIREWORKS SOMEWHERE.

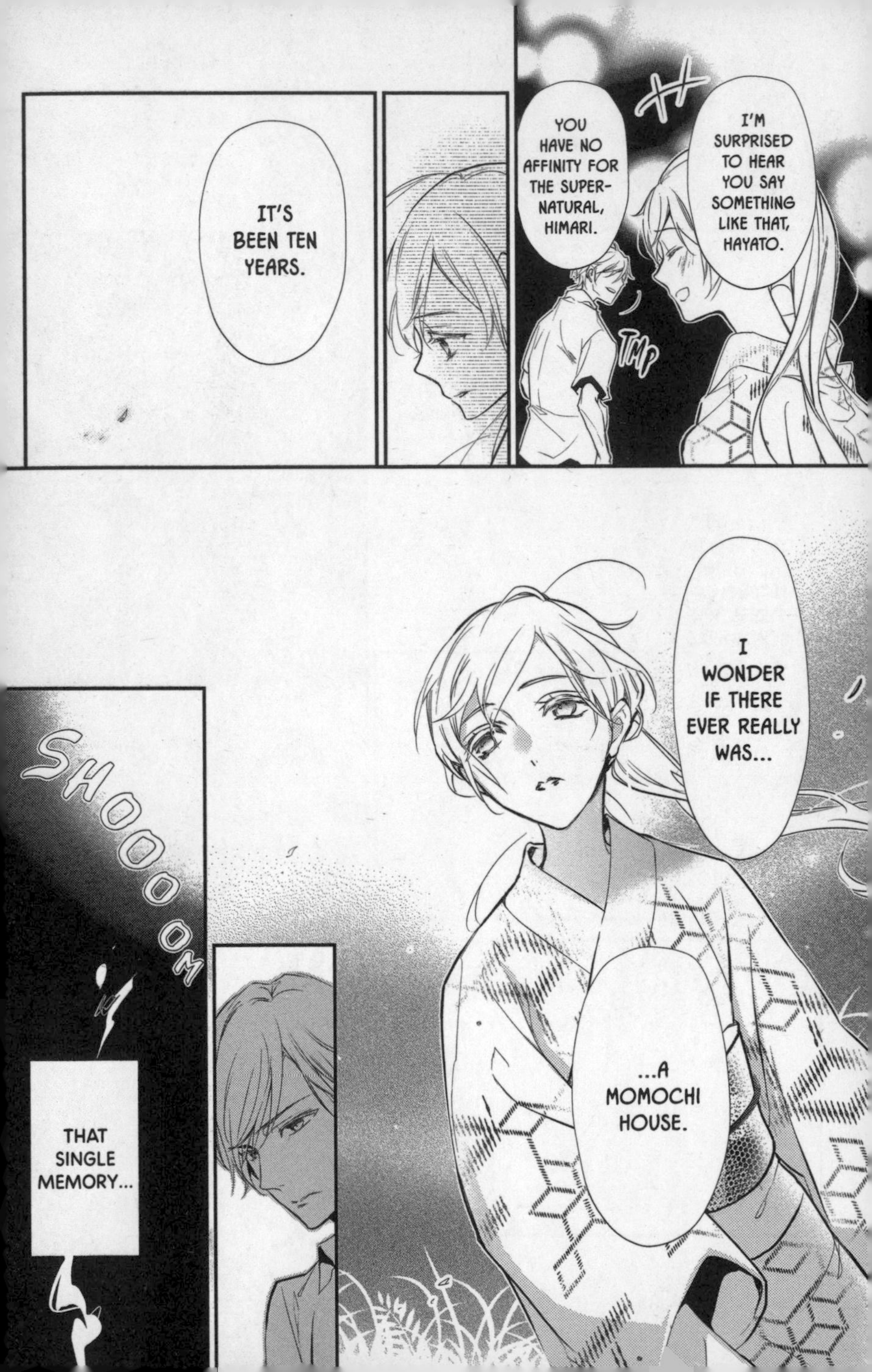
I'M SURPRISED TO HEAR YOU SAY SOMETHING LIKE THAT, HAYATO.
YOU HAVE NO AFFINITY FOR THE SUPER-NATURAL, HIMARI.
TMP
IT'S BEEN TEN YEARS.
I WONDER IF THERE EVER REALLY WAS...
...A MOMOCHI HOUSE.
SHOOOOOM
THAT SINGLE MEMORY...

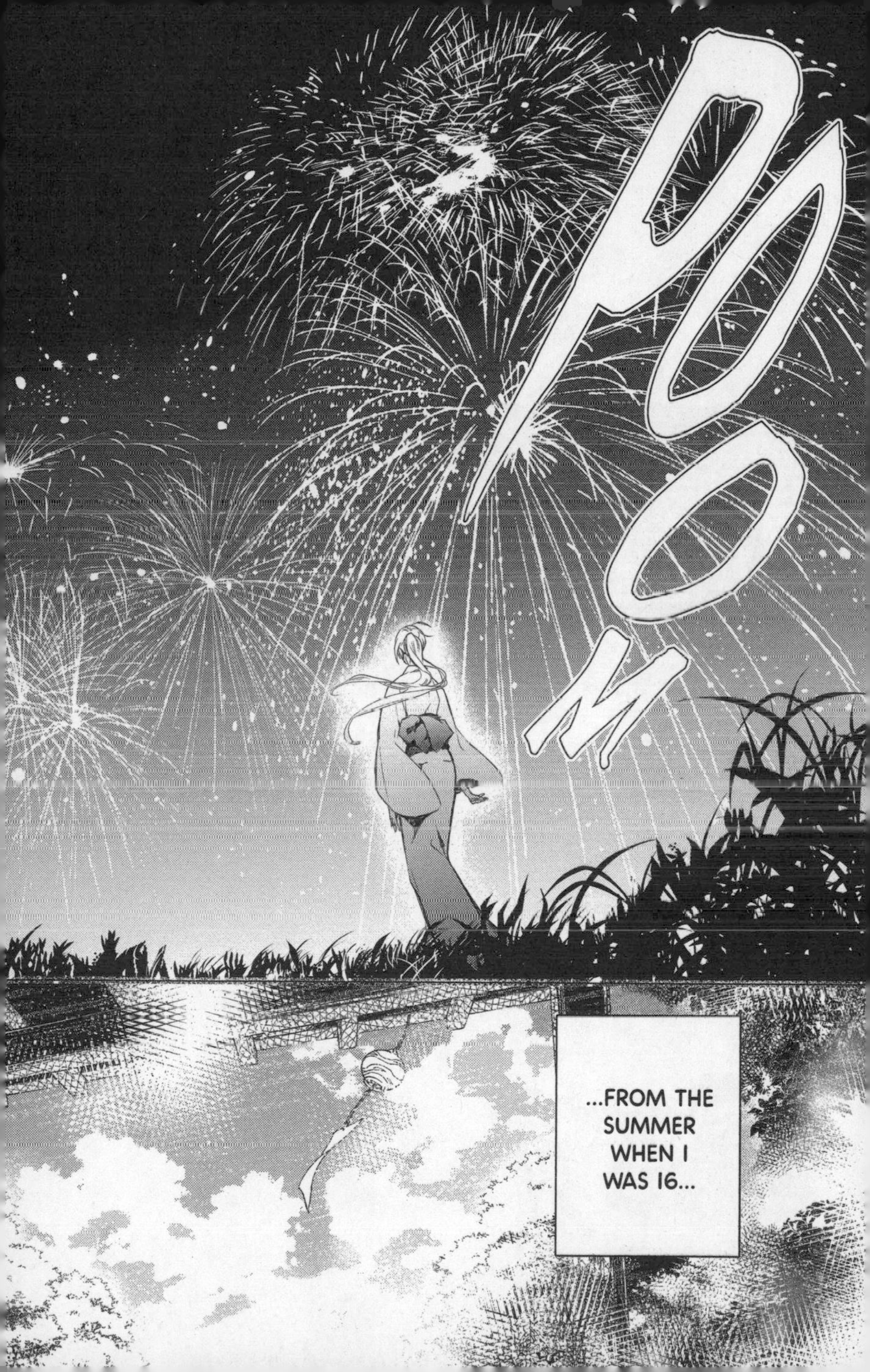
POOM
...FROM THE SUMMER WHEN I WAS 16...

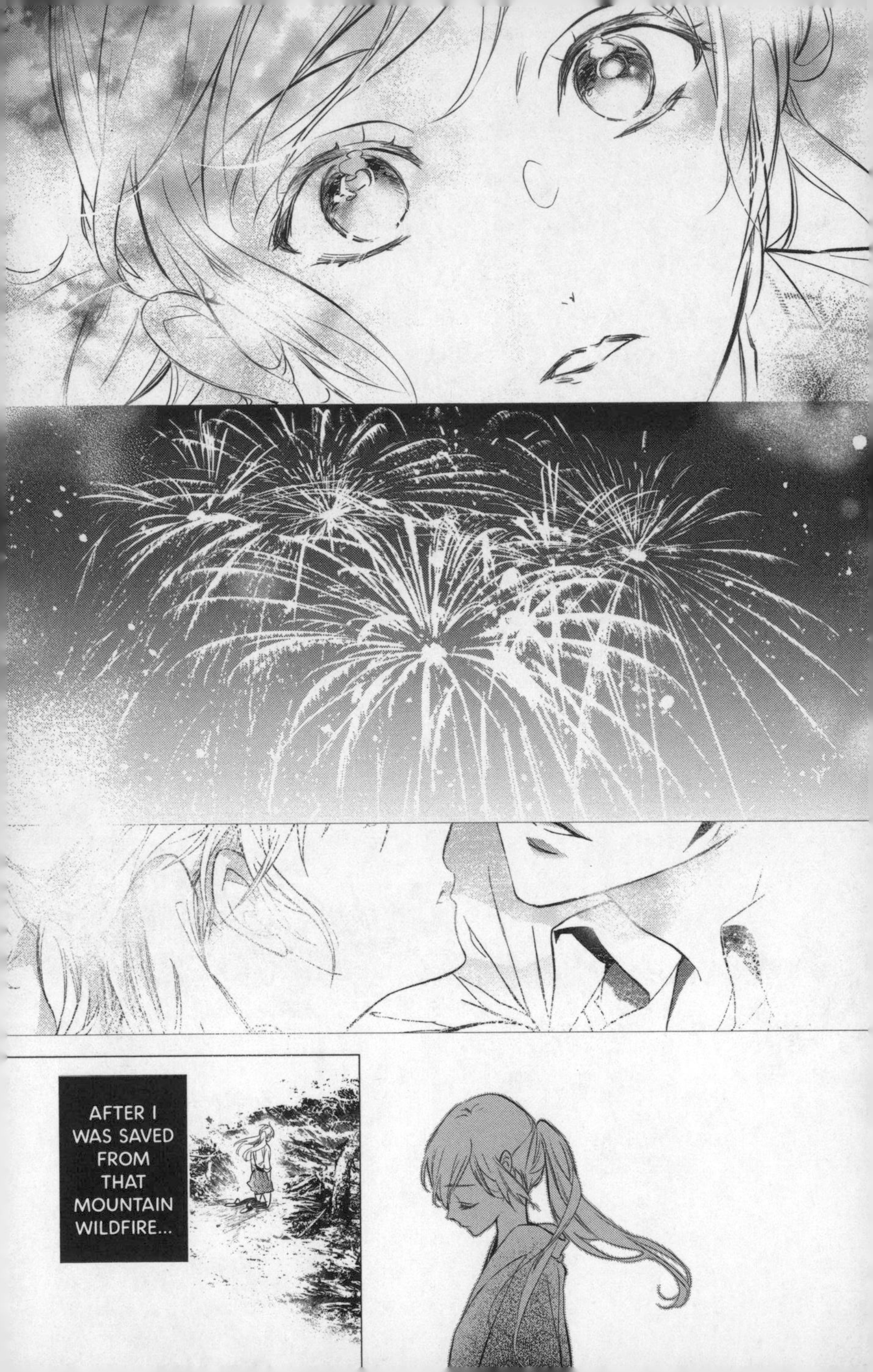
AFTER I WAS SAVED FROM THAT MOUNTAIN WILDFIRE...

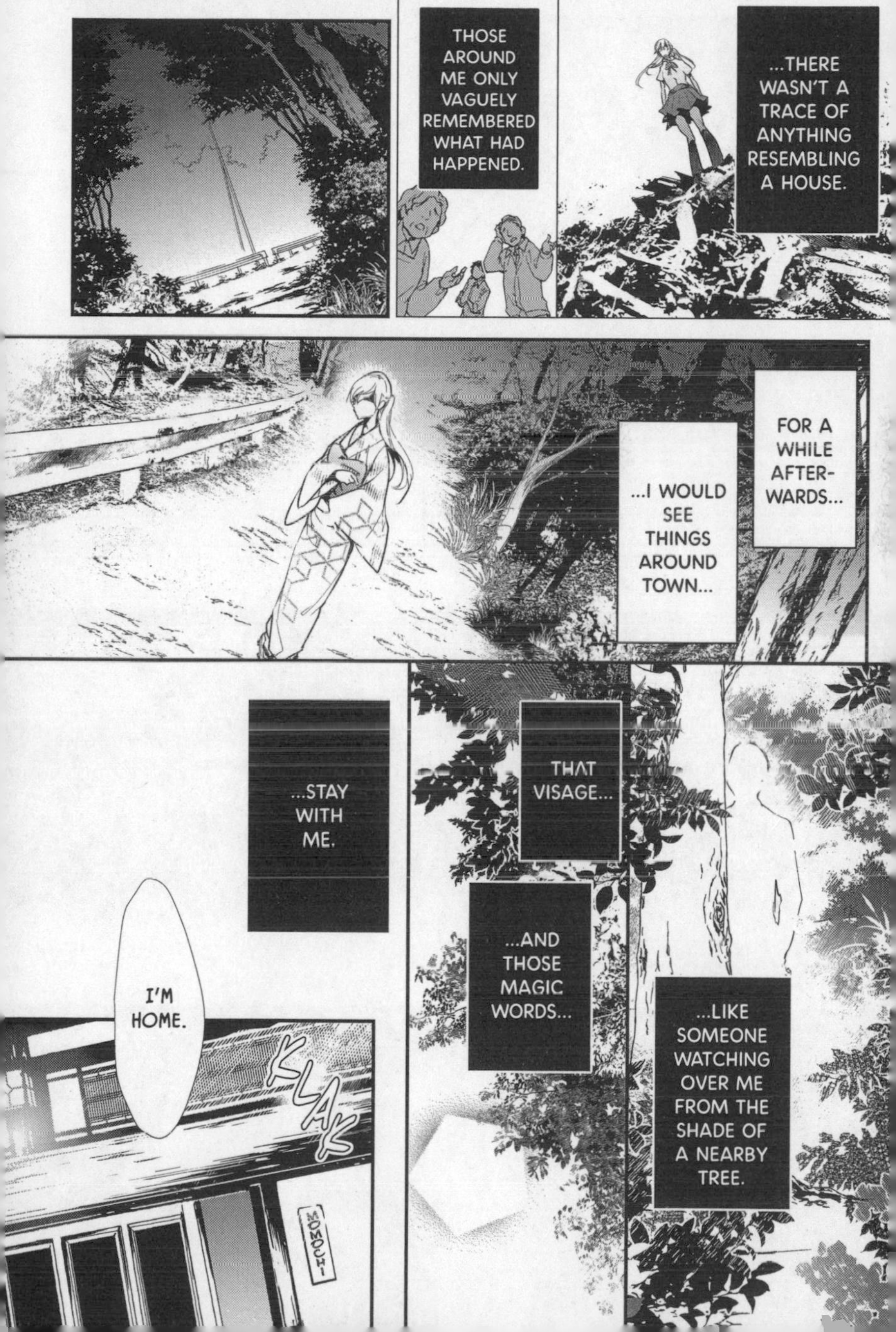
...THERE WASN'T A TRACE OF ANYTHING RESEMBLING A HOUSE.
THOSE AROUND ME ONLY VAGUELY REMEMBERED WHAT HAD HAPPENED.
FOR A WHILE AFTER- WARDS...
...I WOULD SEE THINGS AROUND TOWN...
...LIKE SOMEONE WATCHING OVER ME FROM THE SHADE OF A NEARBY TREE.
THAT VISAGE...
...AND THOSE MAGIC WORDS...
...STAY WITH ME.
I'M HOME.
KLAK
MOMOCHI

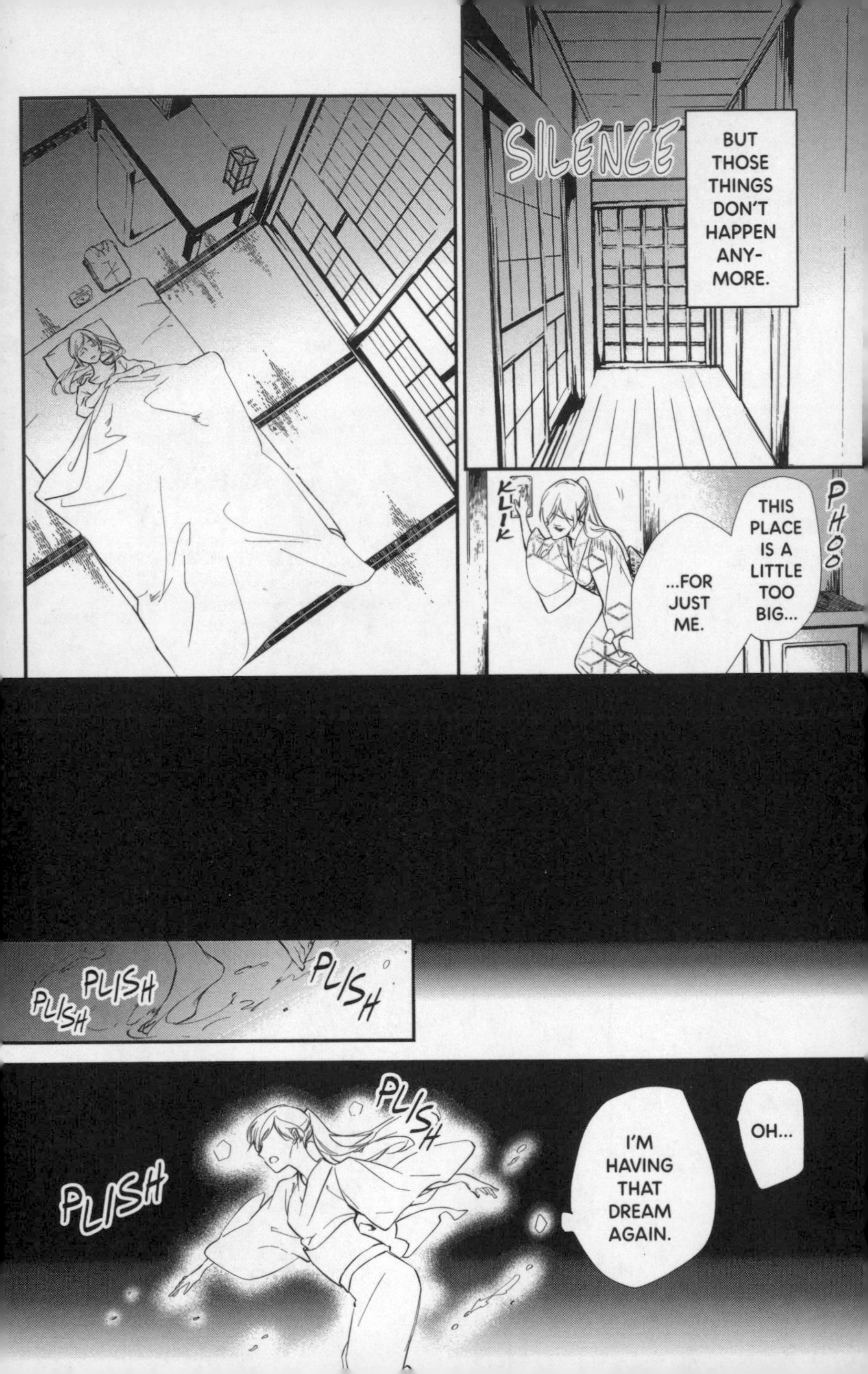
BUT THOSE THINGS DON'T HAPPEN ANYMORE.
SILENCE
PHOO
THIS PLACE IS A LITTLE TOO BIG...
...FOR JUST ME.
KLIK
PLISH
PLISH
PLISH
OH...
I'M HAVING THAT DREAM AGAIN.
PLISH
PLISH

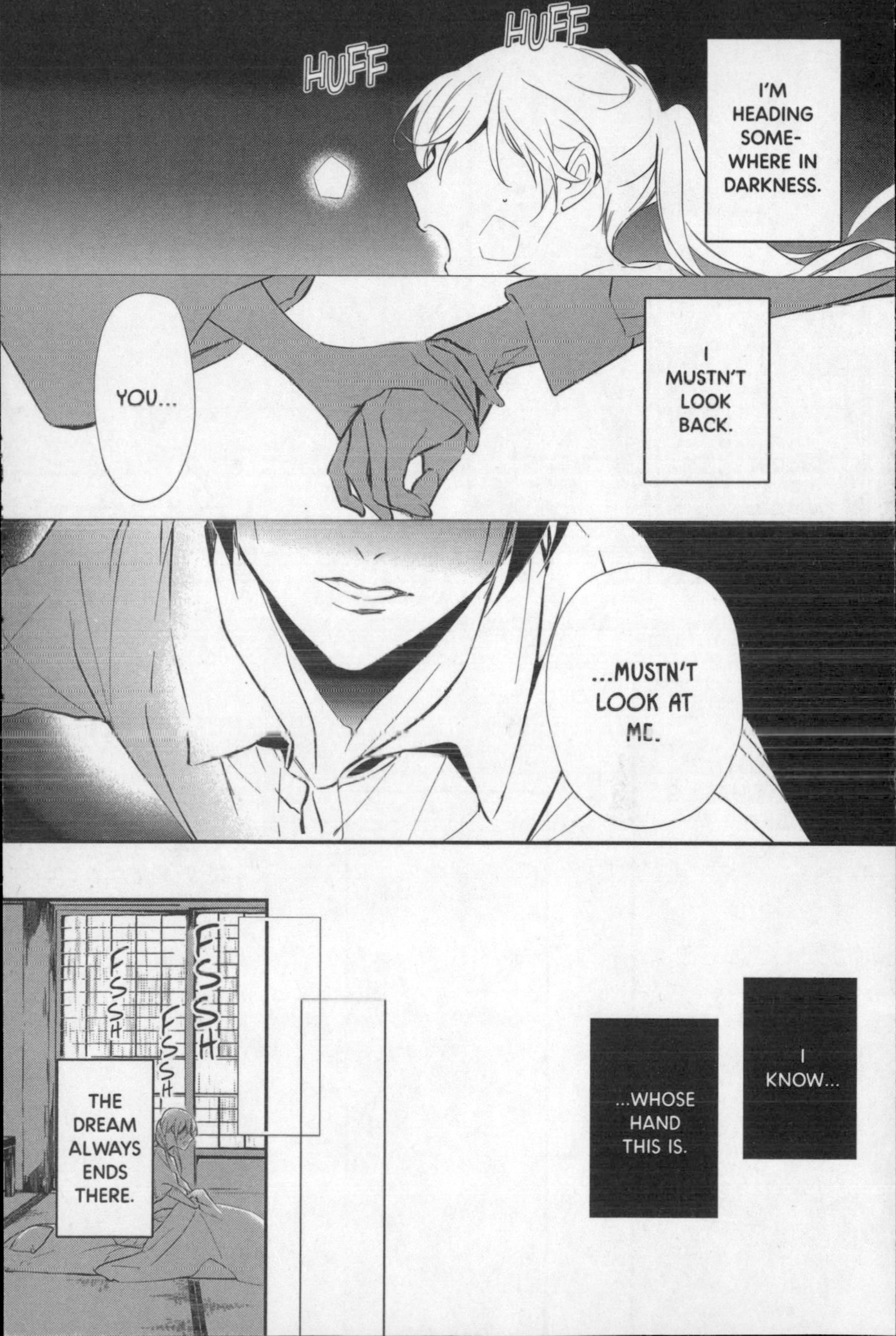
I'M HEADING SOMEWHERE IN DARKNESS.
HUFF
HUFF
I MUSTN'T LOOK BACK.
YOU...
...MUSTN'T LOOK AT ME.
I KNOW...
...WHOSE HAND THIS IS.
FSSH
FSSH
FSSH
THE DREAM ALWAYS ENDS THERE.

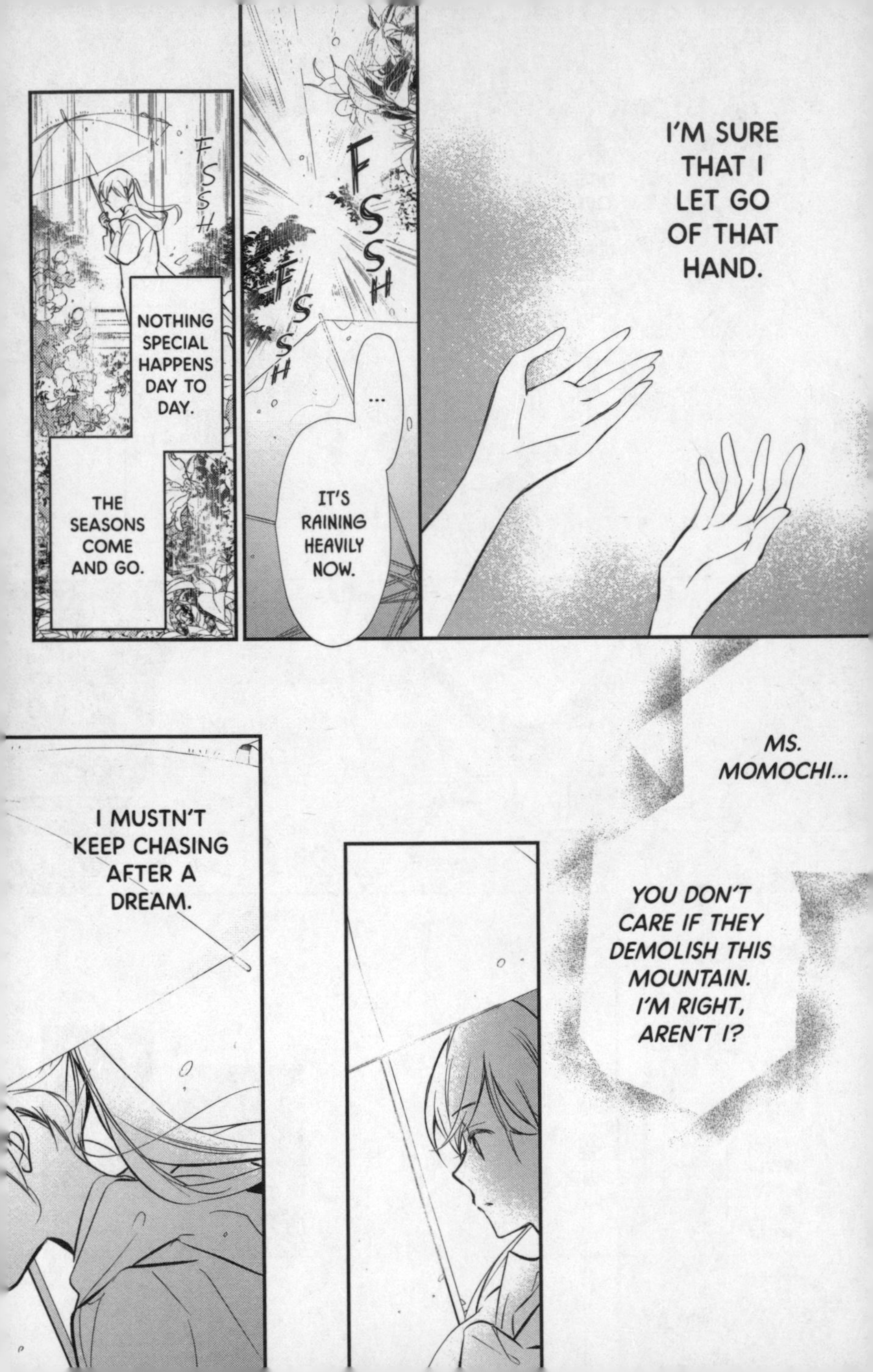
I'M SURE THAT I LET GO OF THAT HAND.
FSSH
...
IT'S RAINING HEAVILY NOW.
FSSH
FSSH
NOTHING SPECIAL HAPPENS DAY TO DAY.
THE SEASONS COME AND GO.
MS. MOMOCHI...
YOU DON'T CARE IF THEY DEMOLISH THIS MOUNTAIN. I'M RIGHT, AREN'T I?
I MUSTN'T KEEP CHASING AFTER A DREAM.

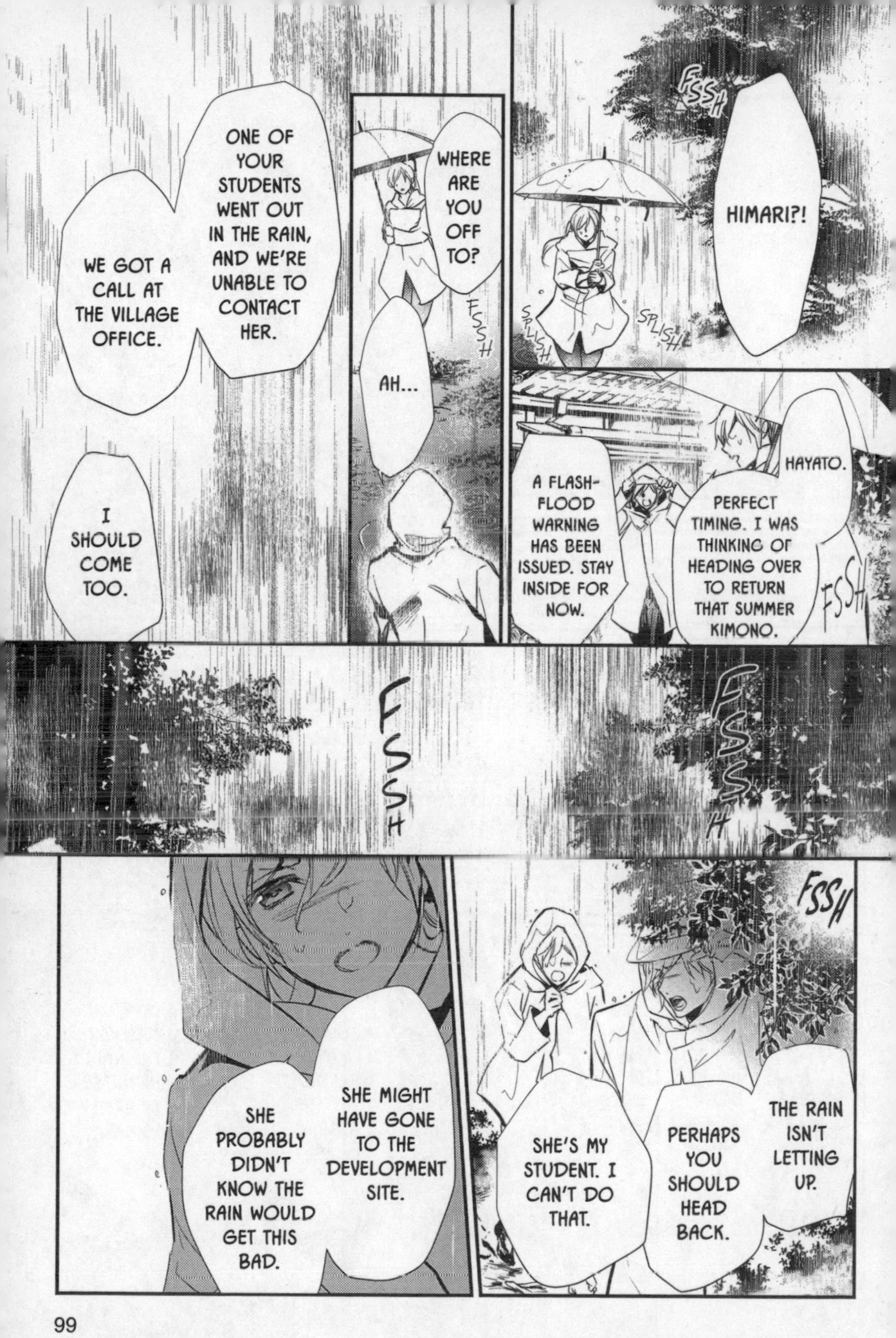
FSSH
HIMARI?!
SPLISH
SPLISH
HAYATO.
PERFECT TIMING. I WAS THINKING OF HEADING OVER TO RETURN THAT SUMMER KIMONO.
A FLASH-FLOOD WARNING HAS BEEN ISSUED. STAY INSIDE FOR NOW.
FSSH
WHERE ARE YOU OFF TO?
FSSH
AH...
ONE OF YOUR STUDENTS WENT OUT IN THE RAIN, AND WE'RE UNABLE TO CONTACT HER.
WE GOT A CALL AT THE VILLAGE OFFICE.
I SHOULD COME TOO.
FSSH
FSSH
FSSH
THE RAIN ISN'T LETTING UP.
PERHAPS YOU SHOULD HEAD BACK.
SHE'S MY STUDENT. I CAN'T DO THAT.
SHE MIGHT HAVE GONE TO THE DEVELOPMENT SITE.
SHE PROBABLY DIDN'T KNOW THE RAIN WOULD GET THIS BAD.

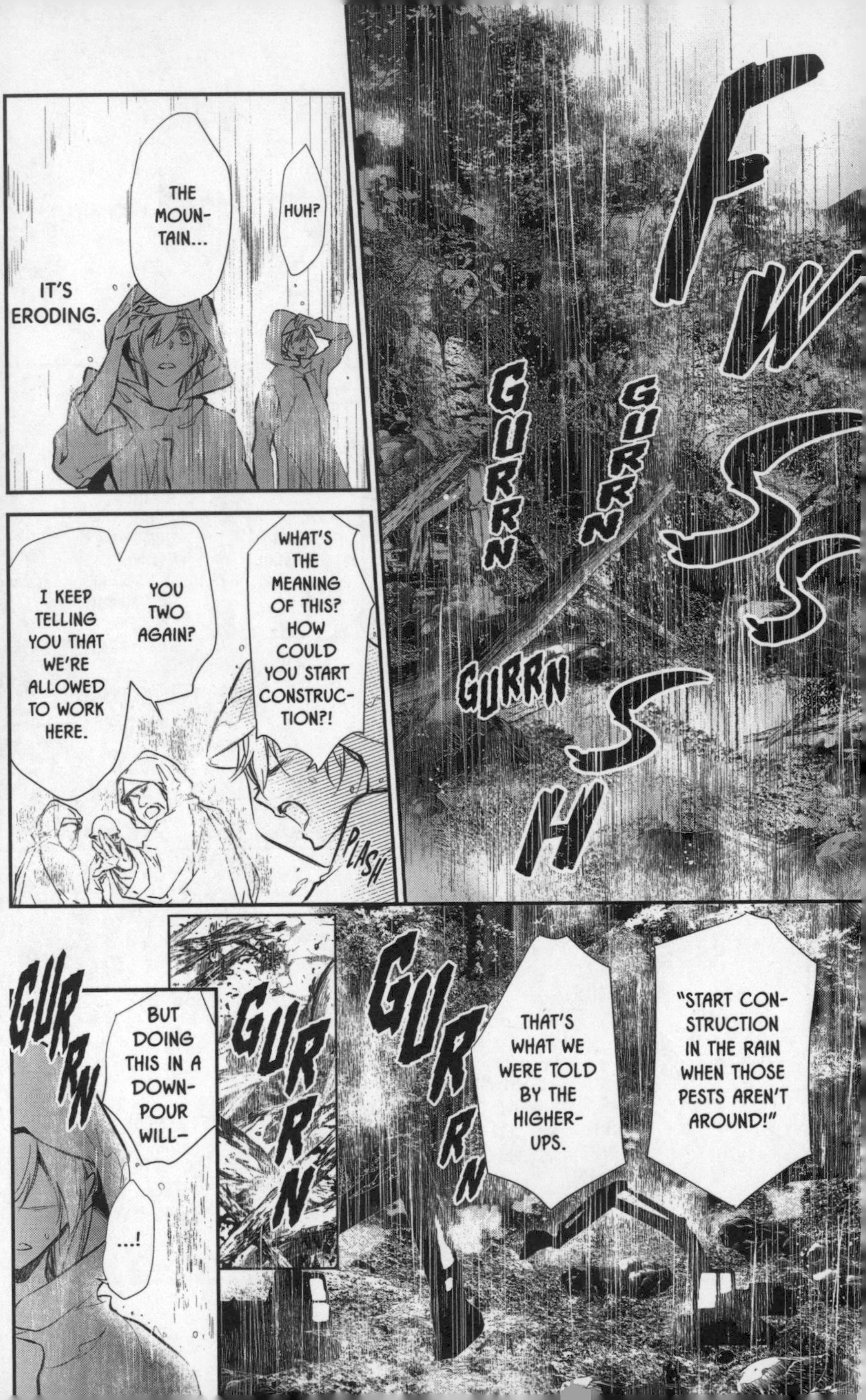
FWSSSH
GURRN
GURRN
GURRN
HUH?
THE MOUNTAIN...
IT'S ERODING.
WHAT'S THE MEANING OF THIS? HOW COULD YOU START CONSTRUCTION?!
YOU TWO AGAIN?
I KEEP TELLING YOU THAT WE'RE ALLOWED TO WORK HERE.
PLASH
"START CONSTRUCTION IN THE RAIN WHEN THOSE PESTS AREN'T AROUND!"
THAT'S WHAT WE WERE TOLD BY THE HIGHER-UPS.
GURRN
GURRN
GURRN
BUT DOING THIS IN A DOWNPOUR WILL—
...!

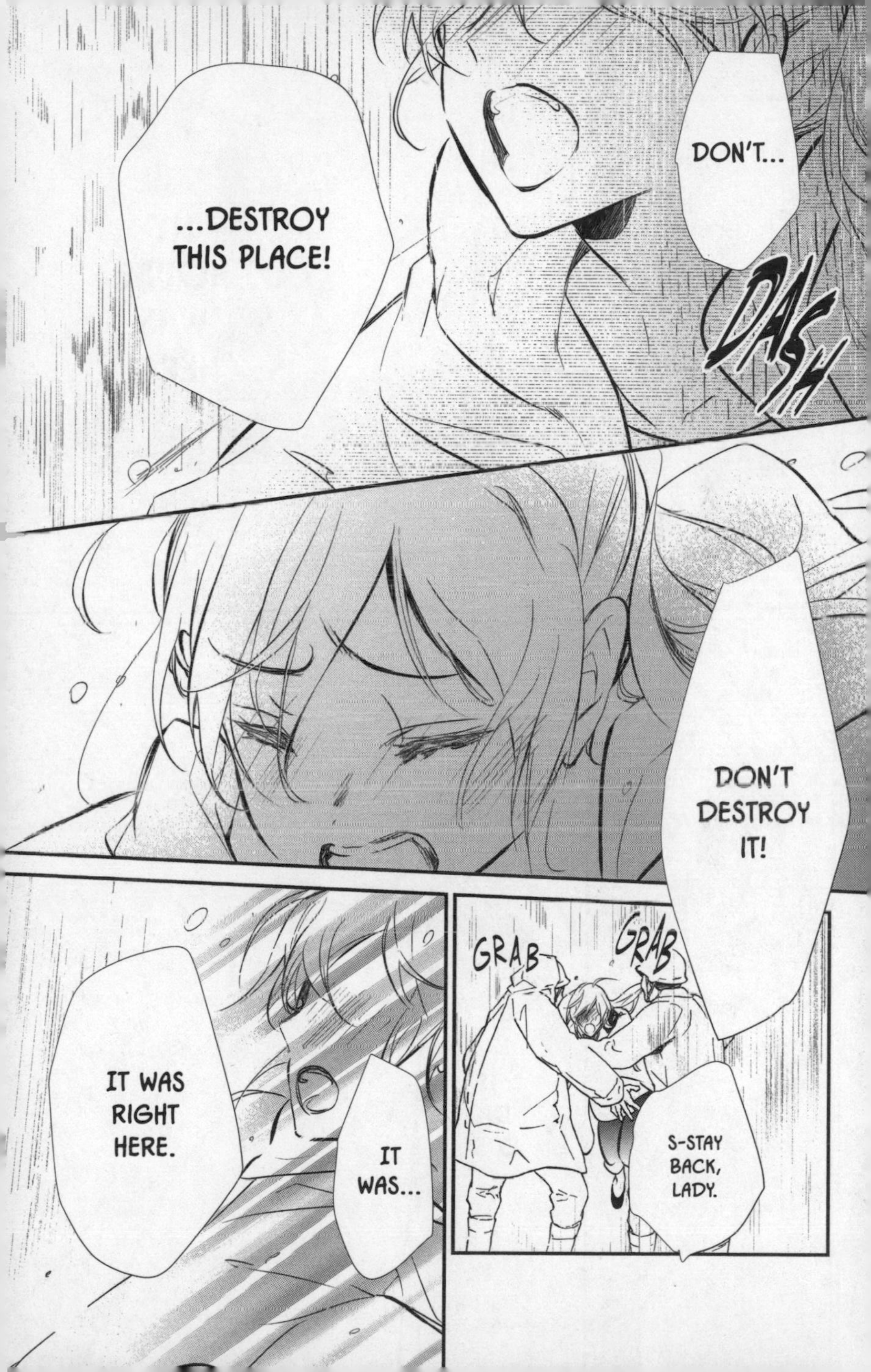
DON'T...
DASH
...DESTROY THIS PLACE!
DON'T DESTROY IT!
GRAB
GRAB
S-STAY BACK, LADY.
IT WAS...
IT WAS RIGHT HERE.

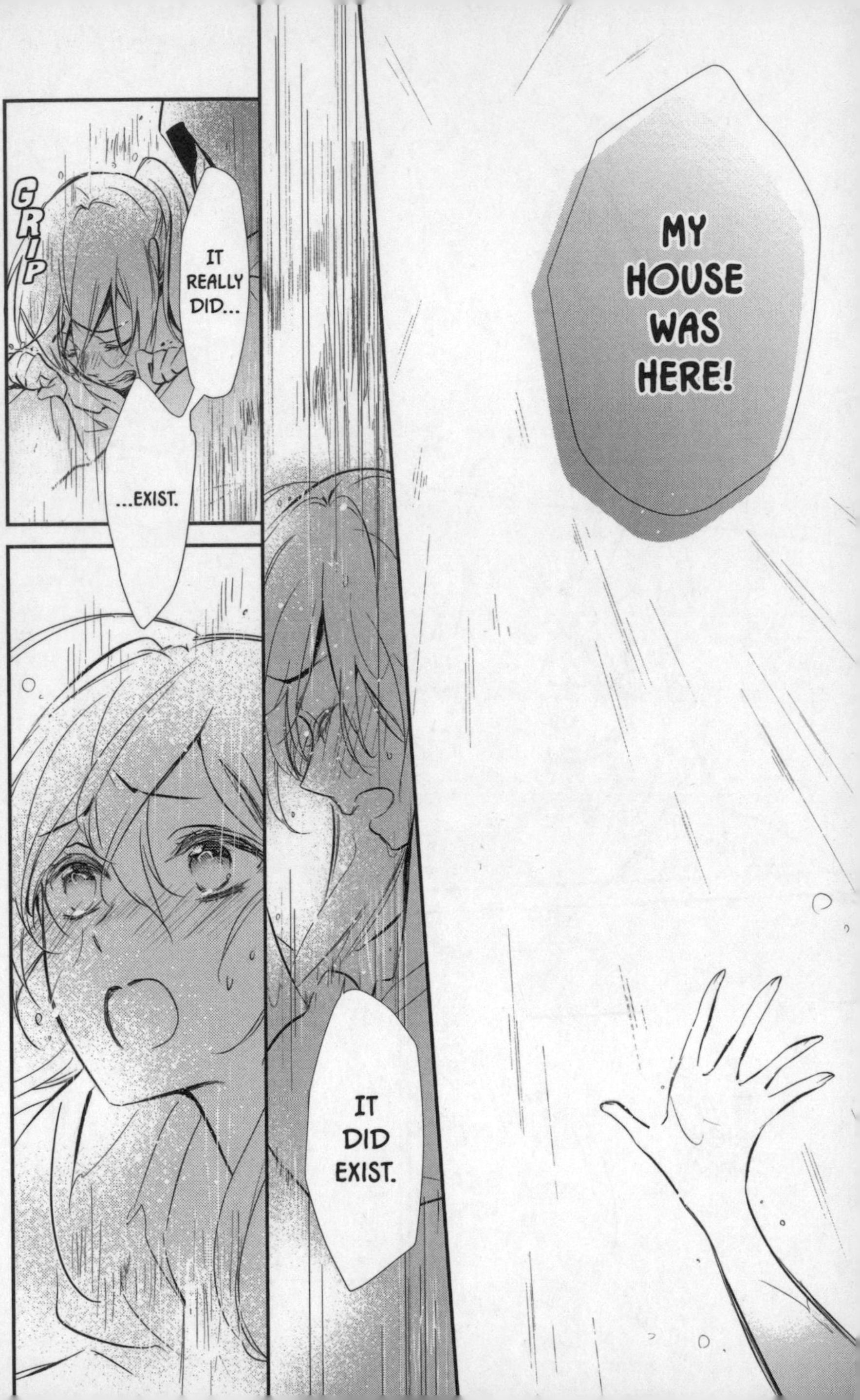
MY HOUSE WAS HERE!
IT DID EXIST.
GRIP
IT REALLY DID...
...EXIST.

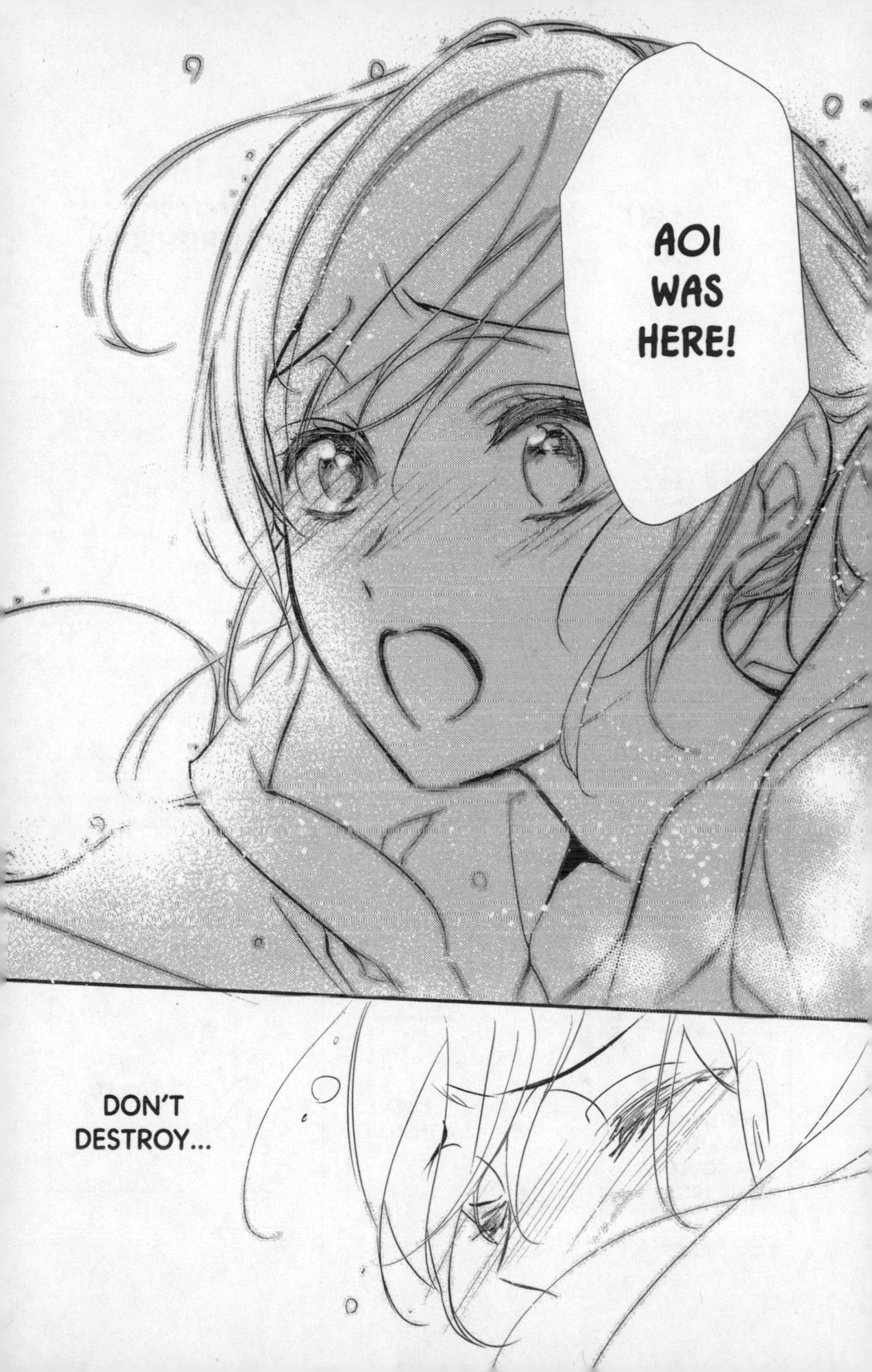
AOI WAS HERE!
DON'T DESTROY...

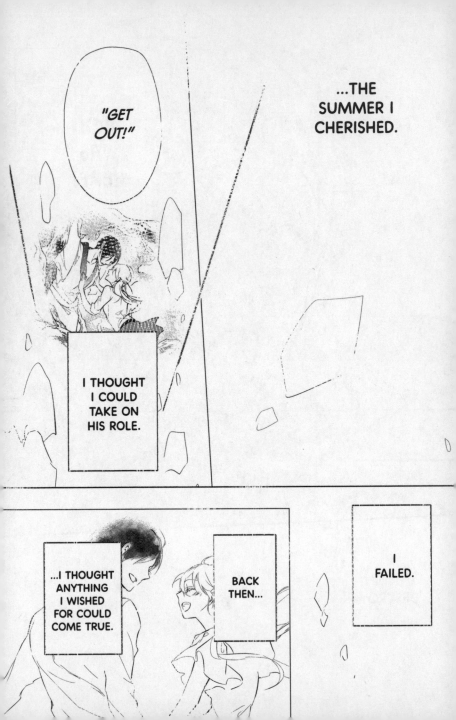

"GET OUT!"

...THE SUMMER I CHERISHED.

I THOUGHT I COULD TAKE ON HIS ROLE.

...I THOUGHT ANYTHING I WISHED FOR COULD COME TRUE.

BACK THEN...

I FAILED.

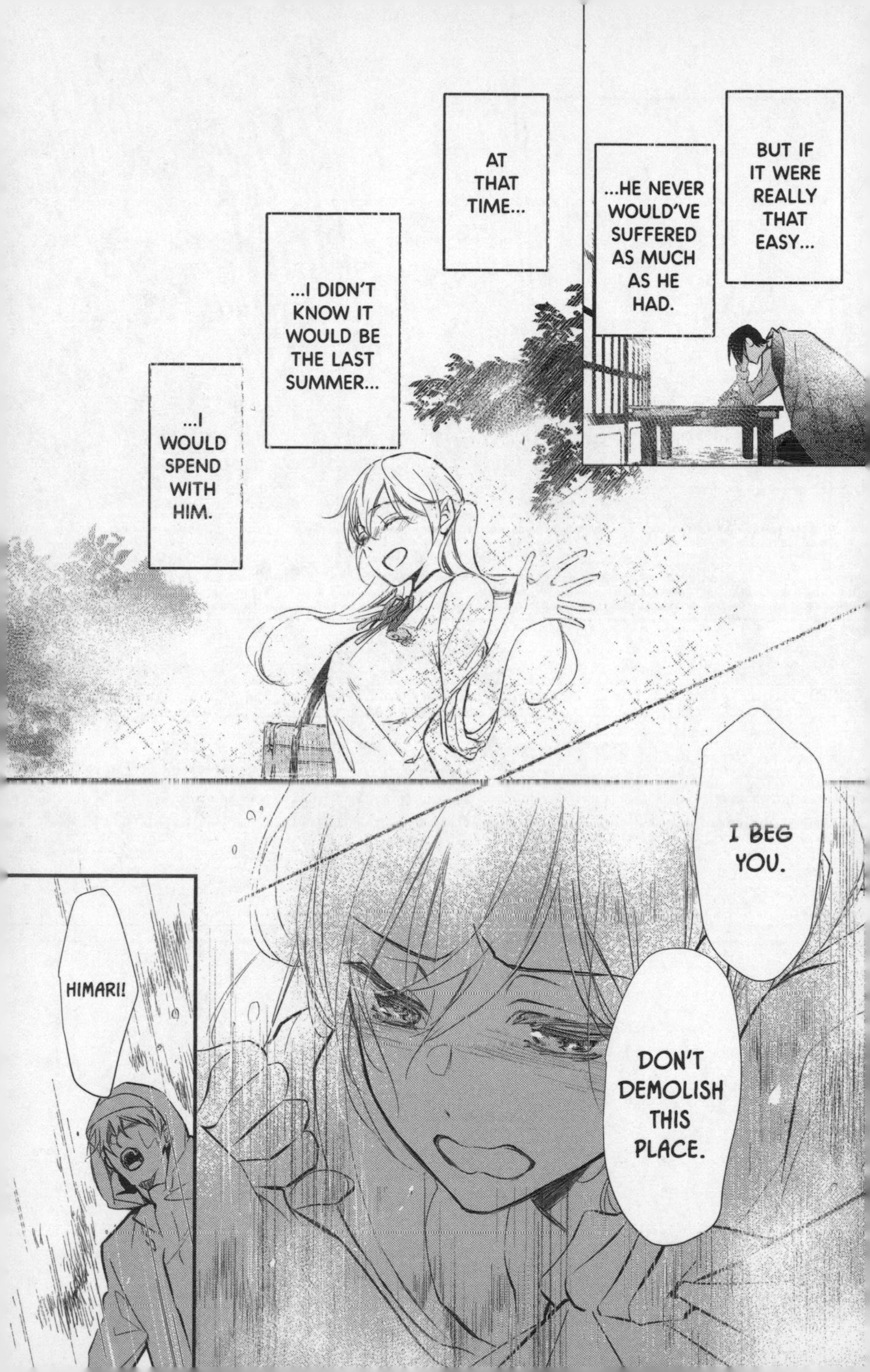
BUT IF IT WERE REALLY THAT EASY...
...HE NEVER WOULD'VE SUFFERED AS MUCH AS HE HAD.
AT THAT TIME...
...I DIDN'T KNOW IT WOULD BE THE LAST SUMMER...
...I WOULD SPEND WITH HIM.
I BEG YOU.
DON'T DEMOLISH THIS PLACE.
HIMARI!

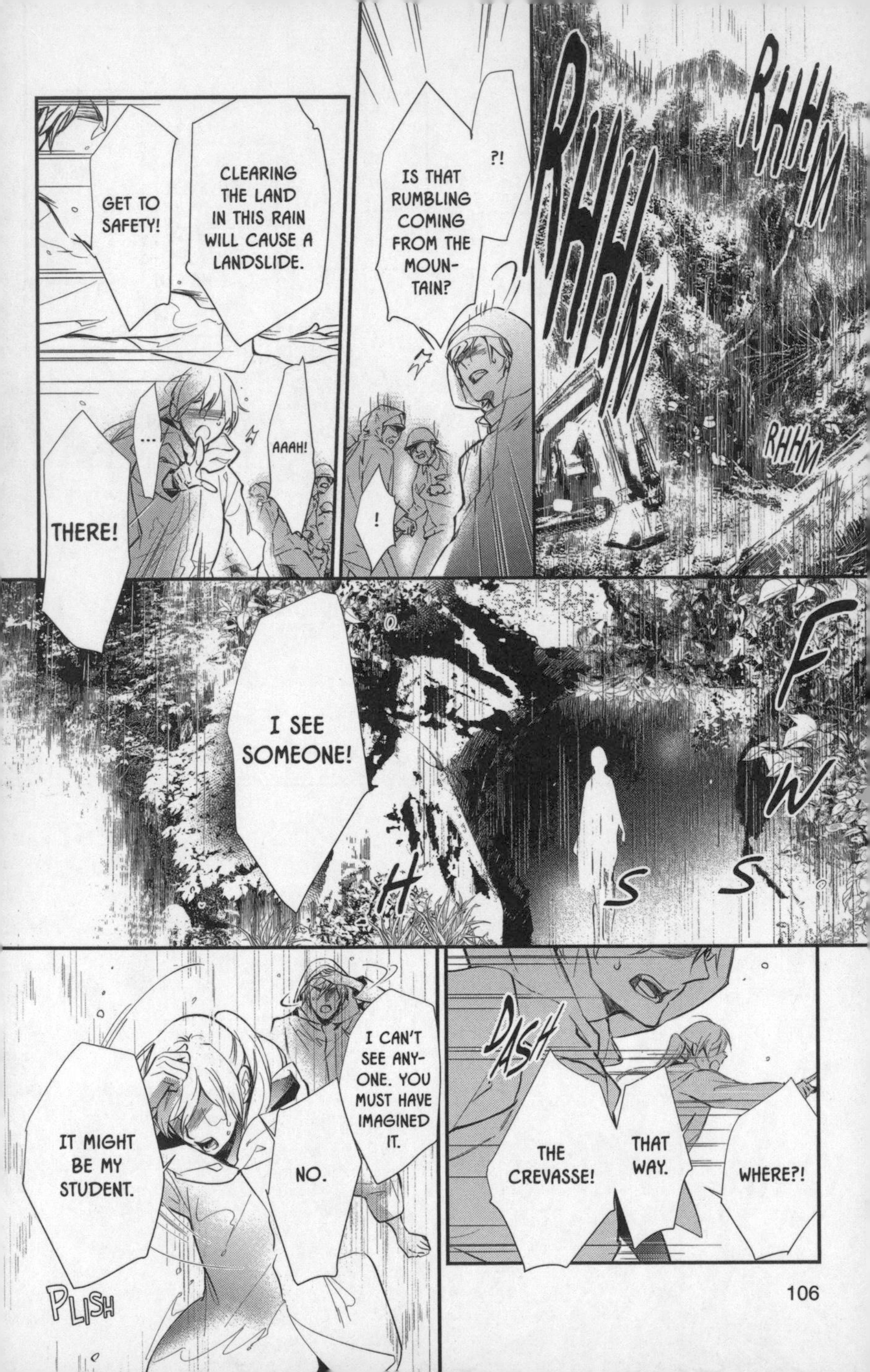
RHHM
RHHM
RHHM
?!
IS THAT RUMBLING COMING FROM THE MOUN-TAIN?
!
CLEARING THE LAND IN THIS RAIN WILL CAUSE A LANDSLIDE.
GET TO SAFETY!
AAAH!
...
THERE!
FWSSH
I SEE SOMEONE!
WHERE?!
THAT WAY.
THE CREVASSE!
DASH
I CAN'T SEE ANY-ONE. YOU MUST HAVE IMAGINED IT.
NO.
IT MIGHT BE MY STUDENT.
PLISH

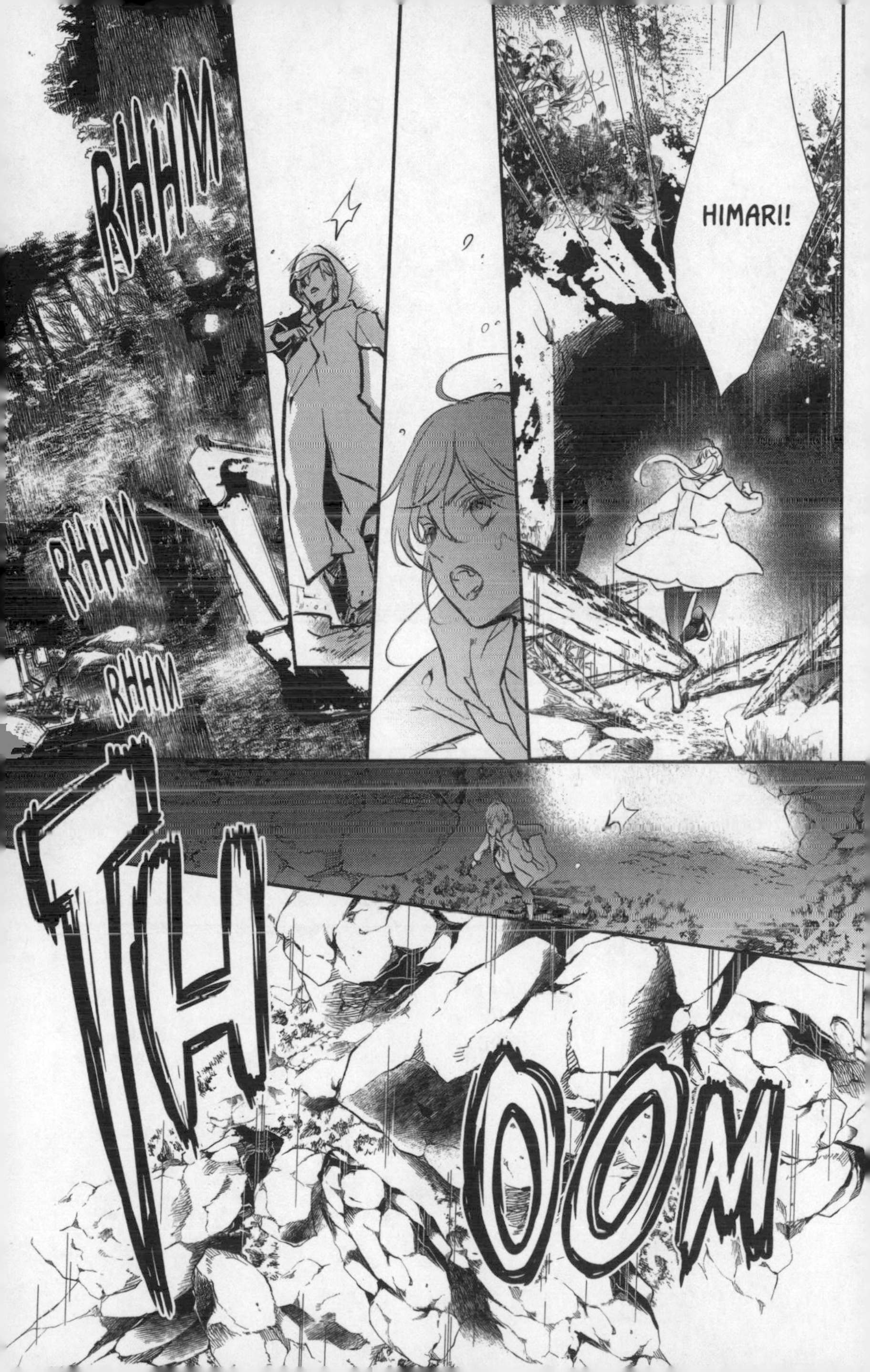
HIMARI!
RHHM
RHHM
RHHM
THOOM

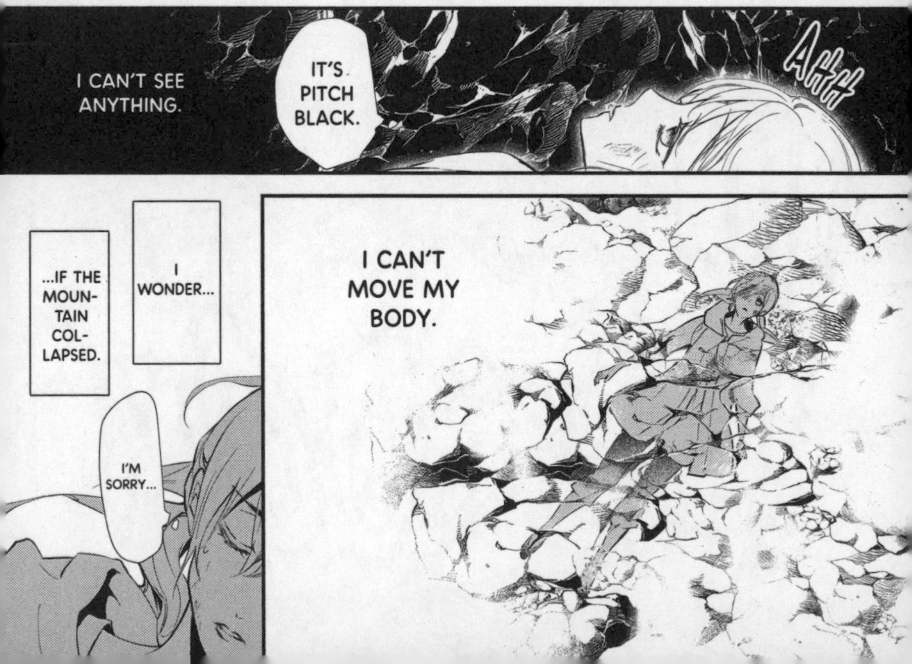
IT'S PITCH BLACK.
I CAN'T SEE ANYTHING.
I CAN'T MOVE MY BODY.
I WONDER...
...IF THE MOUNTAIN COLLAPSED.
I'M SORRY...

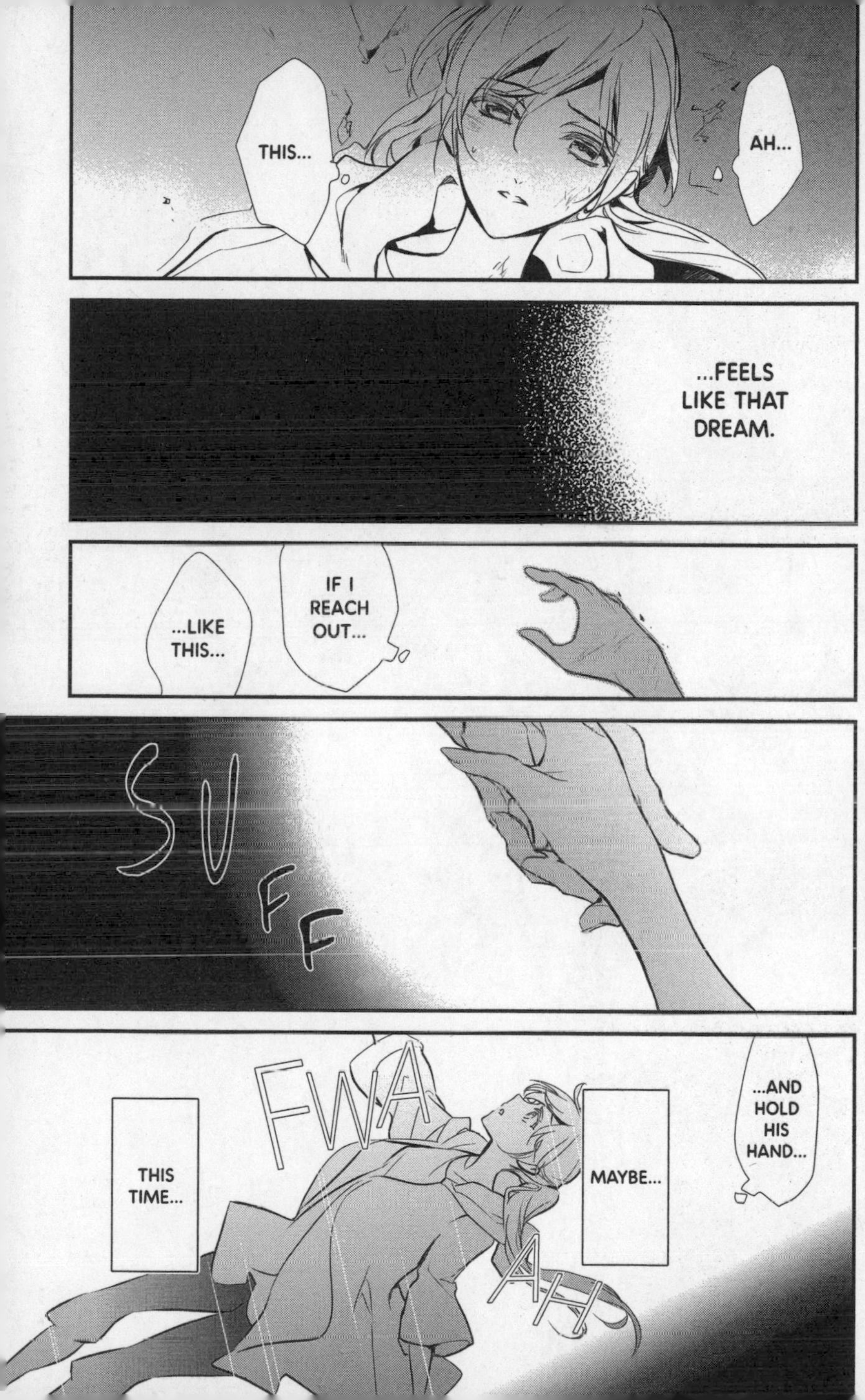
AH...
THIS...
...FEELS LIKE THAT DREAM.
IF I REACH OUT...
...LIKE THIS...
SUFF
...AND HOLD HIS HAND...
FWA
MAYBE...
THIS TIME...
AH

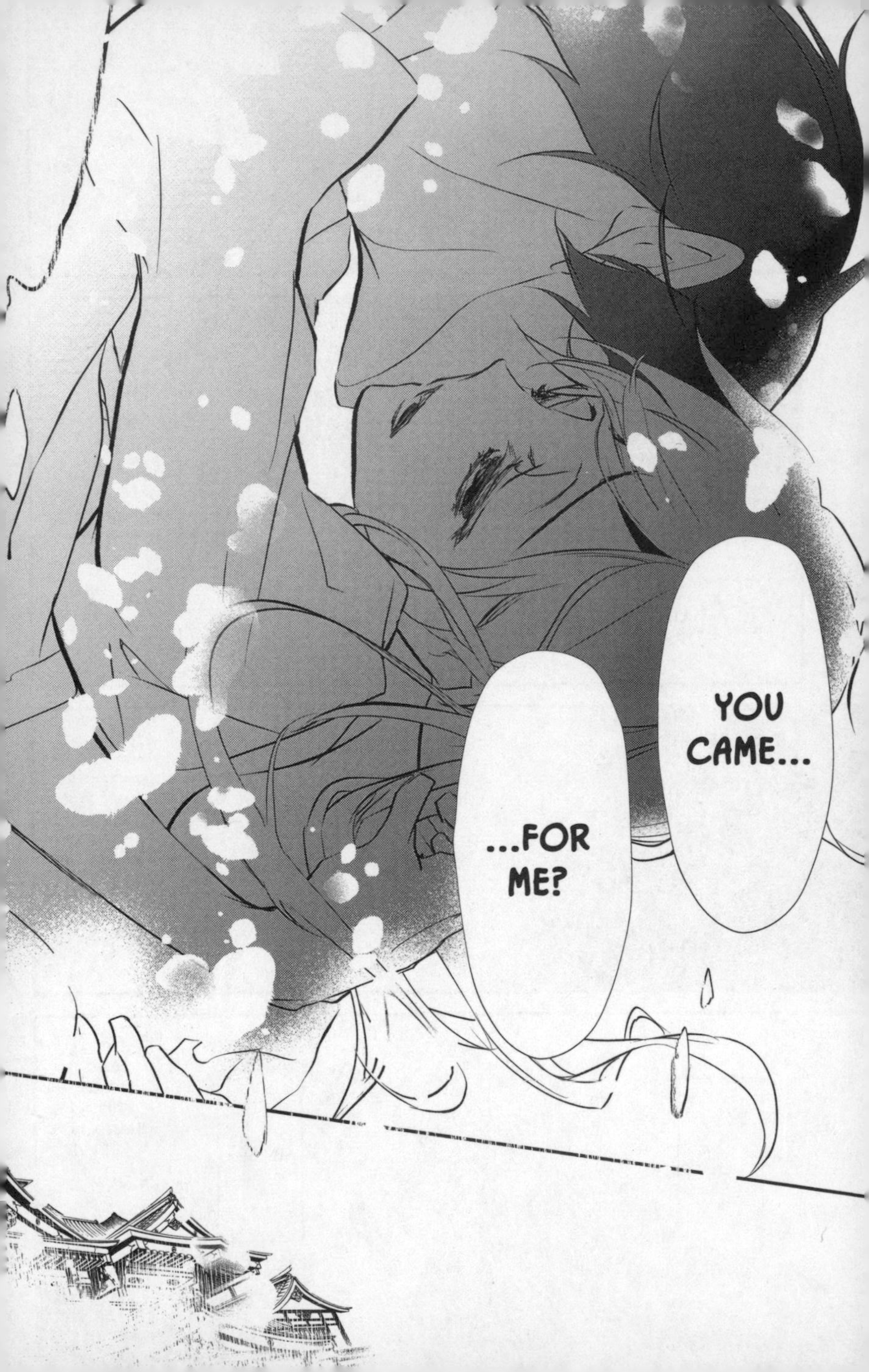
YOU CAME...
...FOR ME?

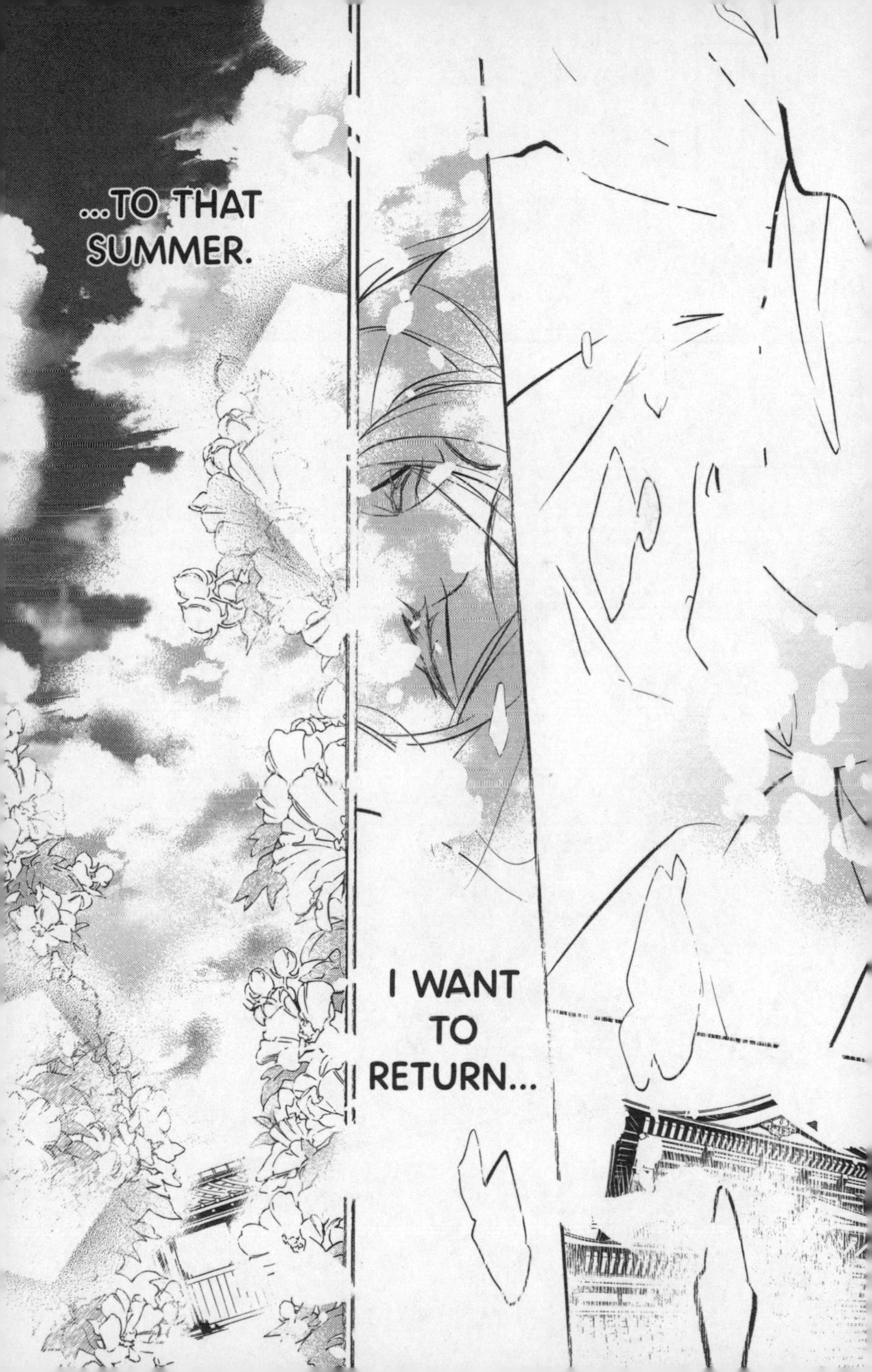
I WANT TO RETURN...
...TO THAT SUMMER.

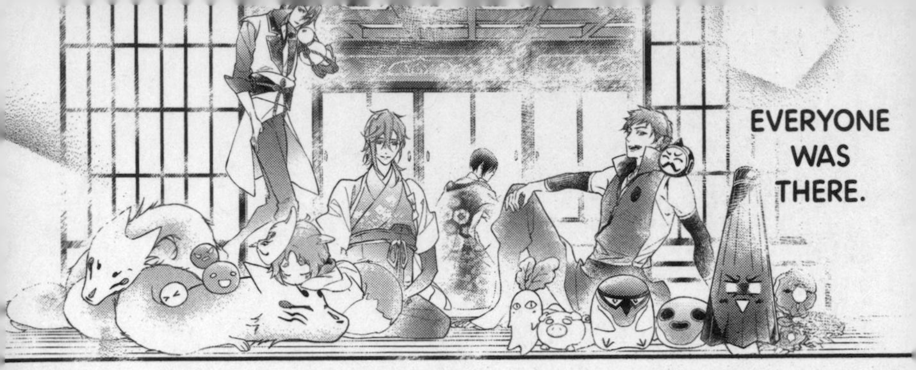
EVERYONE WAS THERE.

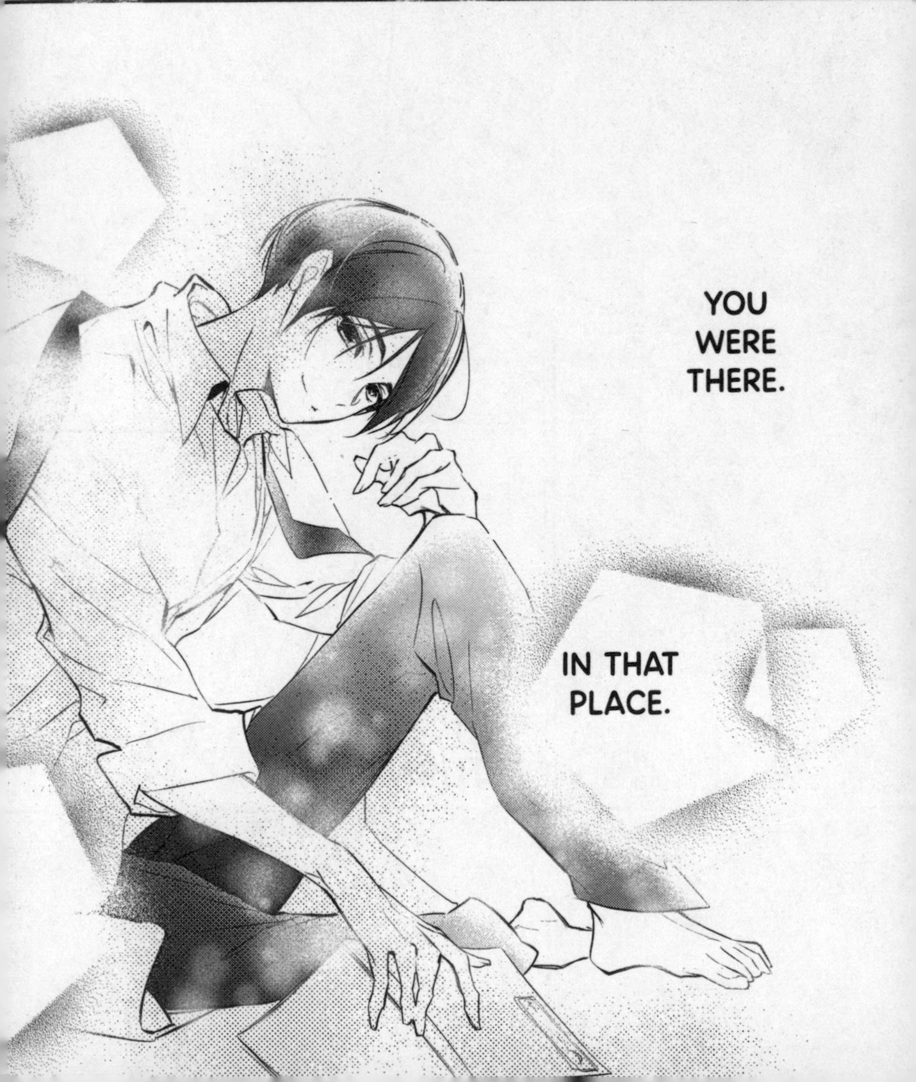
YOU WERE THERE.
IN THAT PLACE.

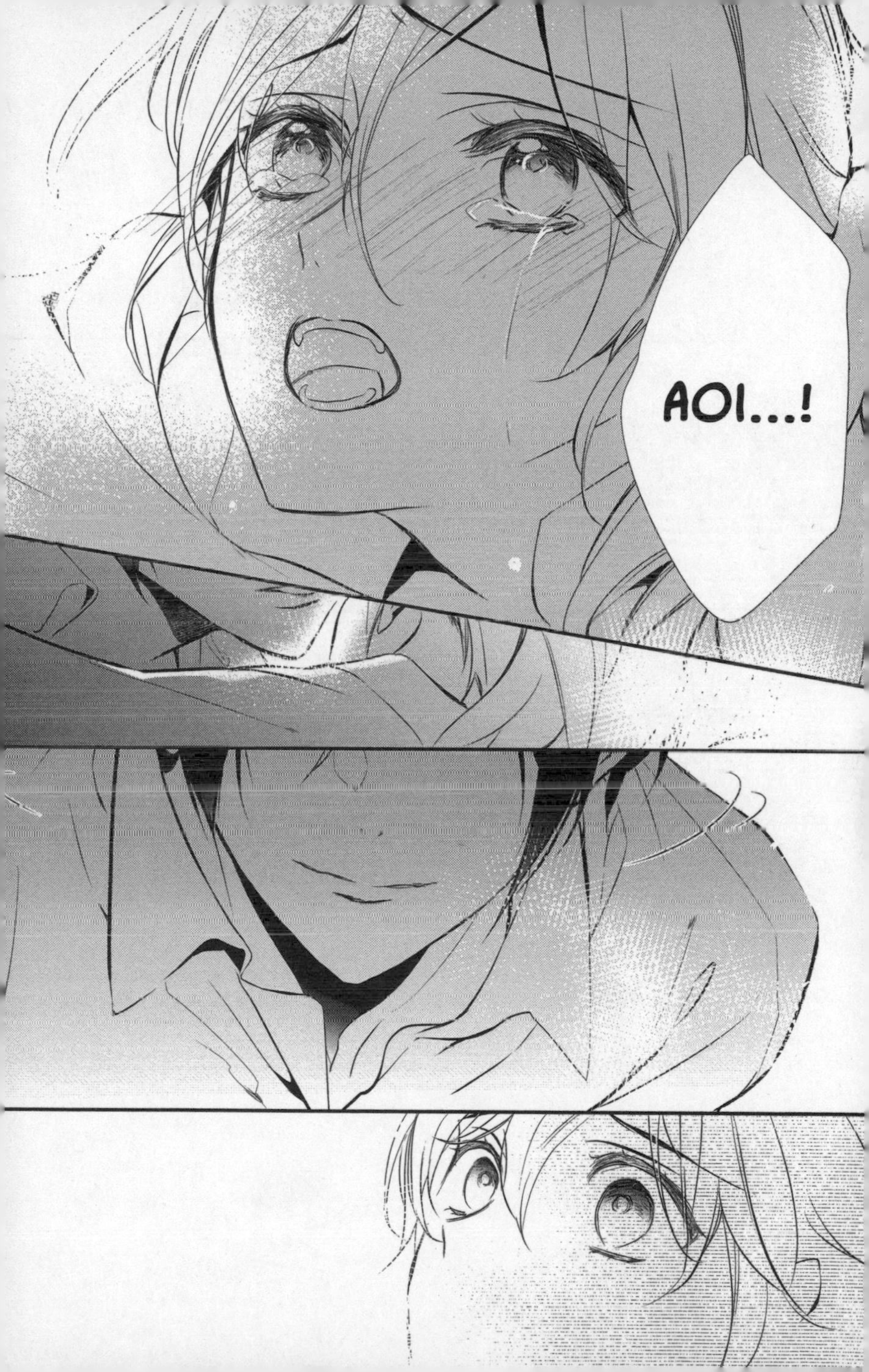
AOI...!

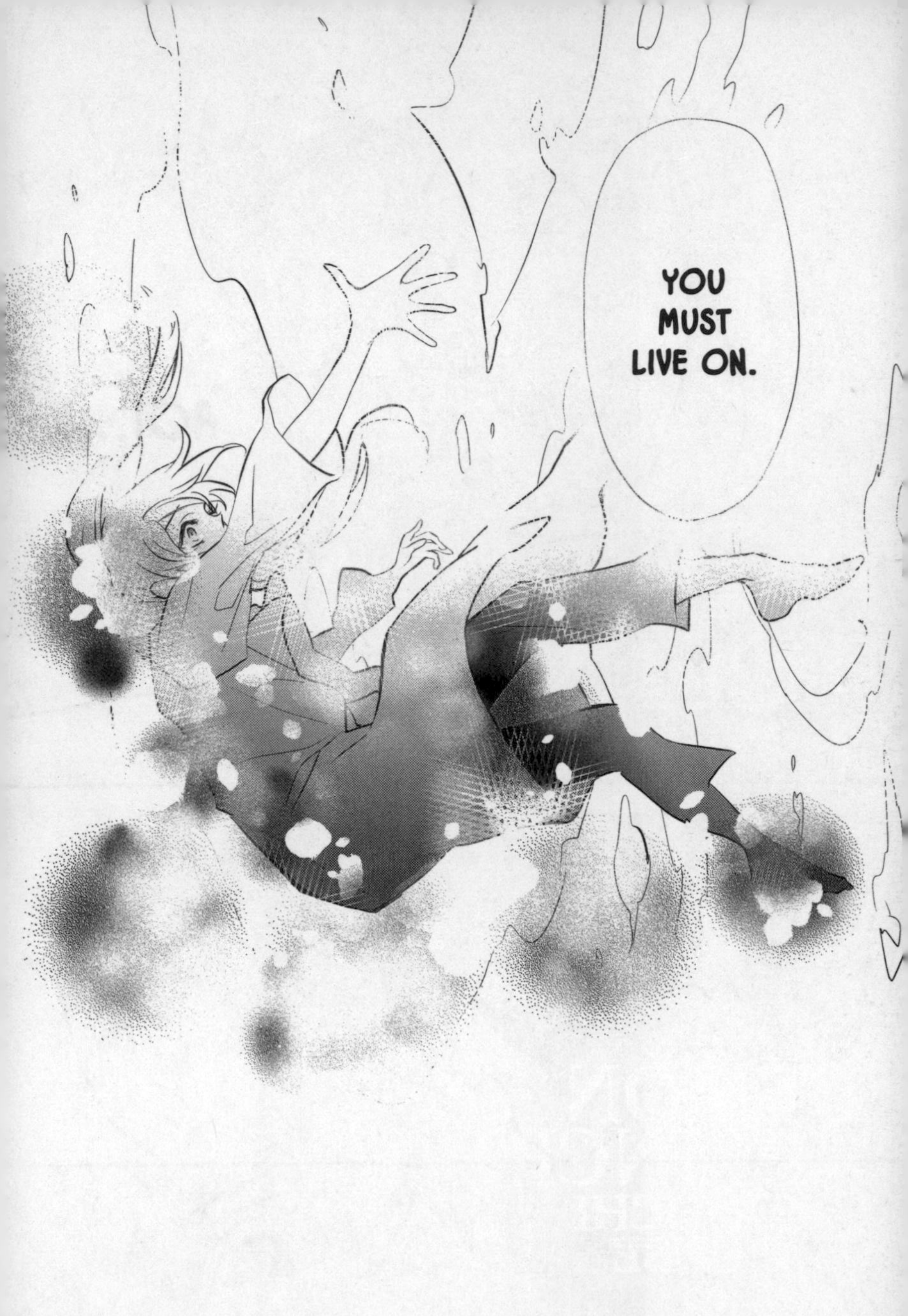
YOU MUST LIVE ON.

Chapter 63/End

The
DEMON
PRINCE
of MOMOCHI
HOUSE

The
DEMON
PRINCE
of MOMOCHI
HOUSE

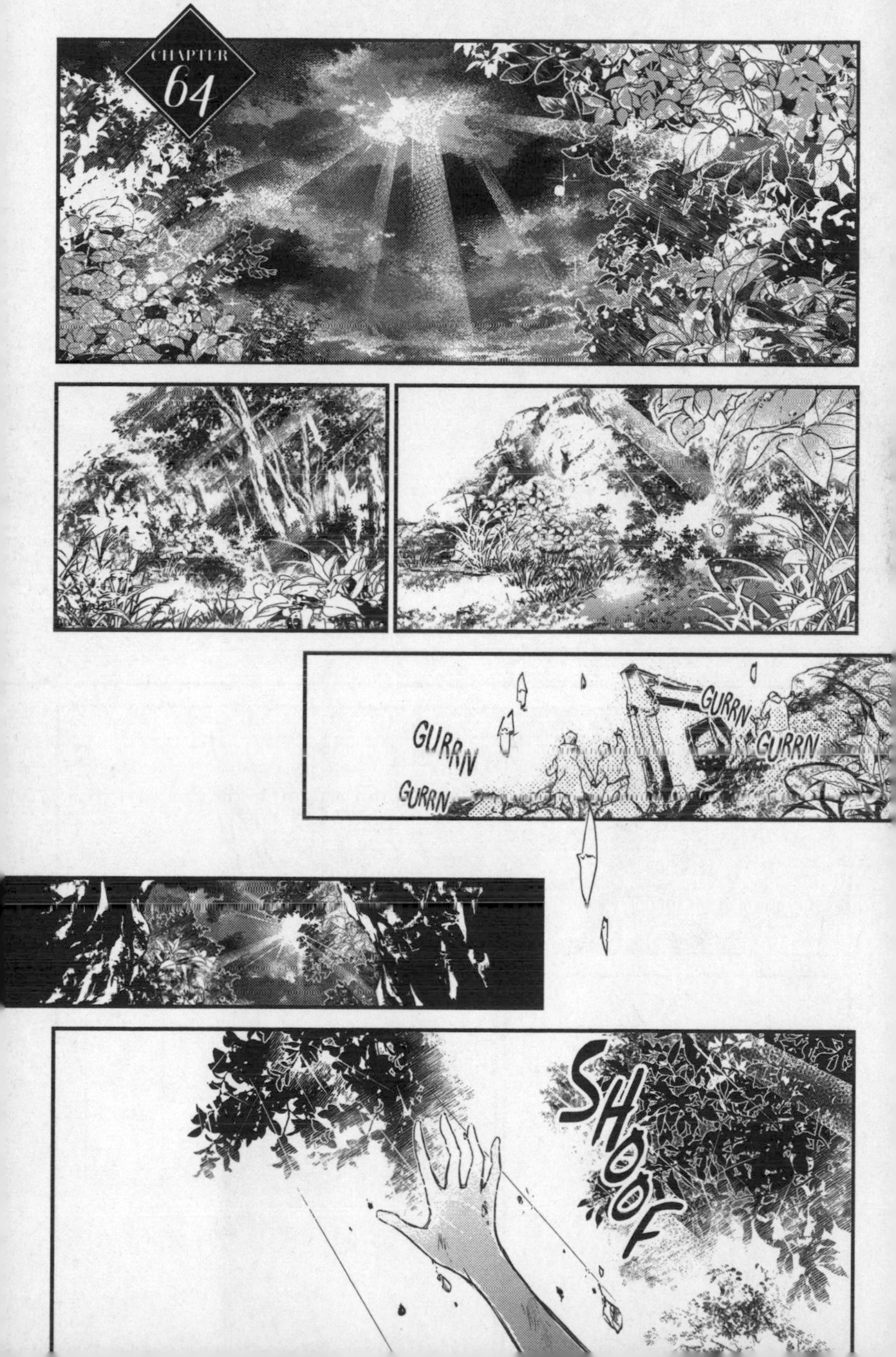
CHAPTER
64
GURRN
GURRN
GURRN
GURRN
SHOOF

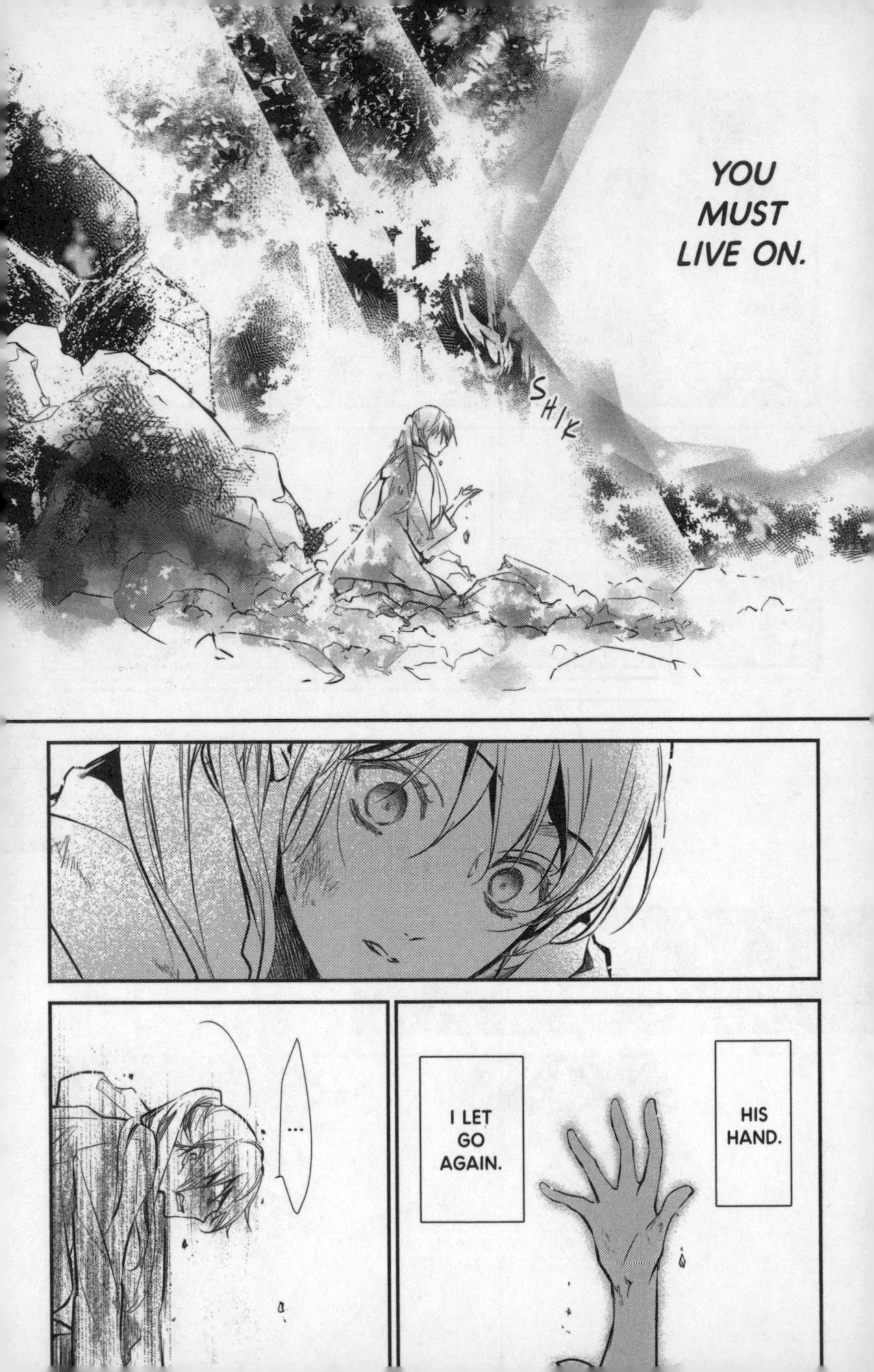
YOU MUST LIVE ON.
SHIK
HIS HAND.
I LET GO AGAIN.
...

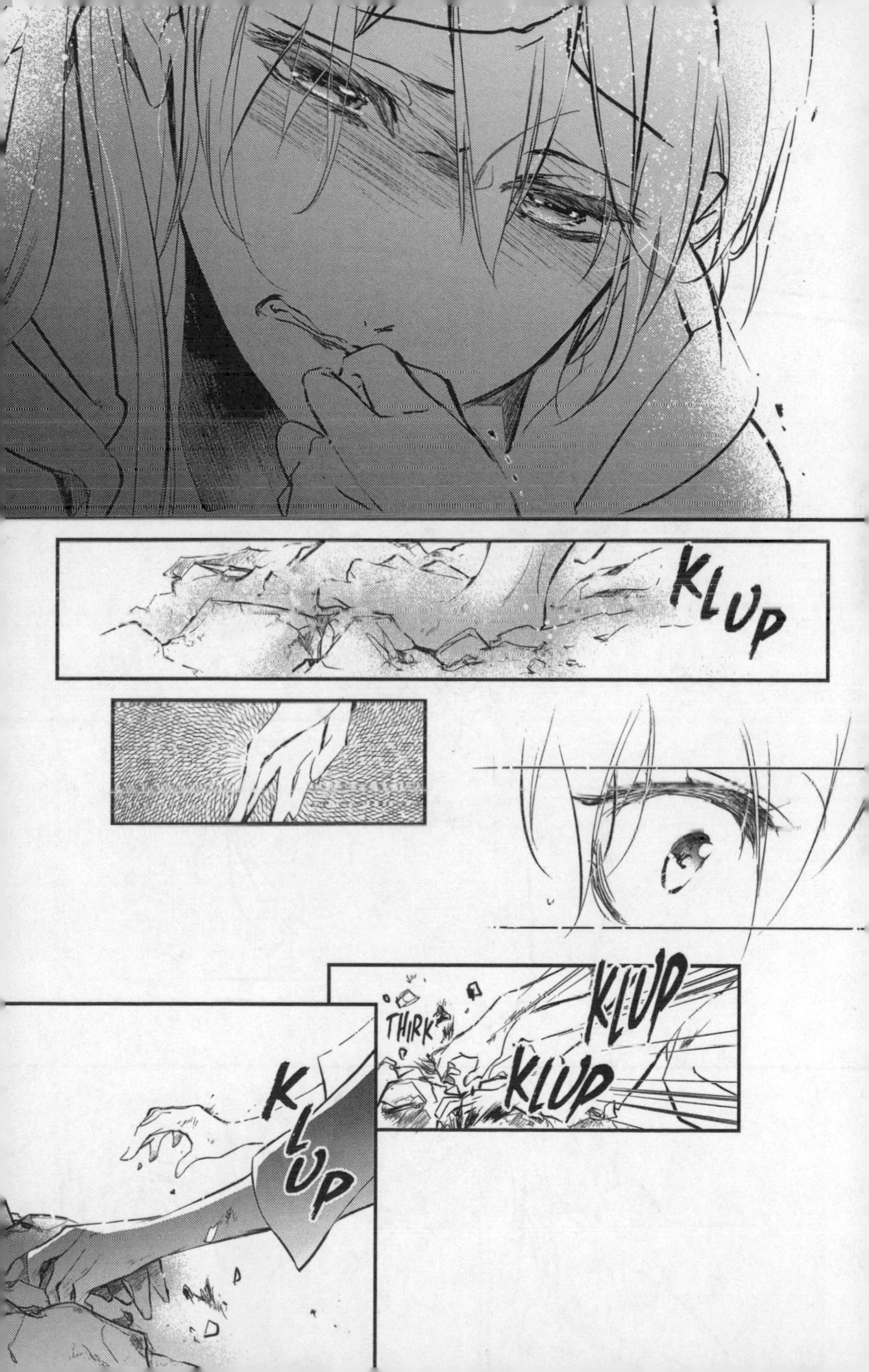
KLUP
KLUP
THIRK
KLUP
KLUP

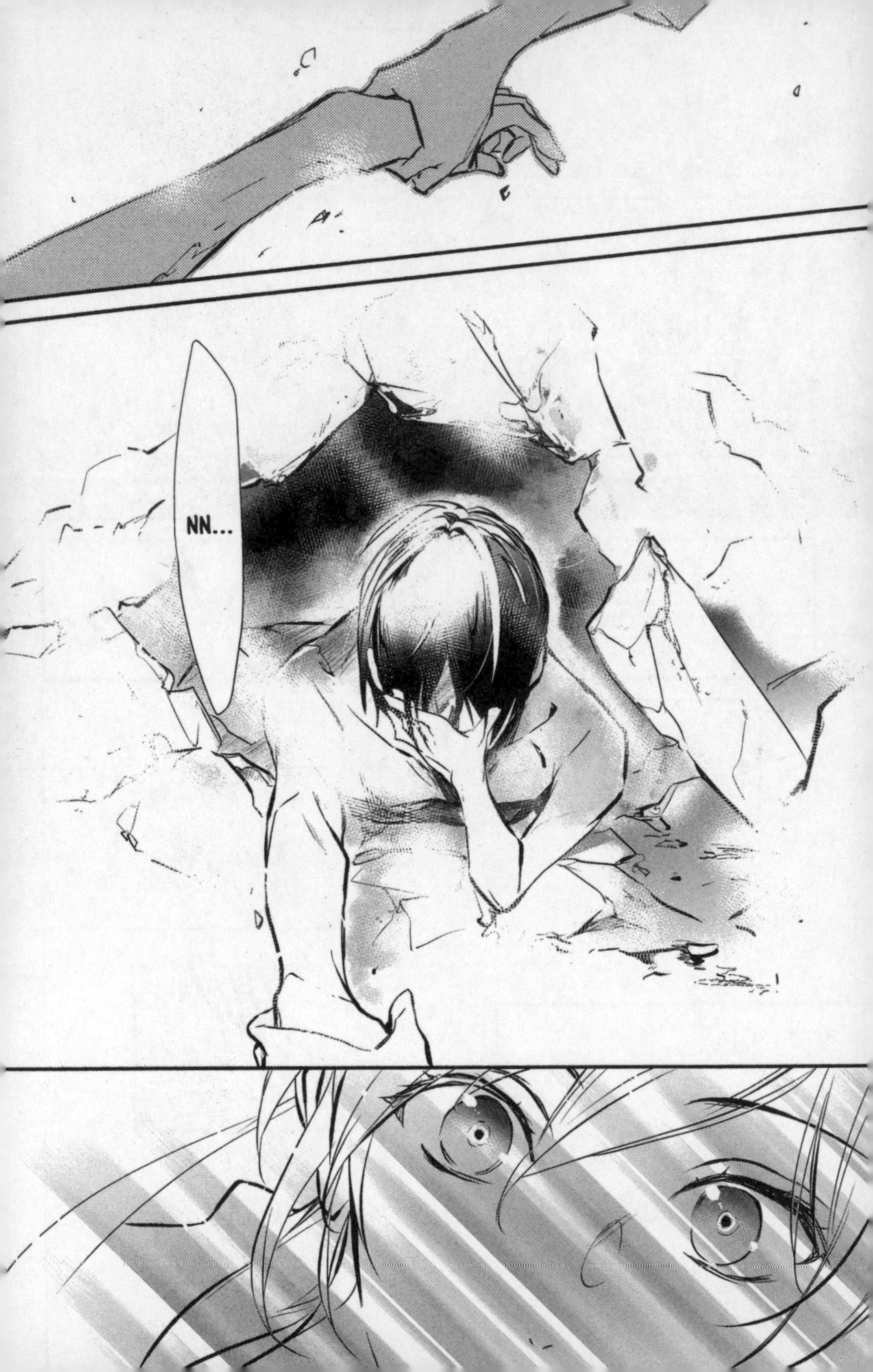
NN...

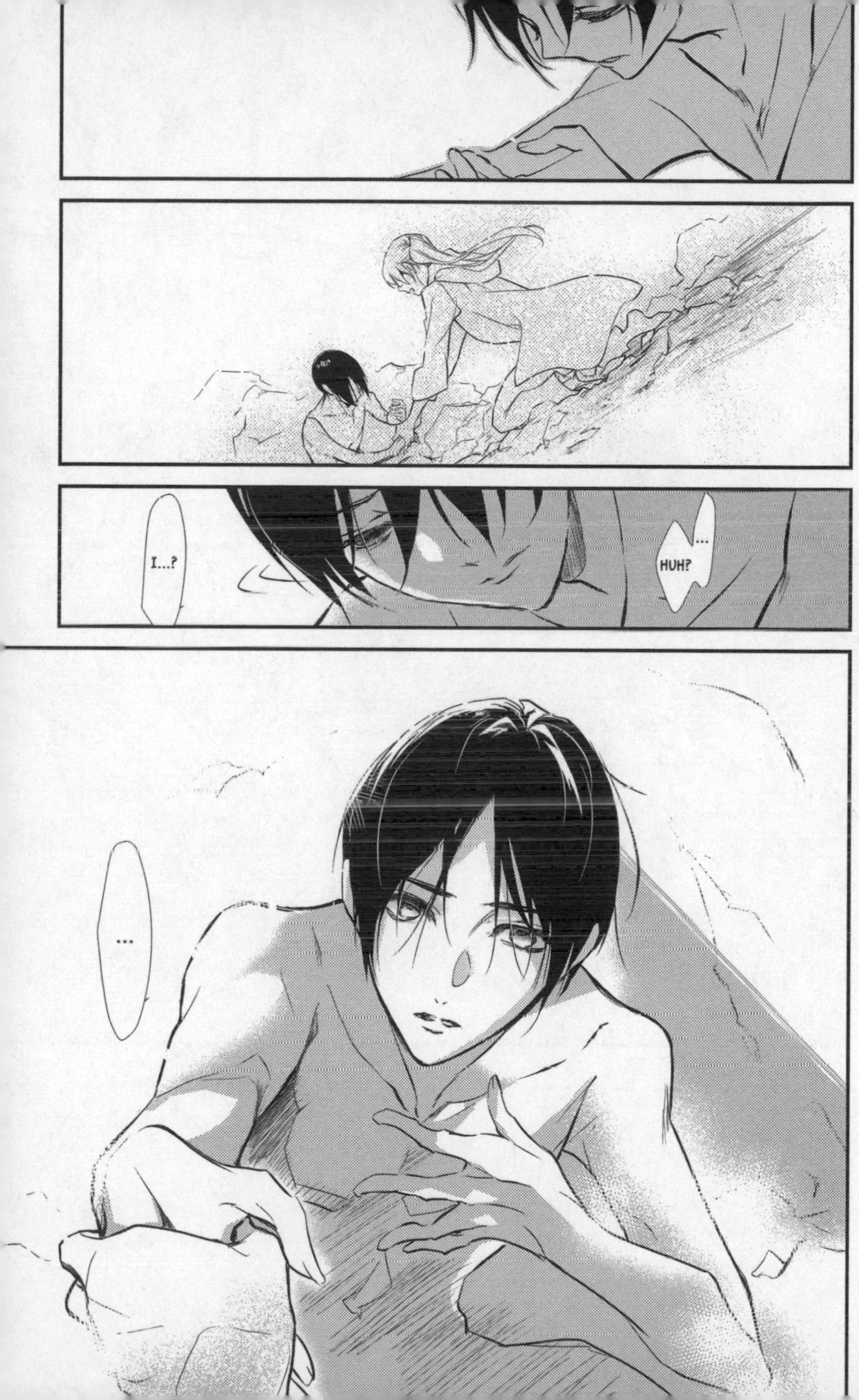
...
HUH?
I...?
...

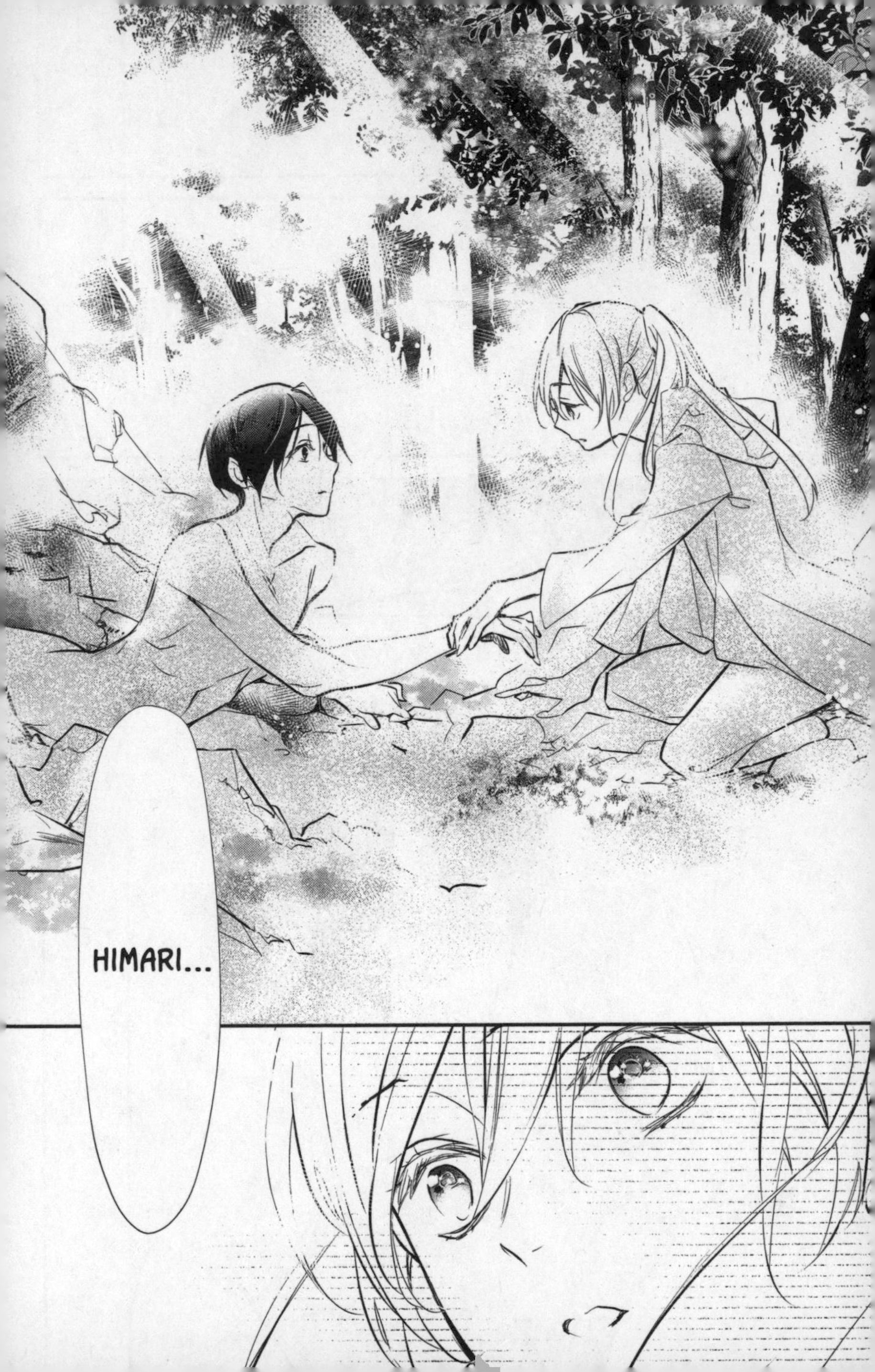
HIMARI...

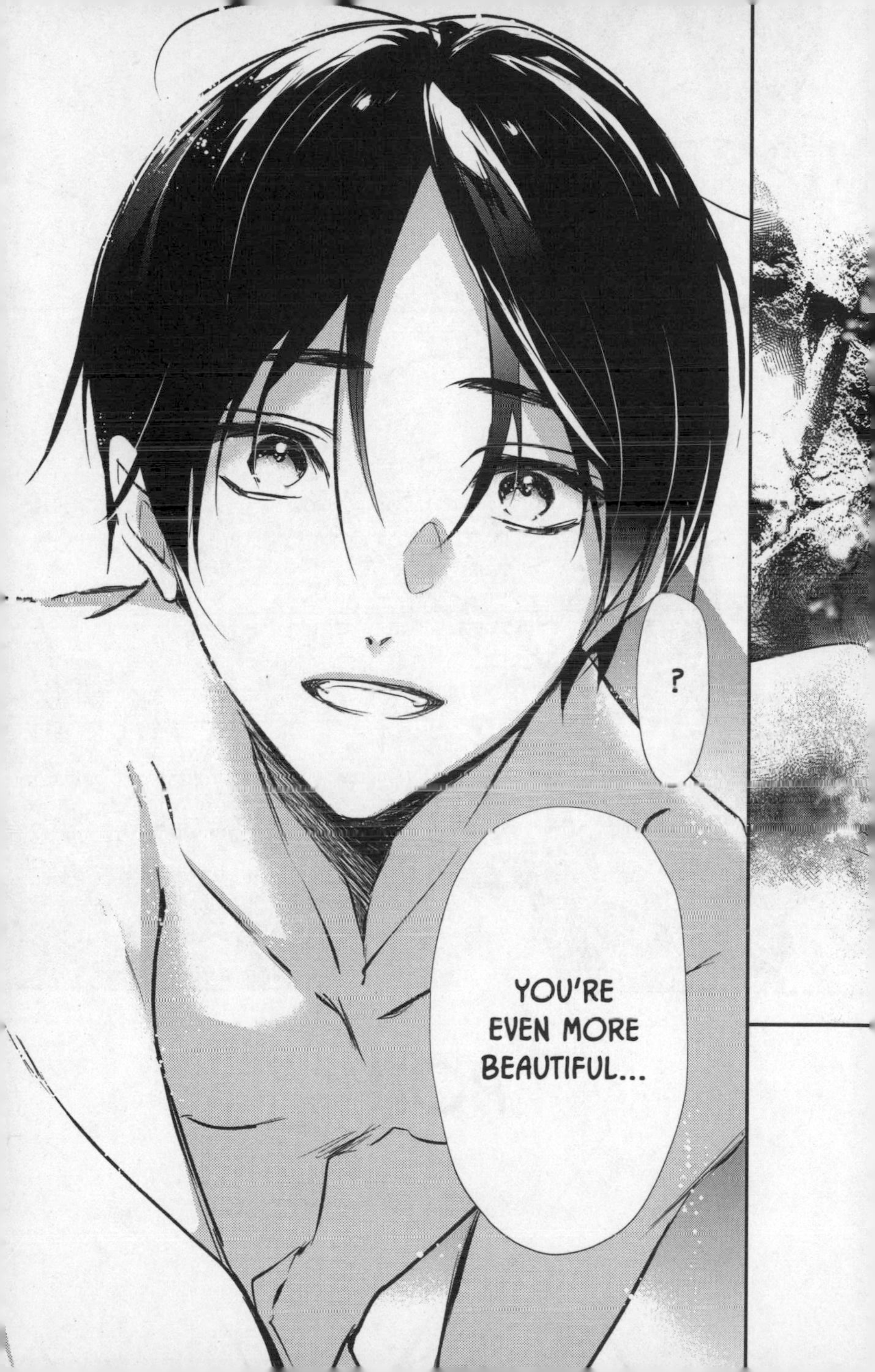
?
YOU'RE EVEN MORE BEAUTIFUL...

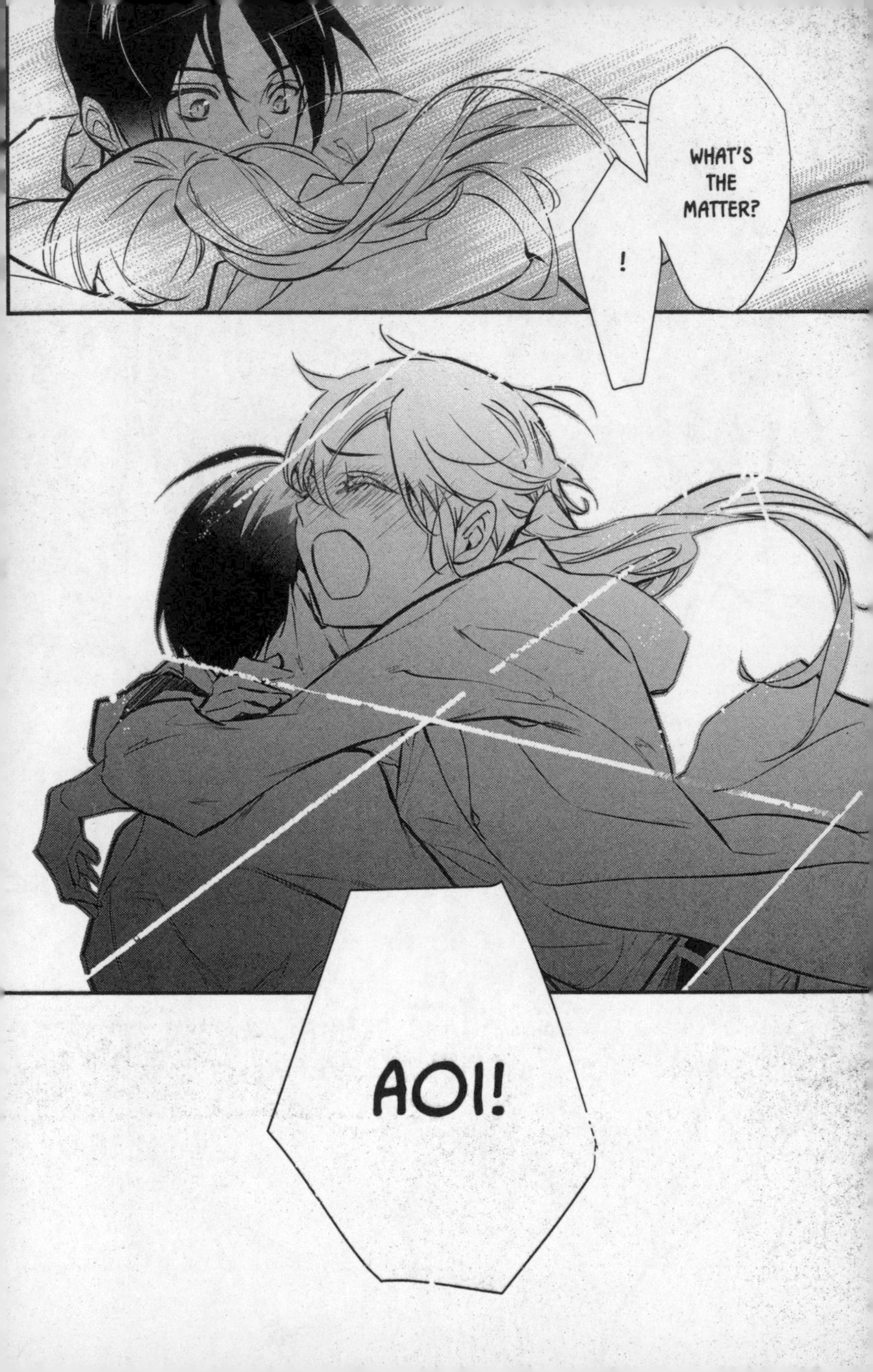
WHAT'S THE MATTER?
!
AOI!

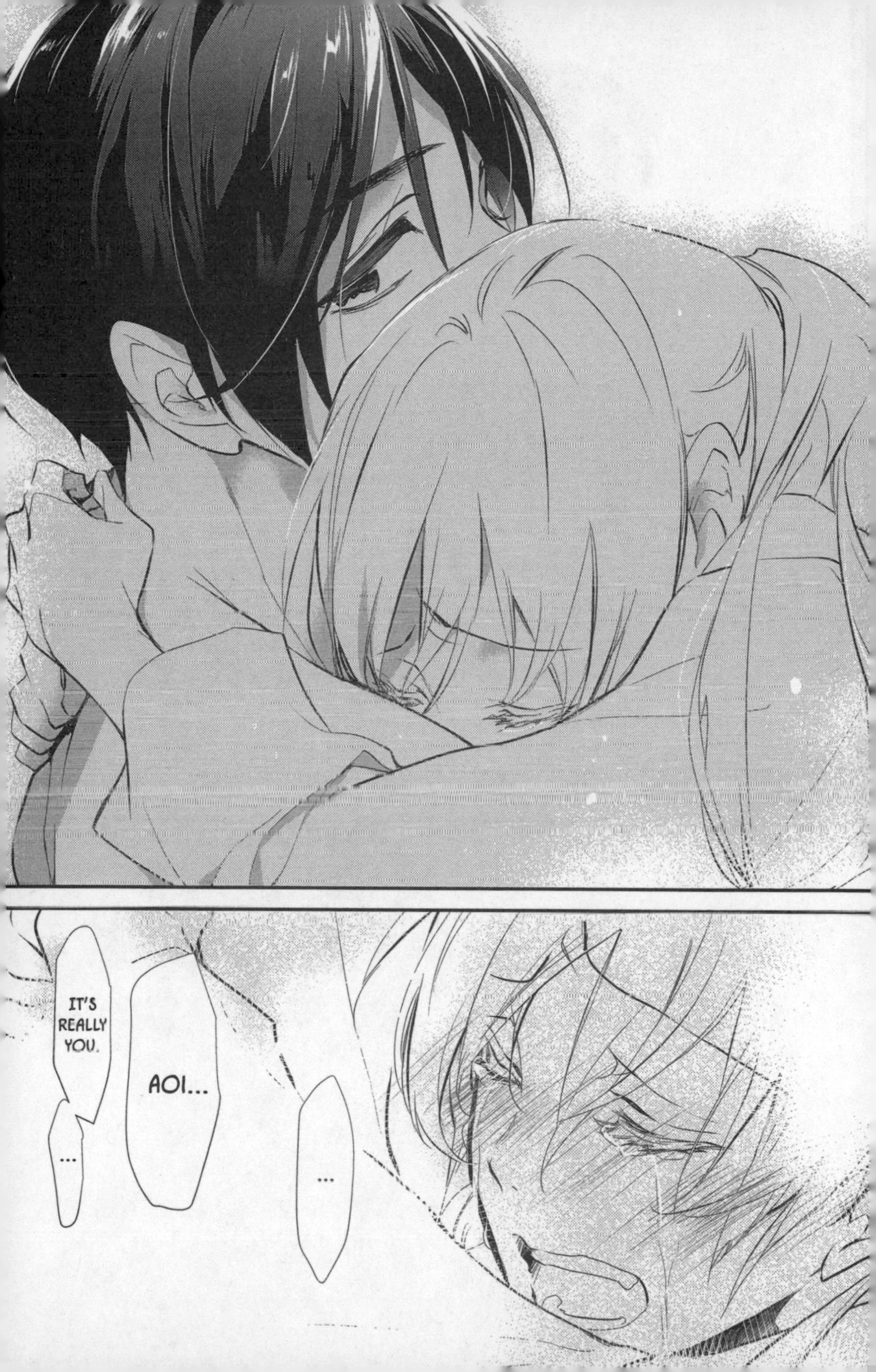
...
AOI...
IT'S REALLY YOU.
...

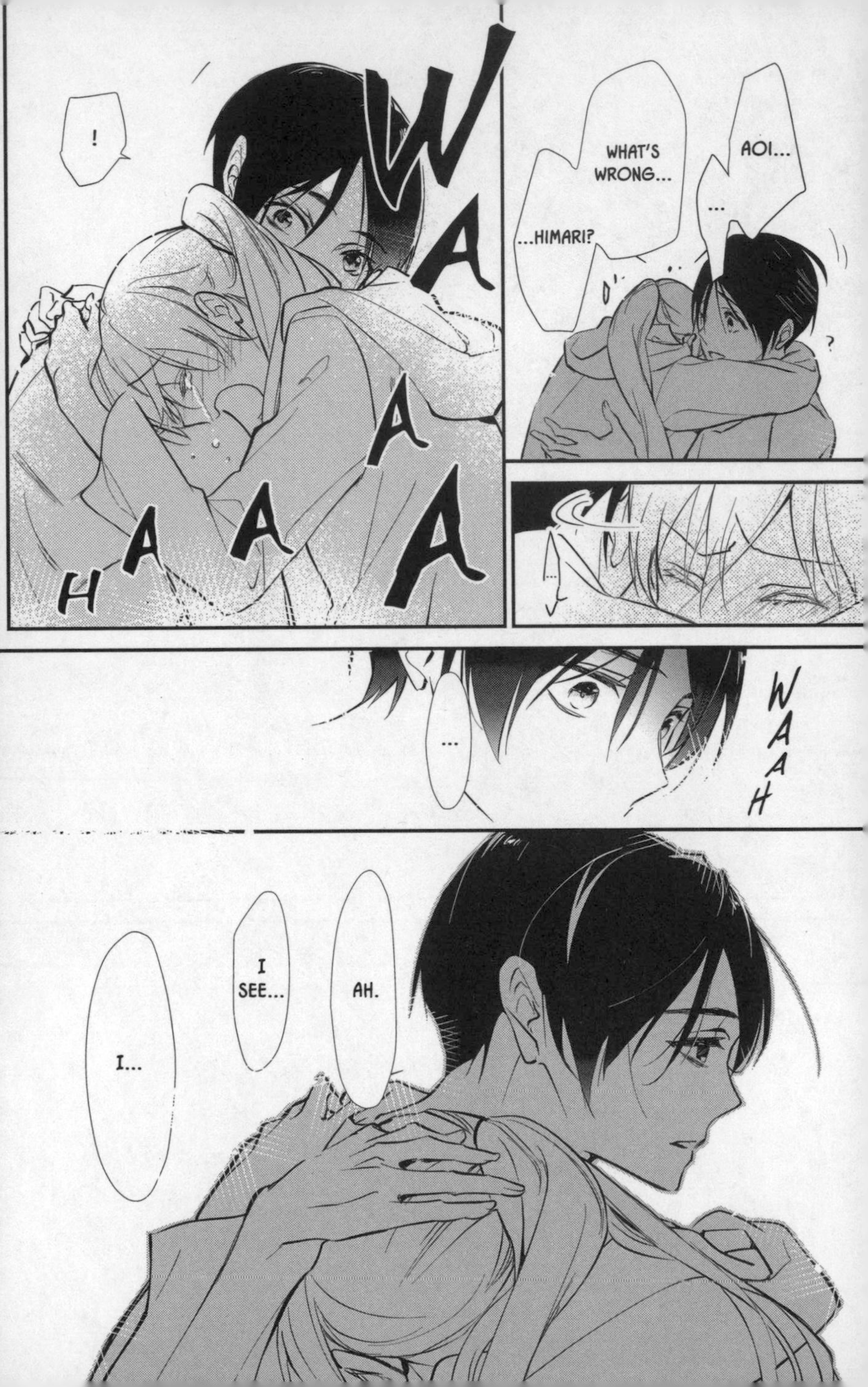
AOI...
...
WHAT'S WRONG...
...HIMARI?
...
!
WAAAAAH
WAAAH
...
AH.
I SEE...
I...

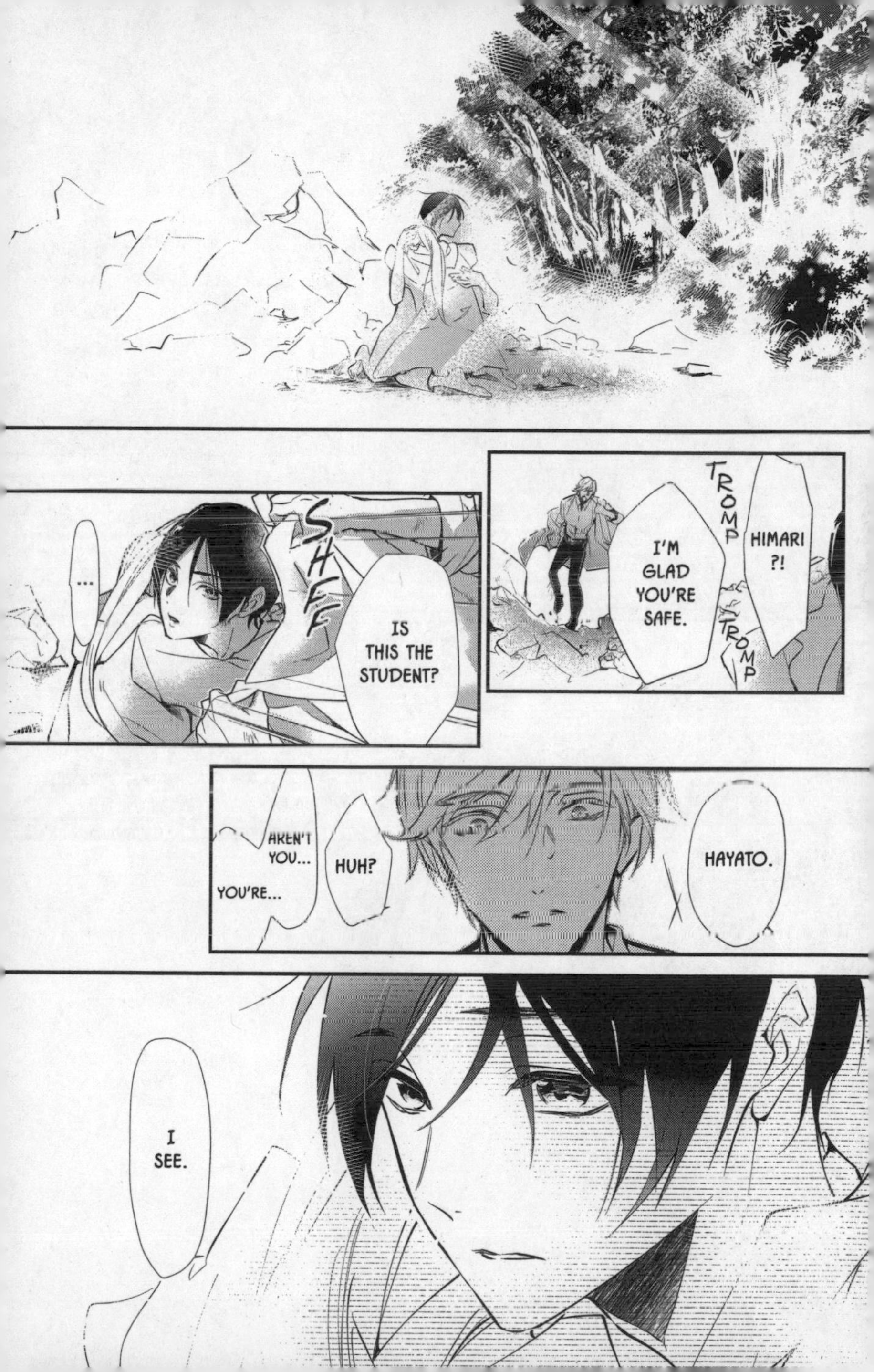

TROMP
HIMARI ?!
I'M GLAD YOU'RE SAFE.
TROMP
SHFF
IS THIS THE STUDENT?
...
HAYATO.
HUH?
AREN'T YOU...
YOU'RE...
I SEE.

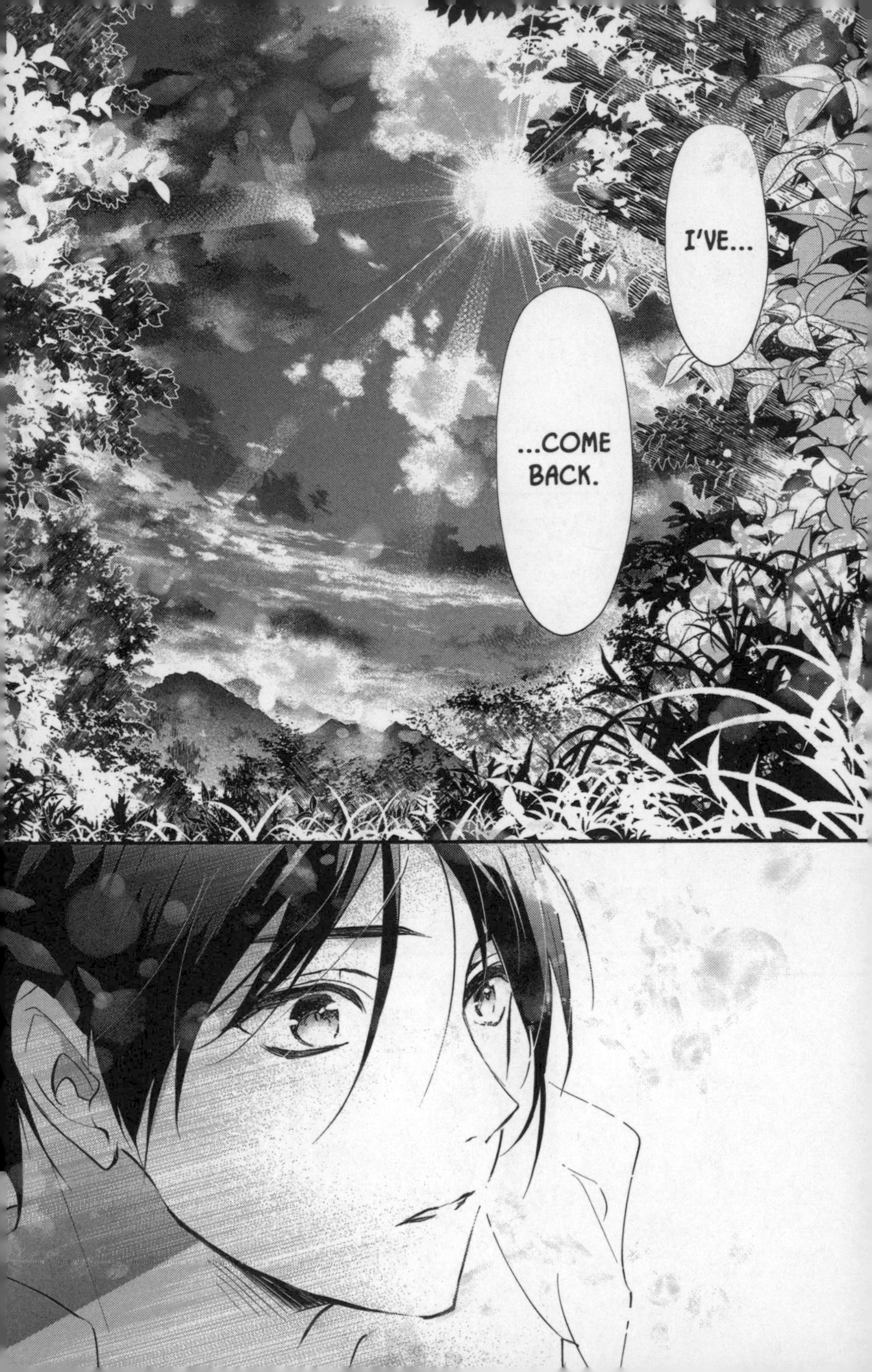
I'VE...
...COME BACK.

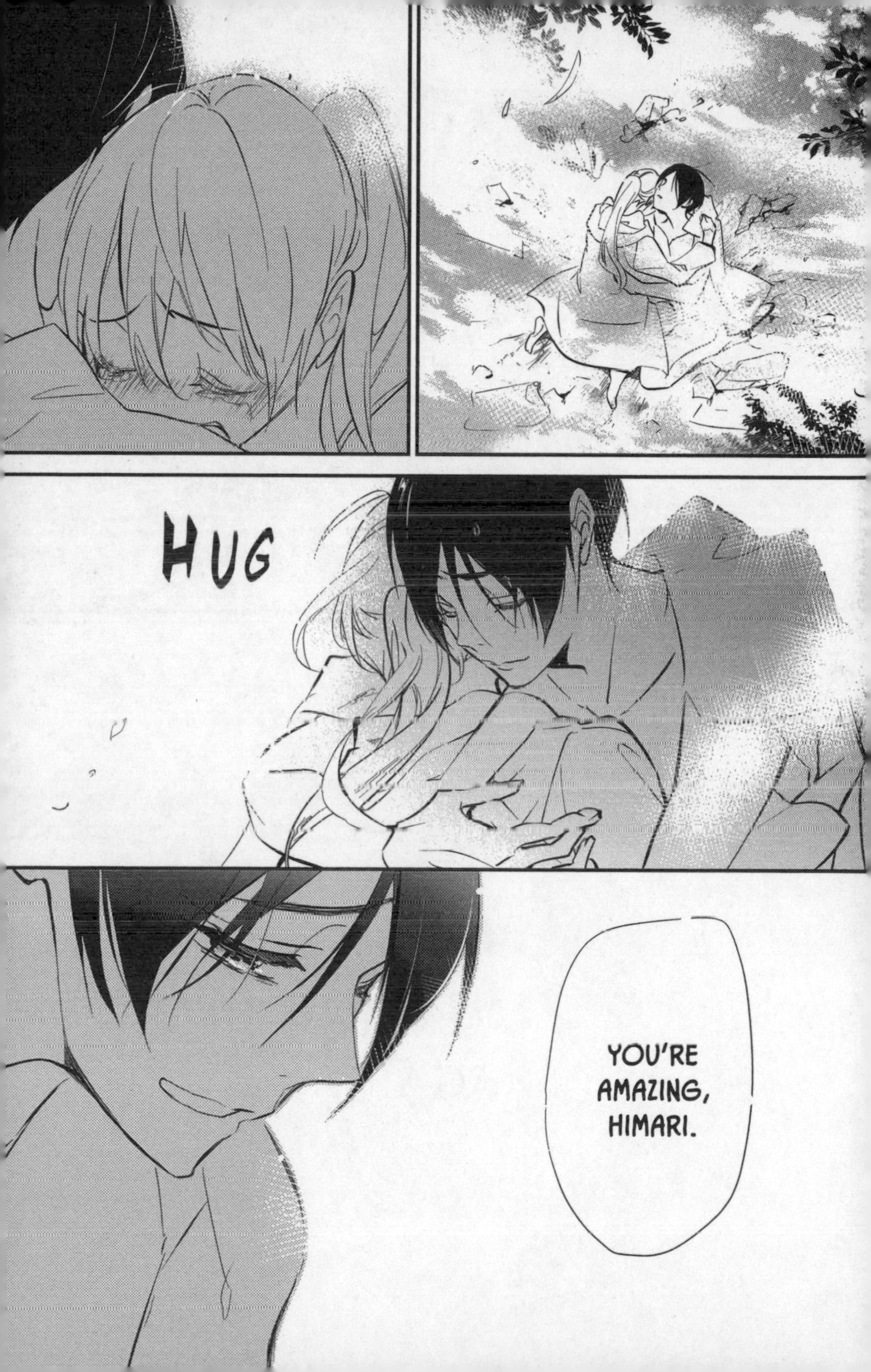
HUG
YOU'RE AMAZING, HIMARI.

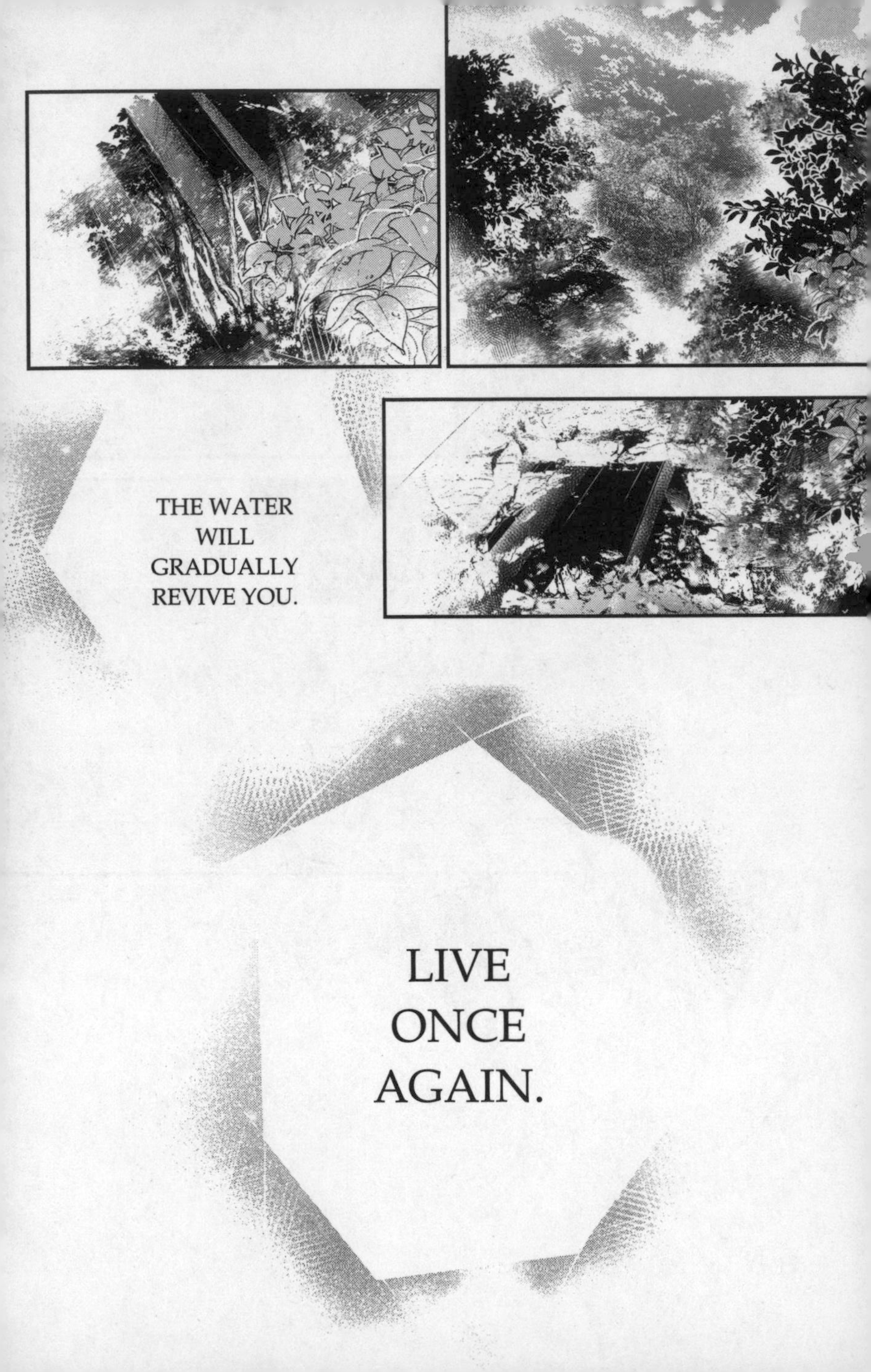
THE WATER WILL GRADUALLY REVIVE YOU.
LIVE ONCE AGAIN.

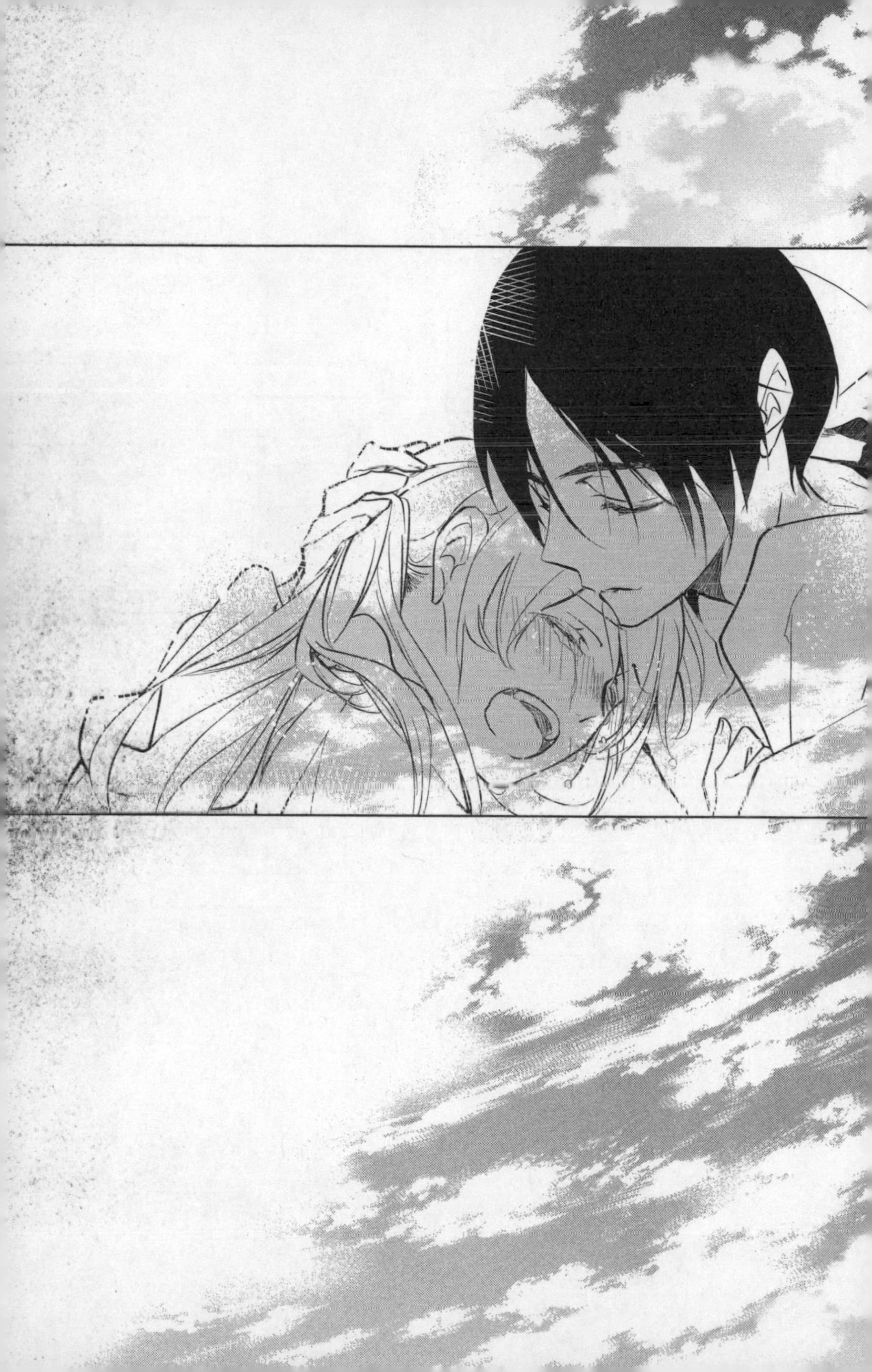

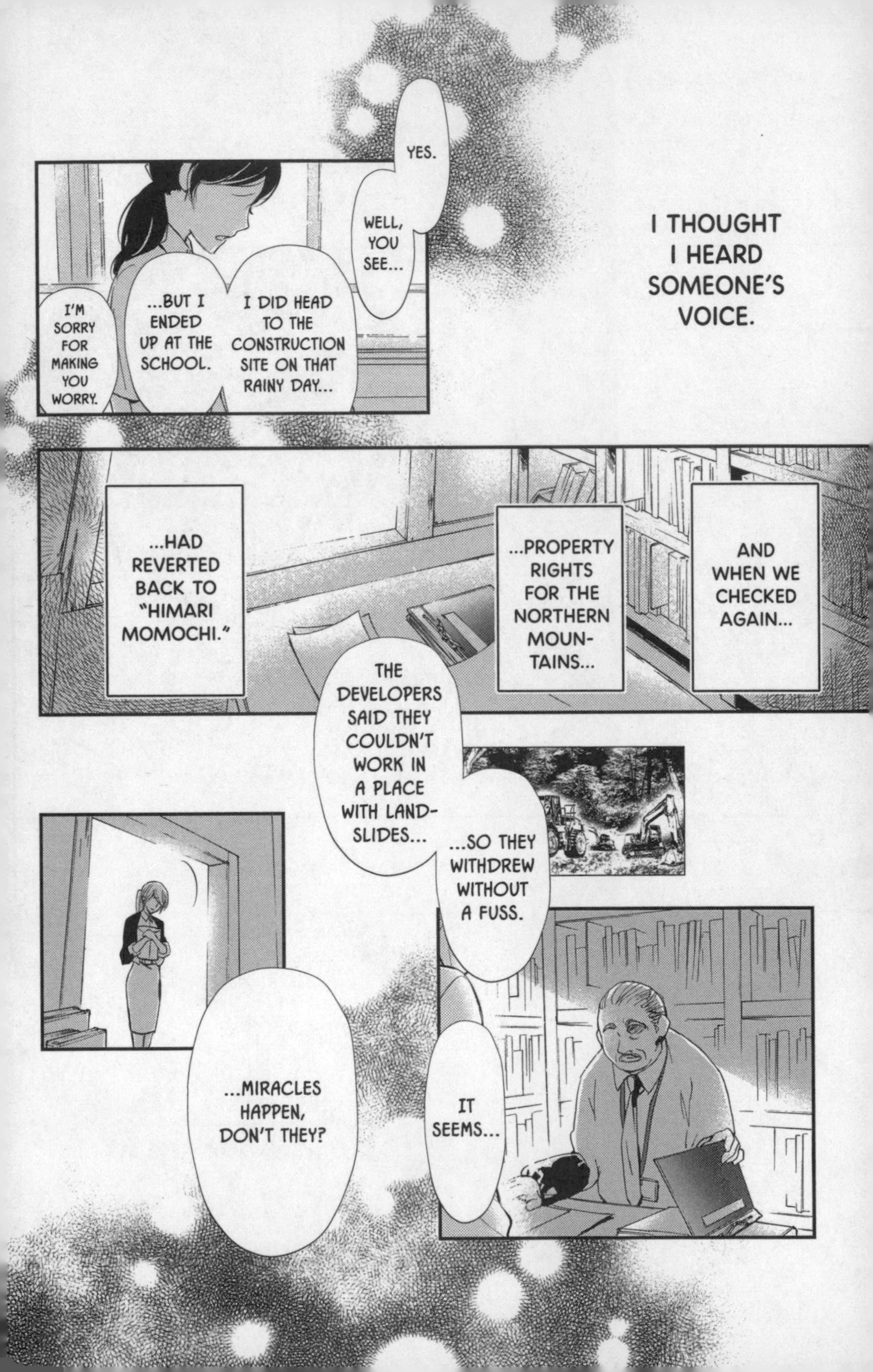
I THOUGHT I HEARD SOMEONE'S VOICE.
YES.
WELL, YOU SEE...
I DID HEAD TO THE CONSTRUCTION SITE ON THAT RAINY DAY...
...BUT I ENDED UP AT THE SCHOOL.
I'M SORRY FOR MAKING YOU WORRY.
AND WHEN WE CHECKED AGAIN...
...PROPERTY RIGHTS FOR THE NORTHERN MOUN-TAINS...
...HAD REVERTED BACK TO "HIMARI MOMOCHI."
THE DEVELOPERS SAID THEY COULDN'T WORK IN A PLACE WITH LAND-SLIDES...
...SO THEY WITHDREW WITHOUT A FUSS.
IT SEEMS...
...MIRACLES HAPPEN, DON'T THEY?

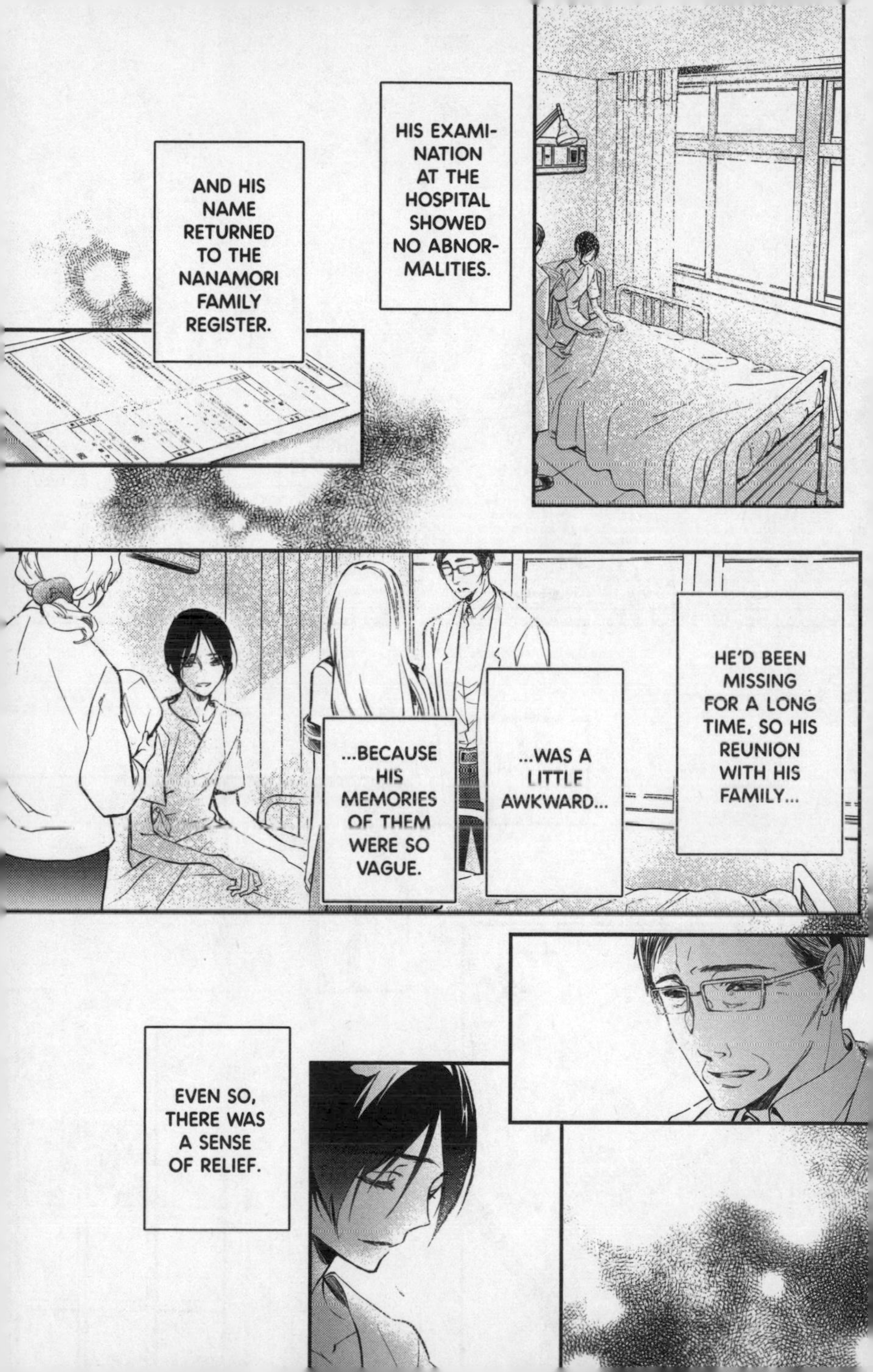
HIS EXAMINATION AT THE HOSPITAL SHOWED NO ABNORMALITIES.
AND HIS NAME RETURNED TO THE NANAMORI FAMILY REGISTER.
HE'D BEEN MISSING FOR A LONG TIME, SO HIS REUNION WITH HIS FAMILY...
...WAS A LITTLE AWKWARD...
...BECAUSE HIS MEMORIES OF THEM WERE SO VAGUE.
EVEN SO, THERE WAS A SENSE OF RELIEF.

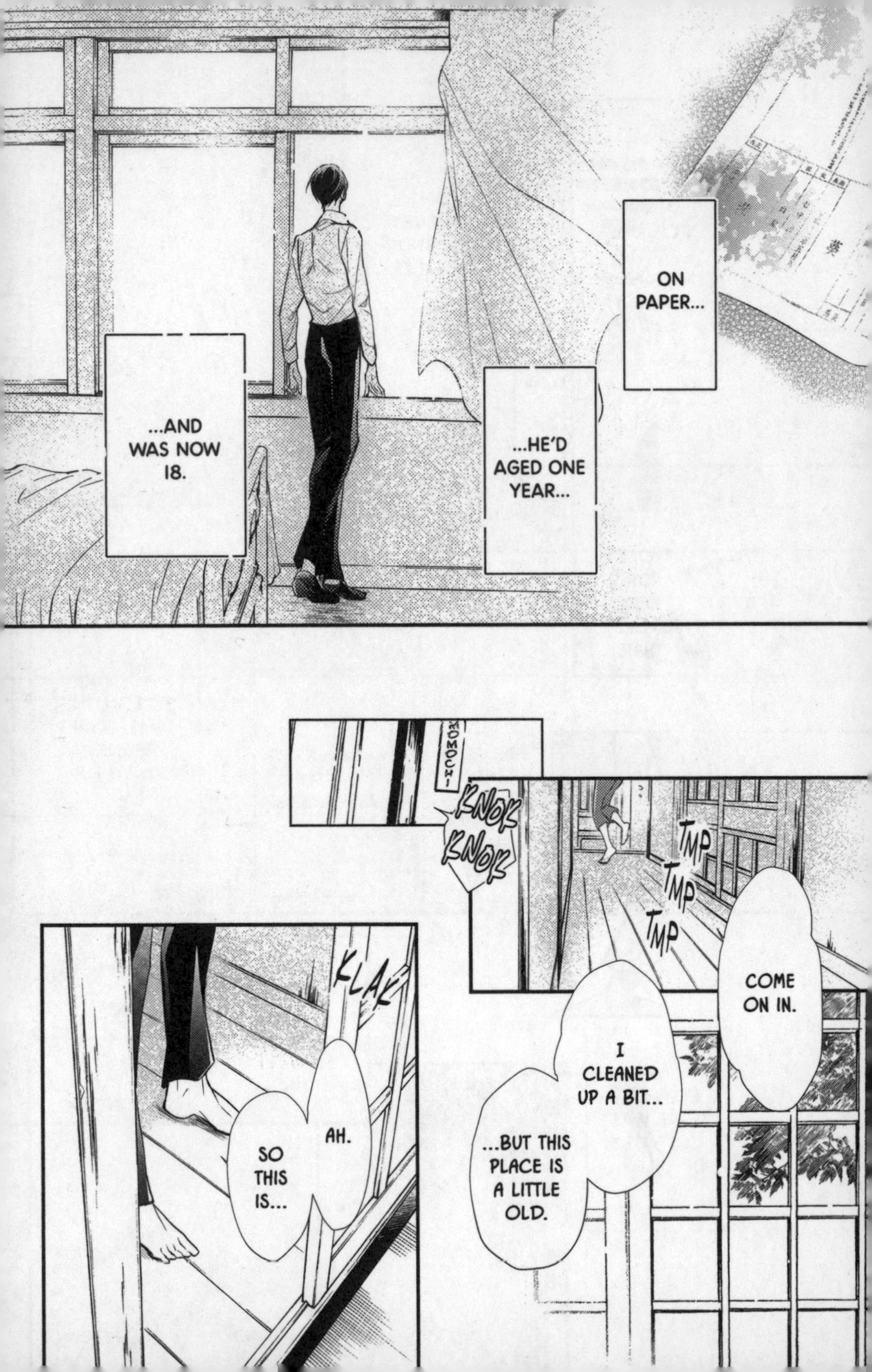
ON PAPER...
...HE'D AGED ONE YEAR...
...AND WAS NOW 18.
MOMOCHI
KNOK KNOK
TMP TMP TMP
COME ON IN.
I CLEANED UP A BIT...
...BUT THIS PLACE IS A LITTLE OLD.
KLAK
AH.
SO THIS IS...

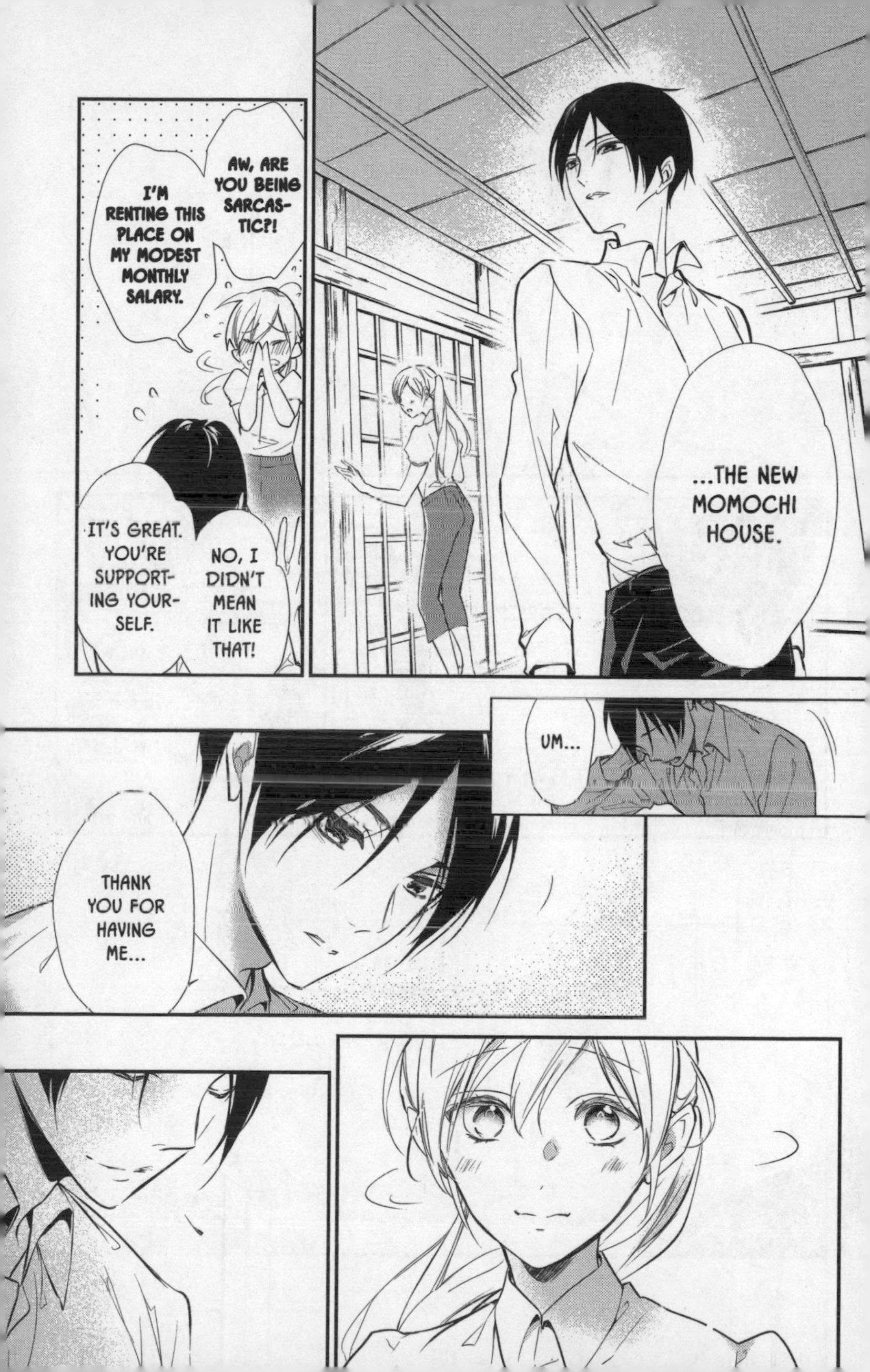
...THE NEW MOMOCHI HOUSE.
AW, ARE YOU BEING SARCASTIC?!
I'M RENTING THIS PLACE ON MY MODEST MONTHLY SALARY.
NO, I DIDN'T MEAN IT LIKE THAT!
IT'S GREAT. YOU'RE SUPPORTING YOURSELF.
UM...
THANK YOU FOR HAVING ME...

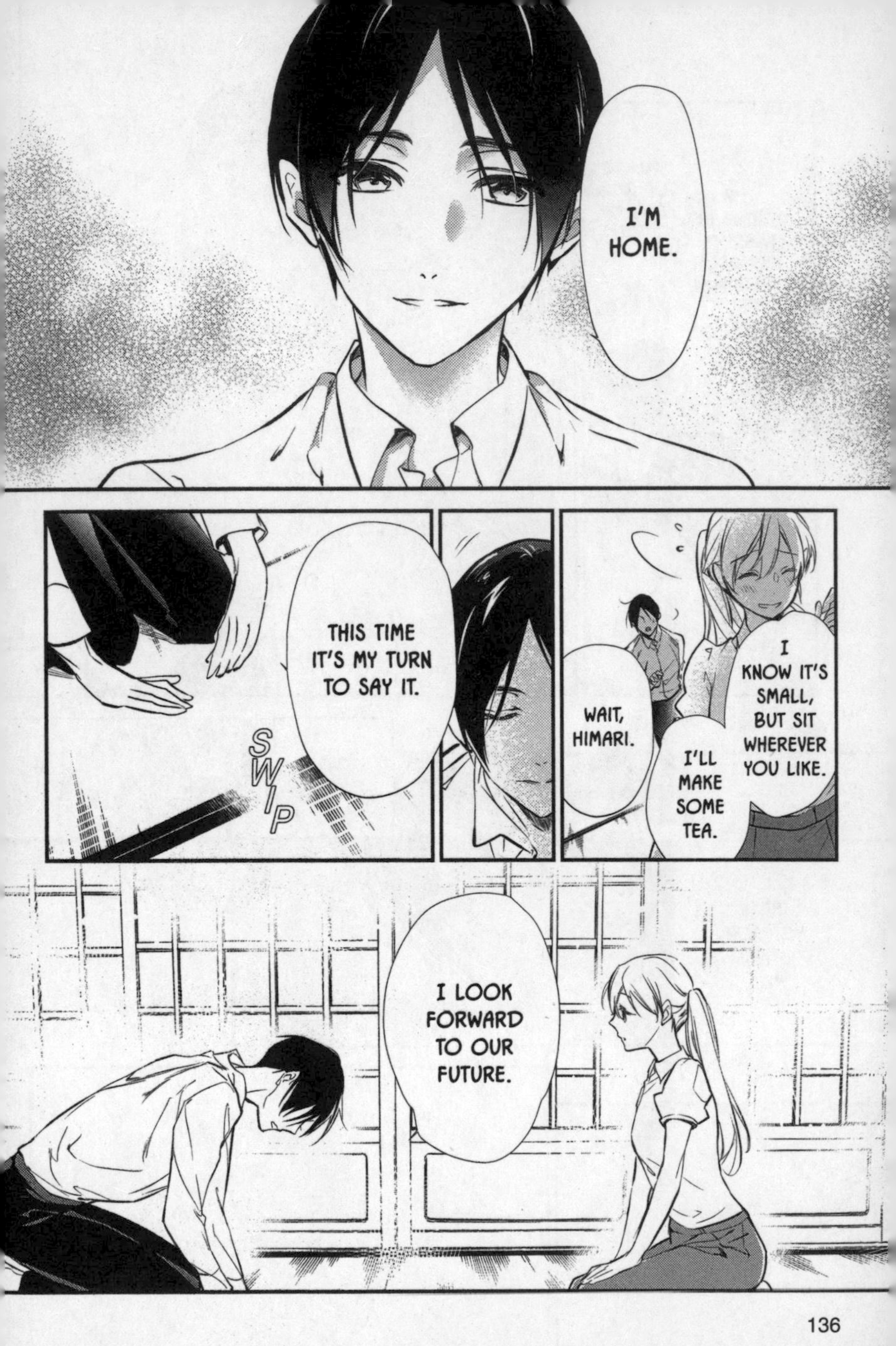
I'M HOME.
I KNOW IT'S SMALL, BUT SIT WHEREVER YOU LIKE.
I'LL MAKE SOME TEA.
WAIT, HIMARI.
THIS TIME IT'S MY TURN TO SAY IT.
SWIP
I LOOK FORWARD TO OUR FUTURE.

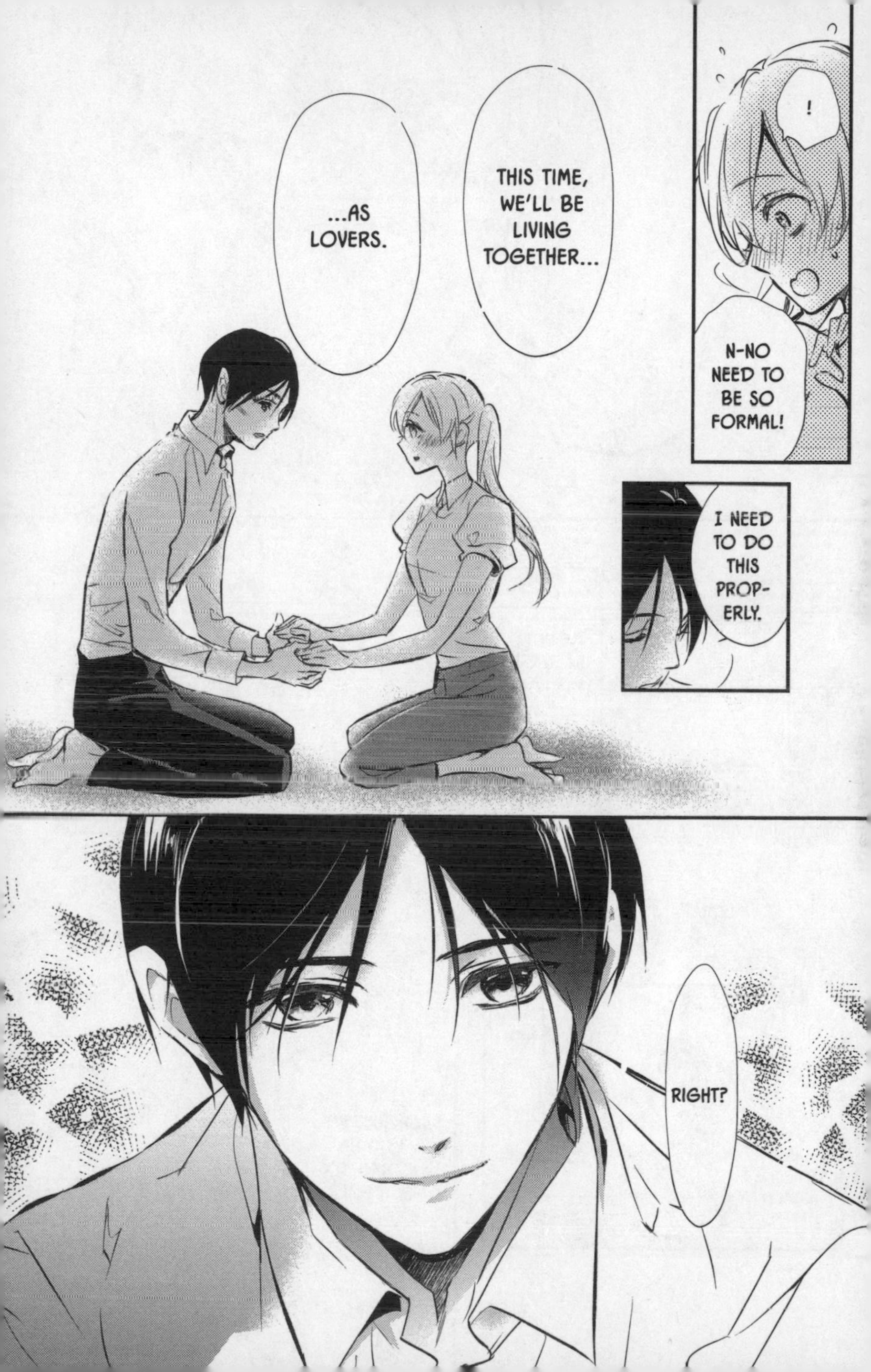
!
N-NO NEED TO BE SO FORMAL!
I NEED TO DO THIS PROPERLY.
THIS TIME, WE'LL BE LIVING TOGETHER...
...AS LOVERS.
RIGHT?

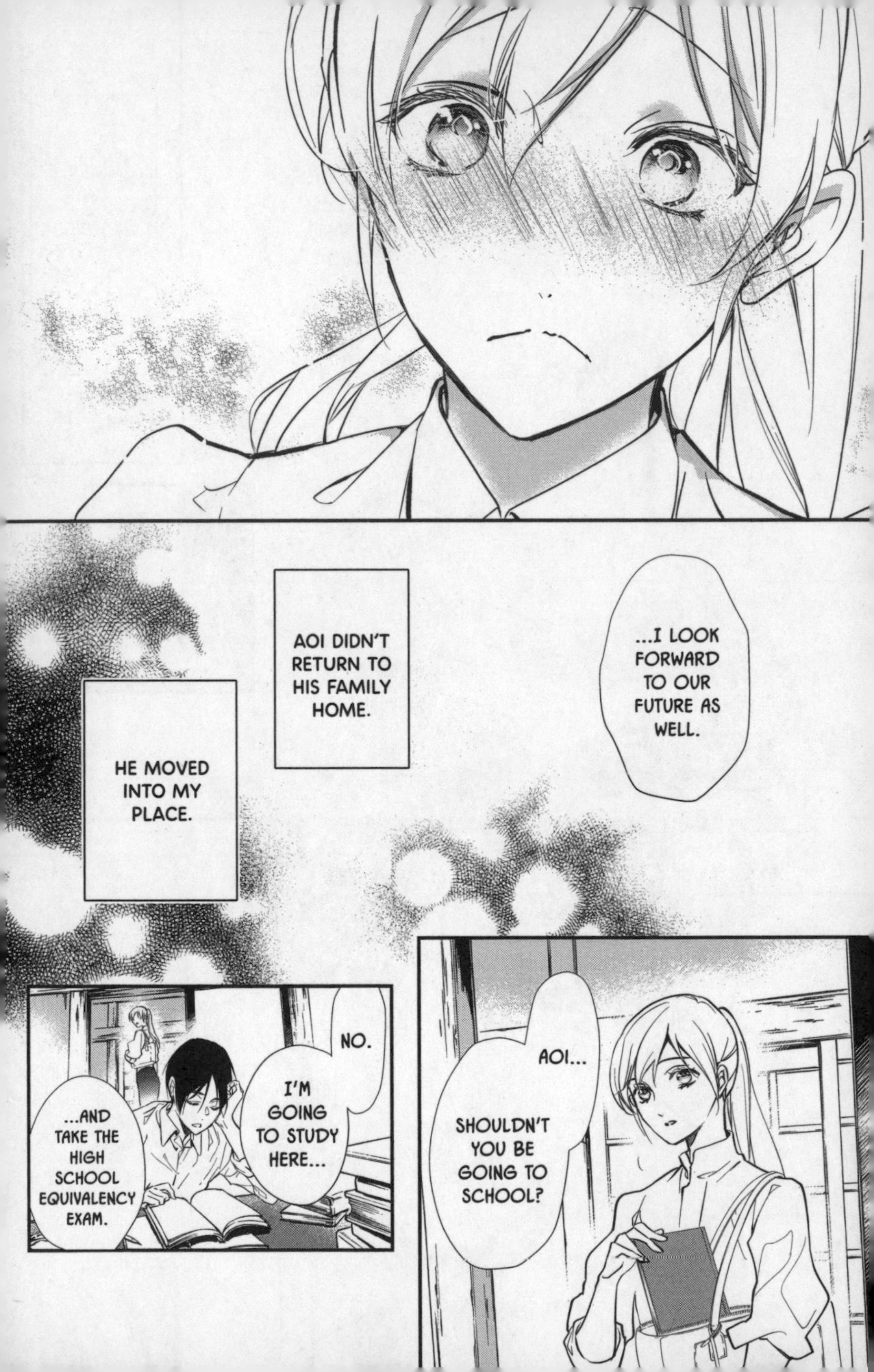
...I LOOK FORWARD TO OUR FUTURE AS WELL.
AOI DIDN'T RETURN TO HIS FAMILY HOME.
HE MOVED INTO MY PLACE.
AOI...
SHOULDN'T YOU BE GOING TO SCHOOL?
NO.
I'M GOING TO STUDY HERE...
...AND TAKE THE HIGH SCHOOL EQUIVALENCY EXAM.

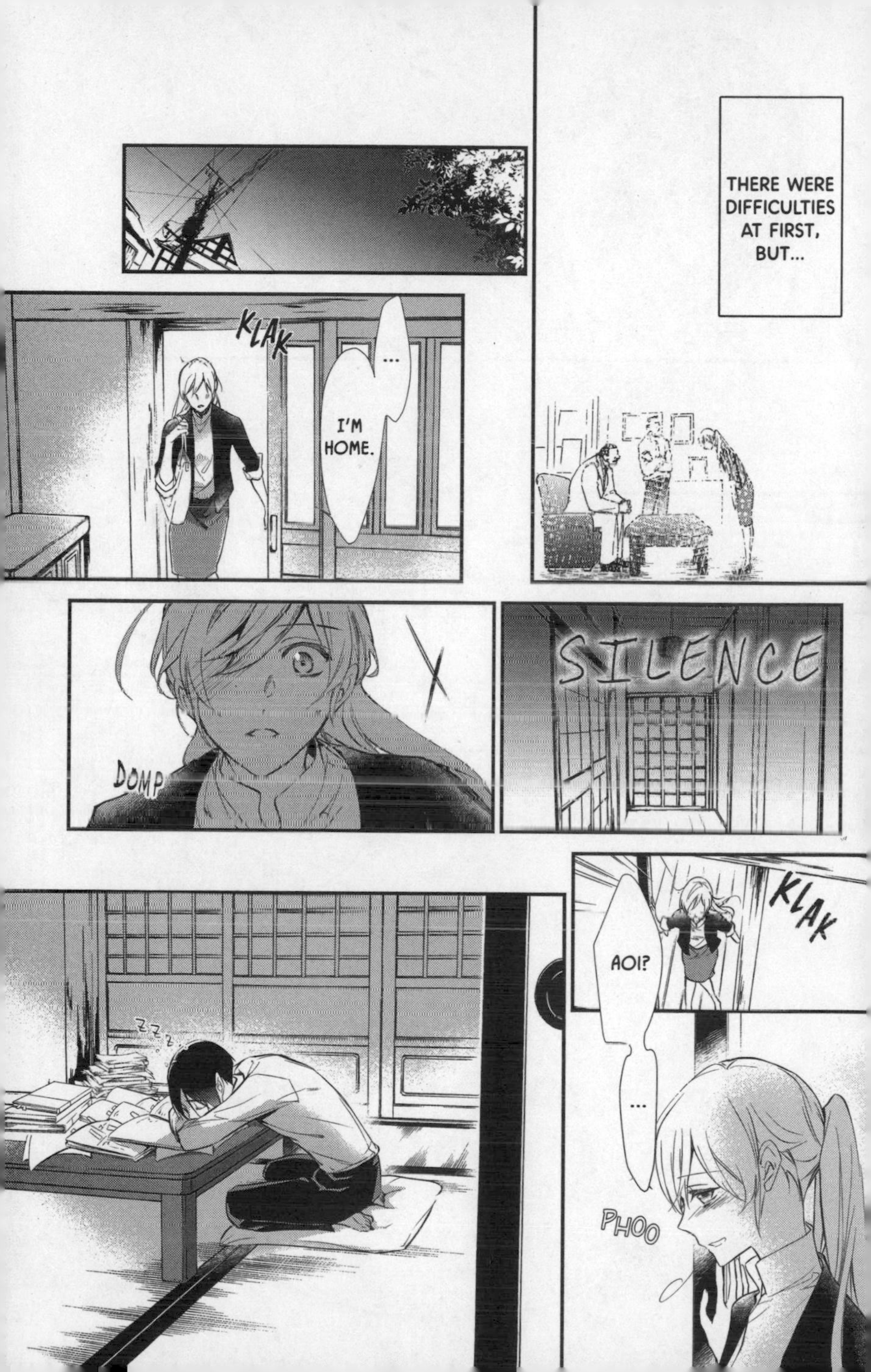
THERE WERE DIFFICULTIES AT FIRST, BUT...
...
I'M HOME.
KLAK
SILENCE
DOMP
KLAK
AOI?
...
PHOO
ZZZ

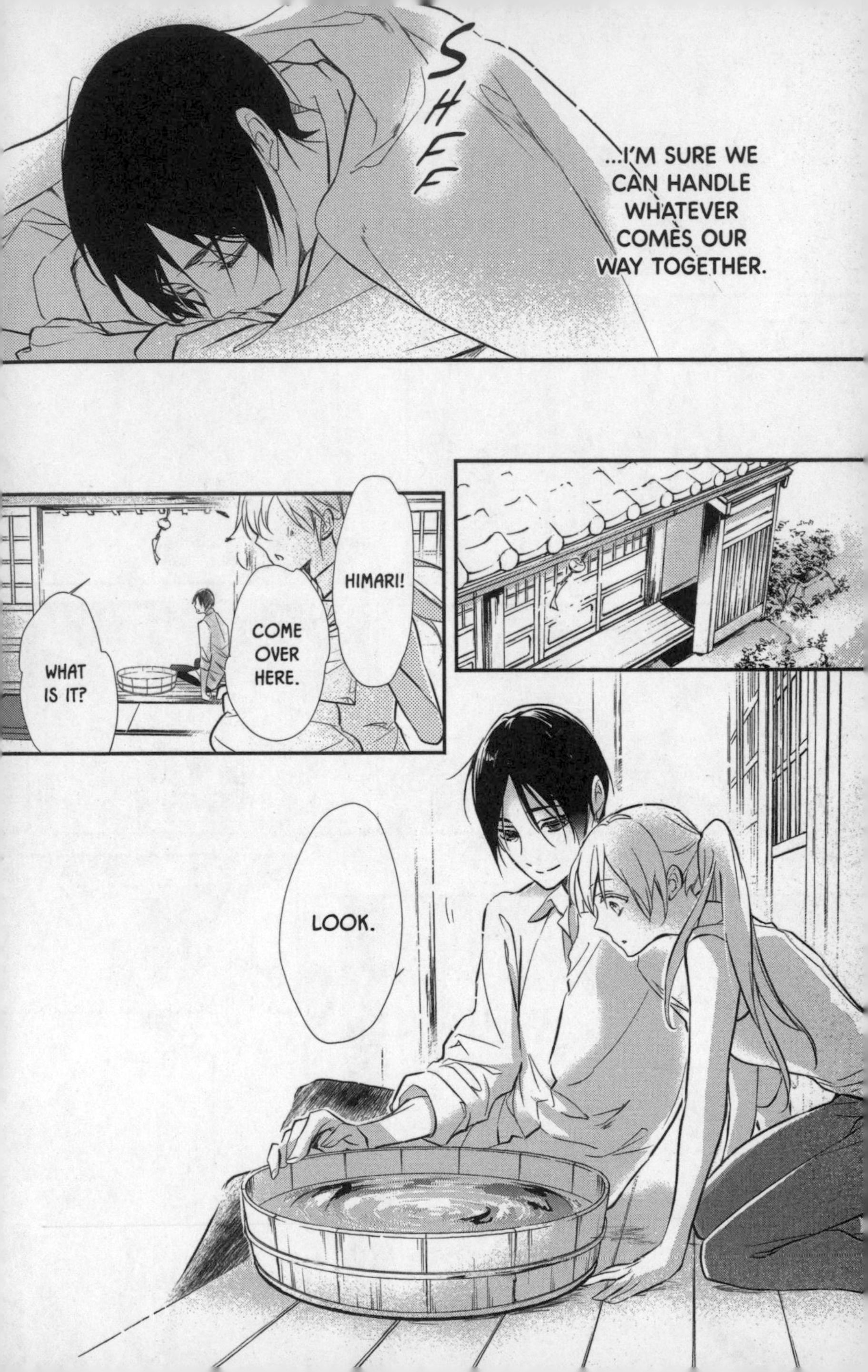
SHFF
...I'M SURE WE CAN HANDLE WHATEVER COMES OUR WAY TOGETHER.
HIMARI!
COME OVER HERE.
WHAT IS IT?
LOOK.

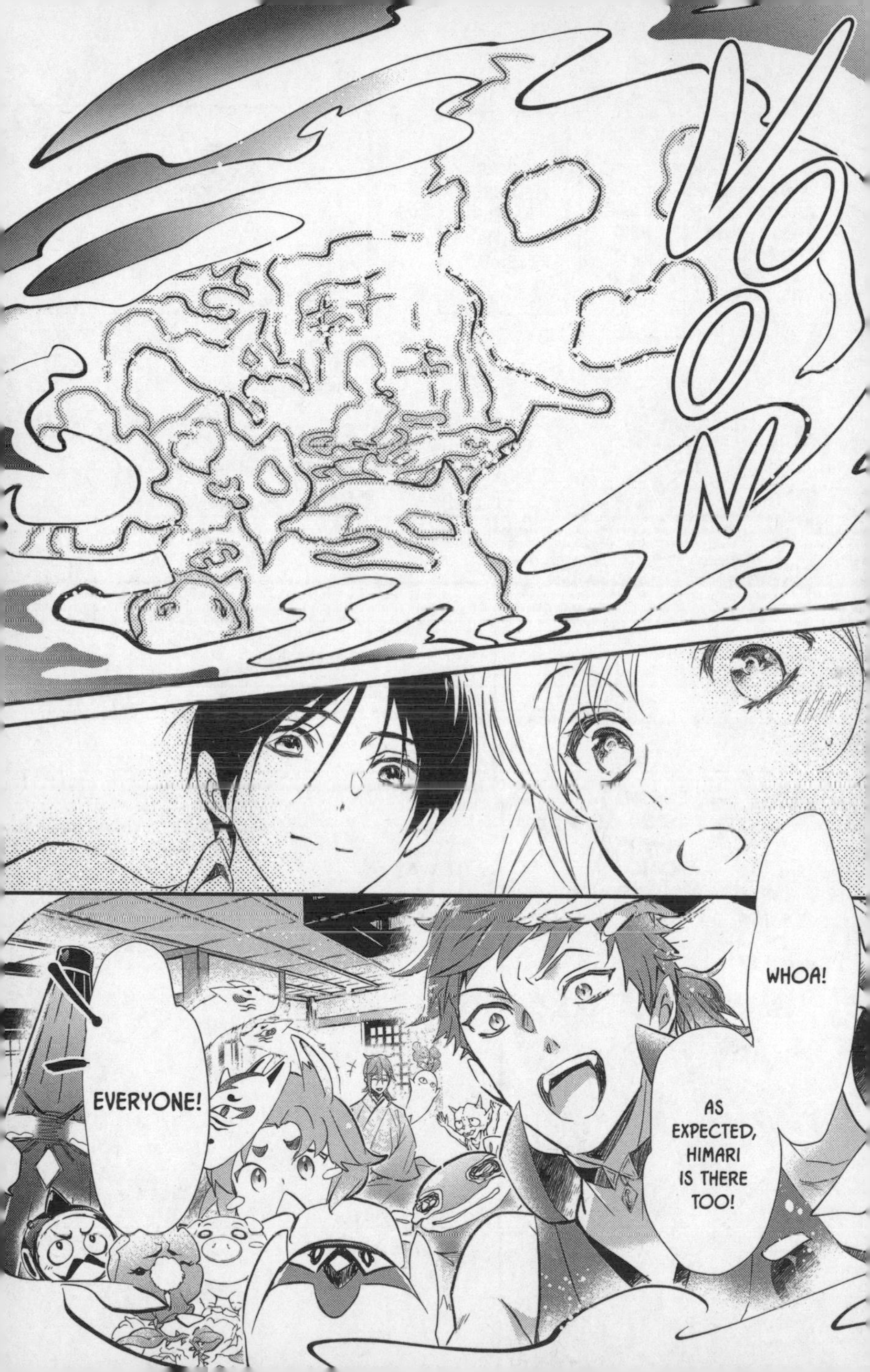
VOON
WHOA!
AS EXPECTED, HIMARI IS THERE TOO!
EVERYONE!

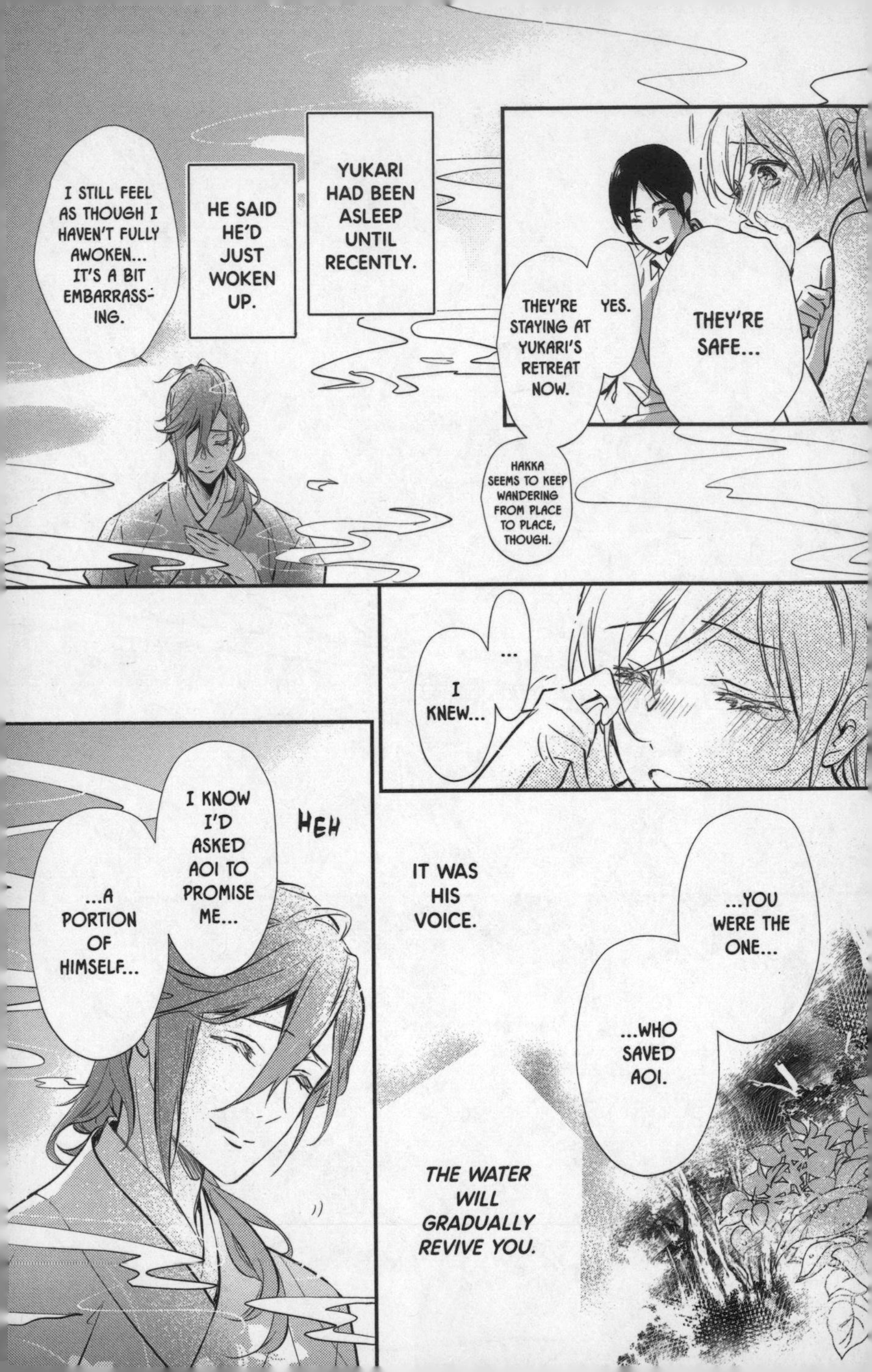
THEY'RE SAFE...
YES. THEY'RE STAYING AT YUKARI'S RETREAT NOW.
HAKKA SEEMS TO KEEP WANDERING FROM PLACE TO PLACE, THOUGH.
YUKARI HAD BEEN ASLEEP UNTIL RECENTLY.
HE SAID HE'D JUST WOKEN UP.
I STILL FEEL AS THOUGH I HAVEN'T FULLY AWOKEN... IT'S A BIT EMBARRASSING.
... I KNEW...
...YOU WERE THE ONE...
...WHO SAVED AOI.
IT WAS HIS VOICE.
THE WATER WILL GRADUALLY REVIVE YOU.
I KNOW I'D ASKED AOI TO PROMISE ME...
HEH
...A PORTION OF HIMSELF...

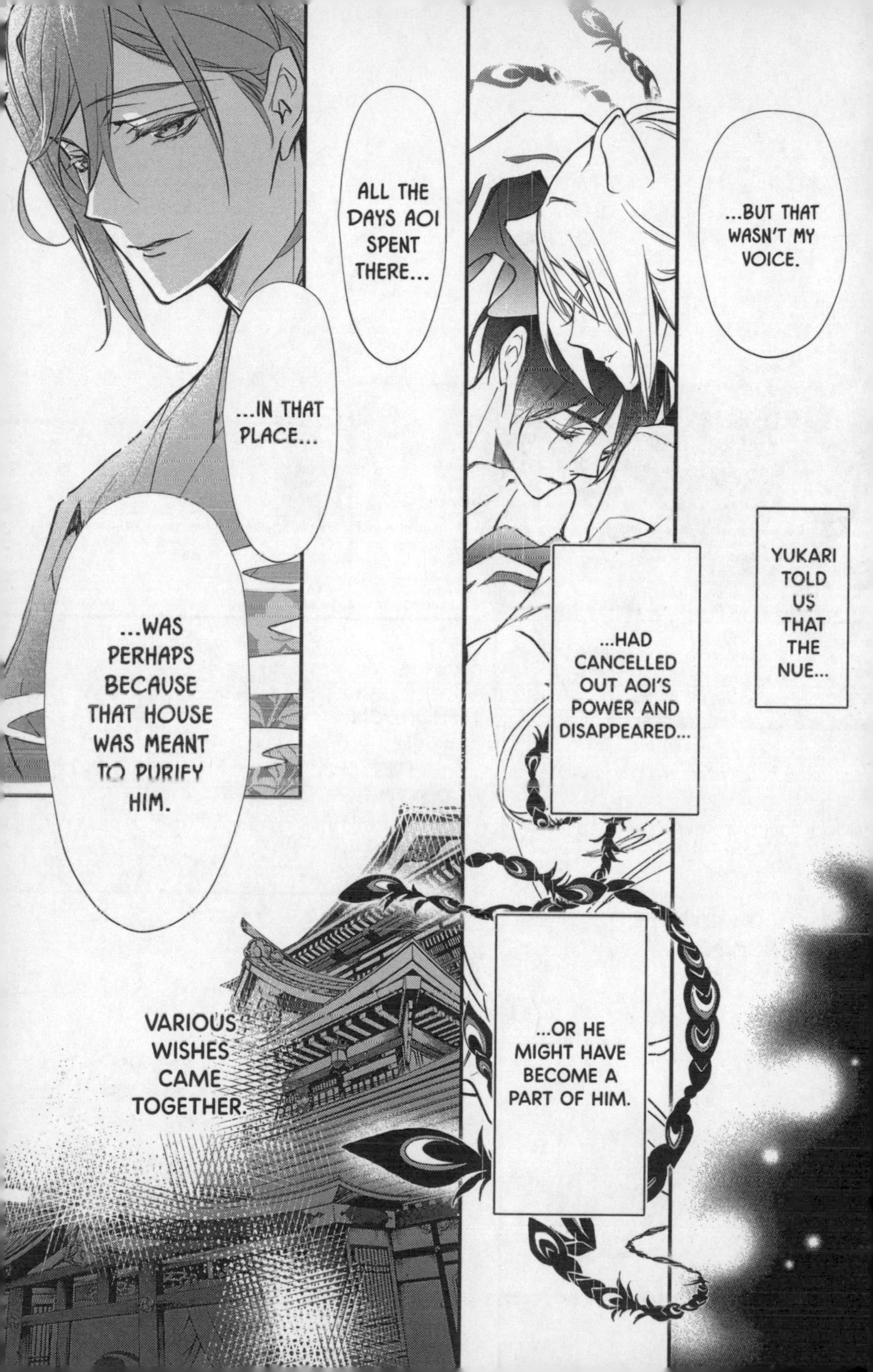
...BUT THAT WASN'T MY VOICE.
YUKARI TOLD US THAT THE NUE...
...HAD CANCELLED OUT AOI'S POWER AND DISAPPEARED...
...OR HE MIGHT HAVE BECOME A PART OF HIM.
ALL THE DAYS AOI SPENT THERE...
...IN THAT PLACE...
...WAS PERHAPS BECAUSE THAT HOUSE WAS MEANT TO PURIFY HIM.
VARIOUS WISHES CAME TOGETHER.

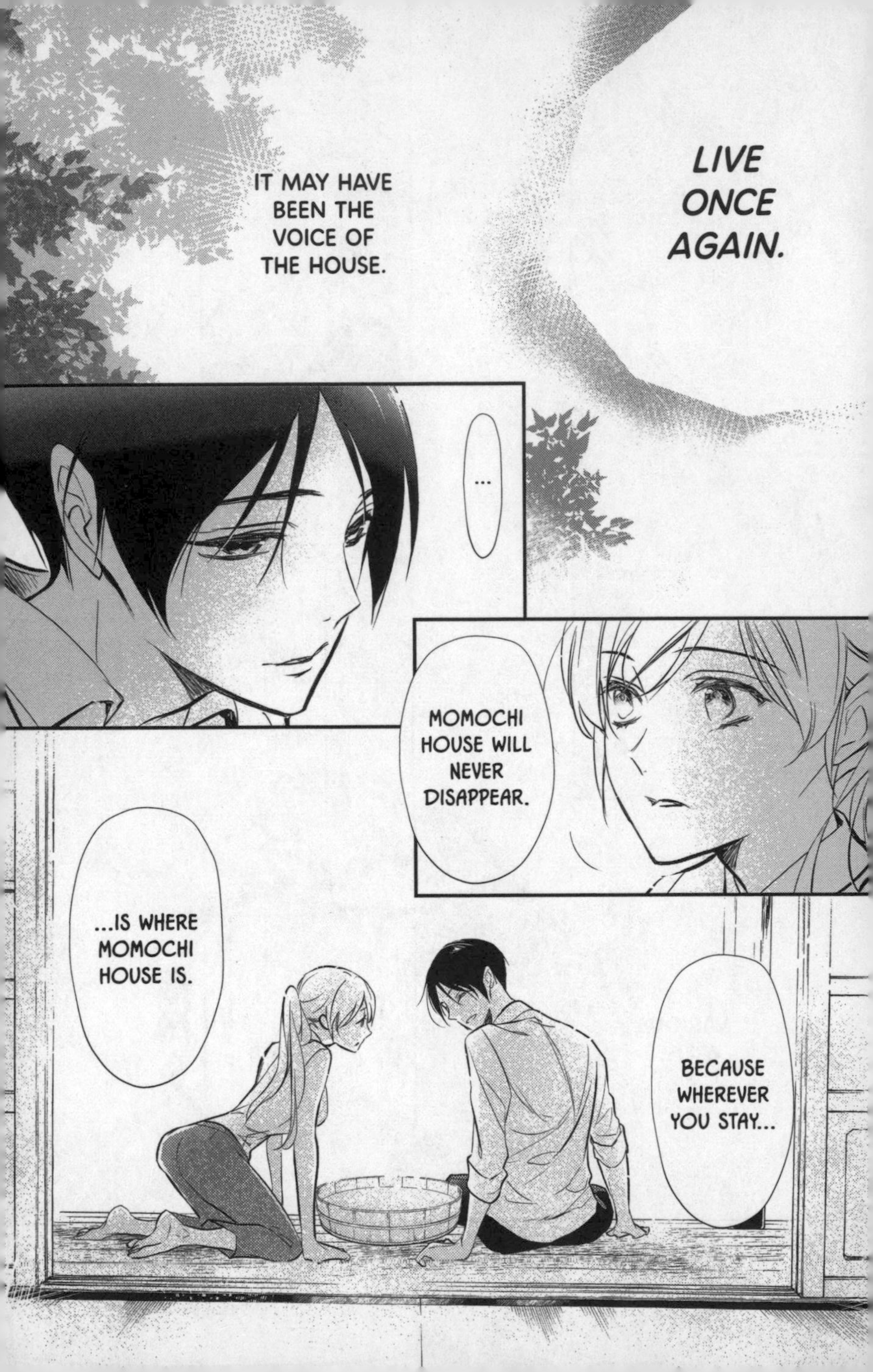
LIVE ONCE AGAIN.
IT MAY HAVE BEEN THE VOICE OF THE HOUSE.
...
MOMOCHI HOUSE WILL NEVER DISAPPEAR.
BECAUSE WHEREVER YOU STAY...
...IS WHERE MOMOCHI HOUSE IS.

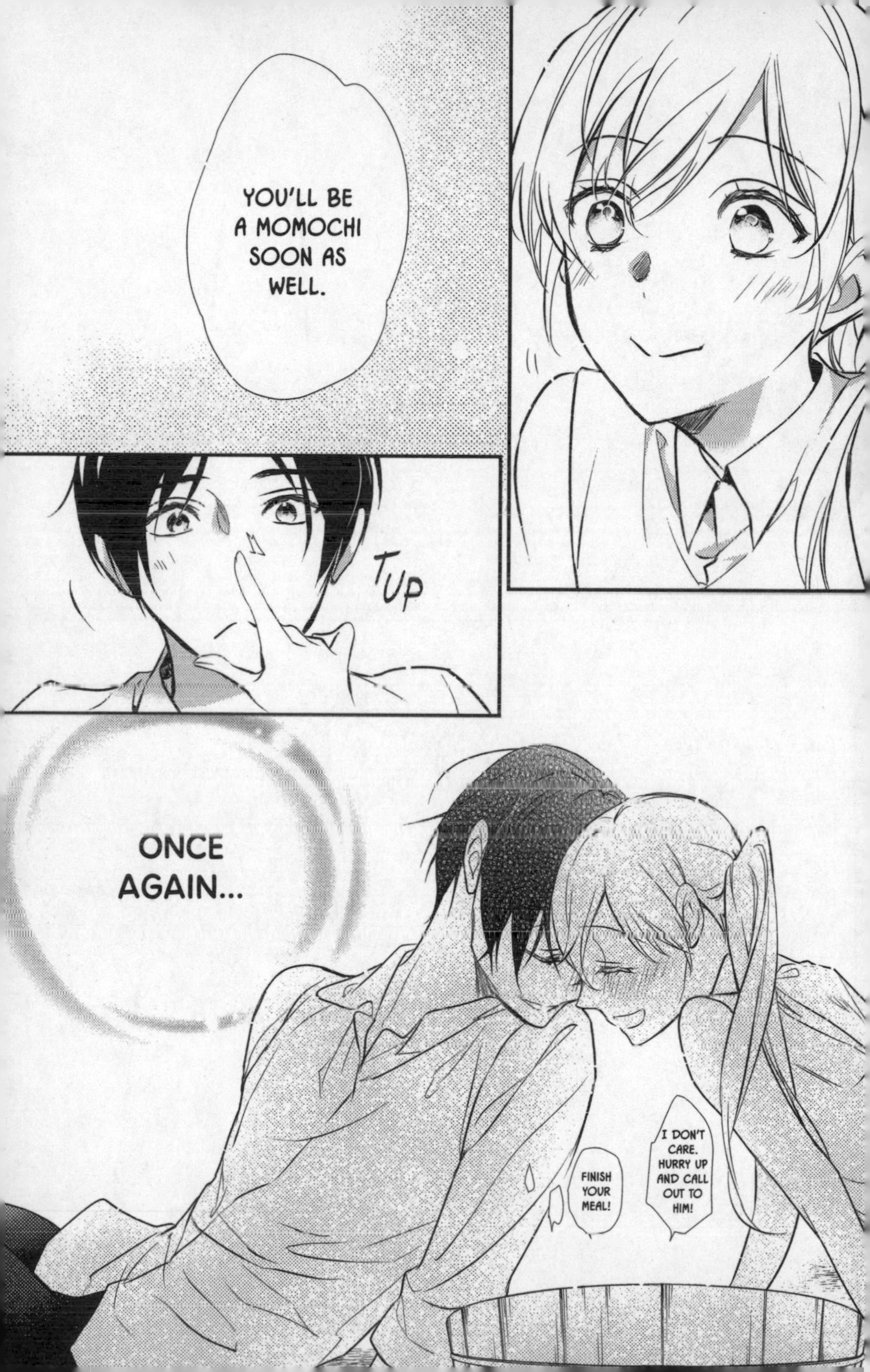
YOU'LL BE A MOMOCHI SOON AS WELL.
TUP
ONCE AGAIN...
I DON'T CARE. HURRY UP AND CALL OUT TO HIM!
FINISH YOUR MEAL!

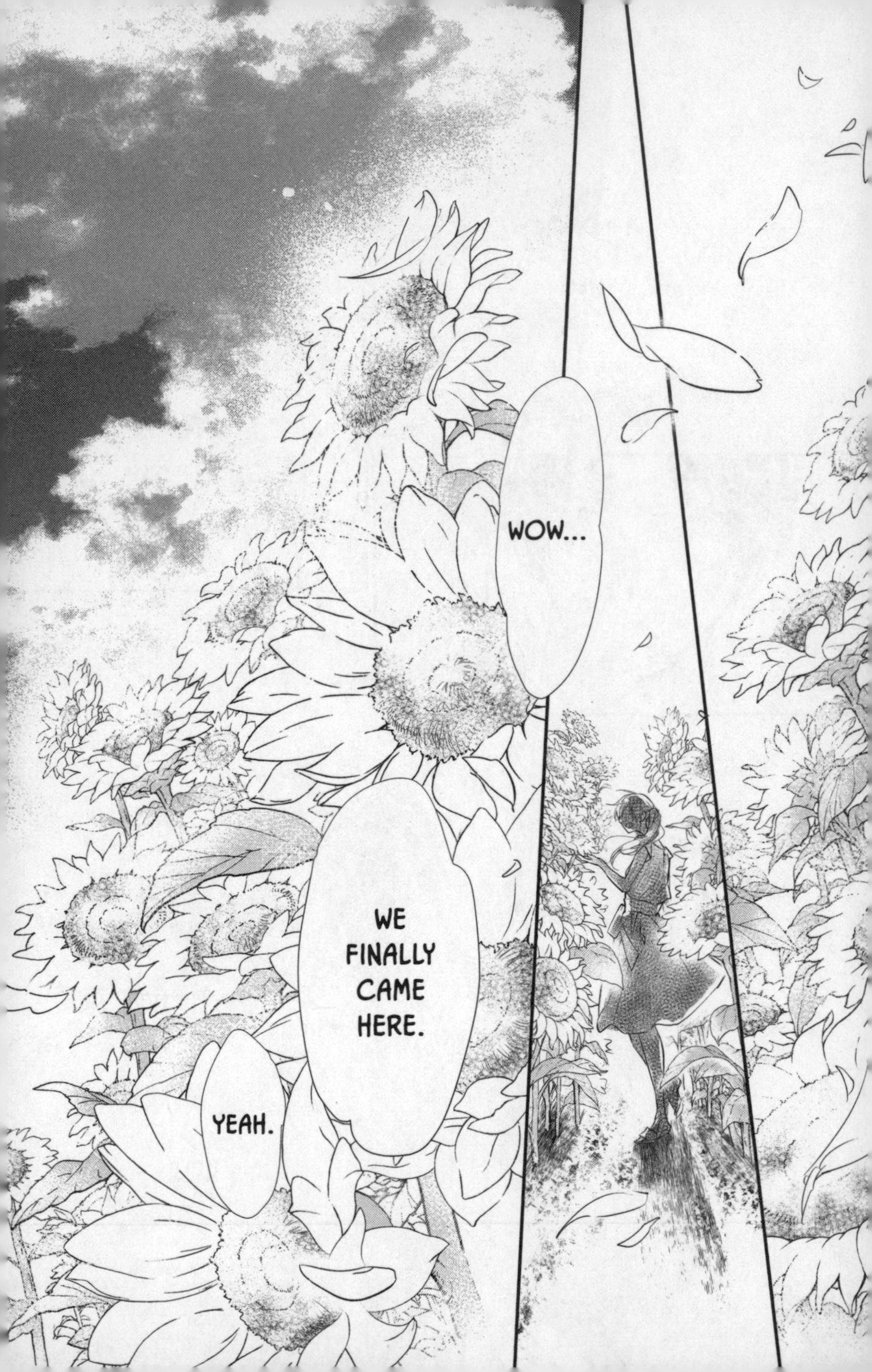
WOW...
WE FINALLY CAME HERE.
YEAH.

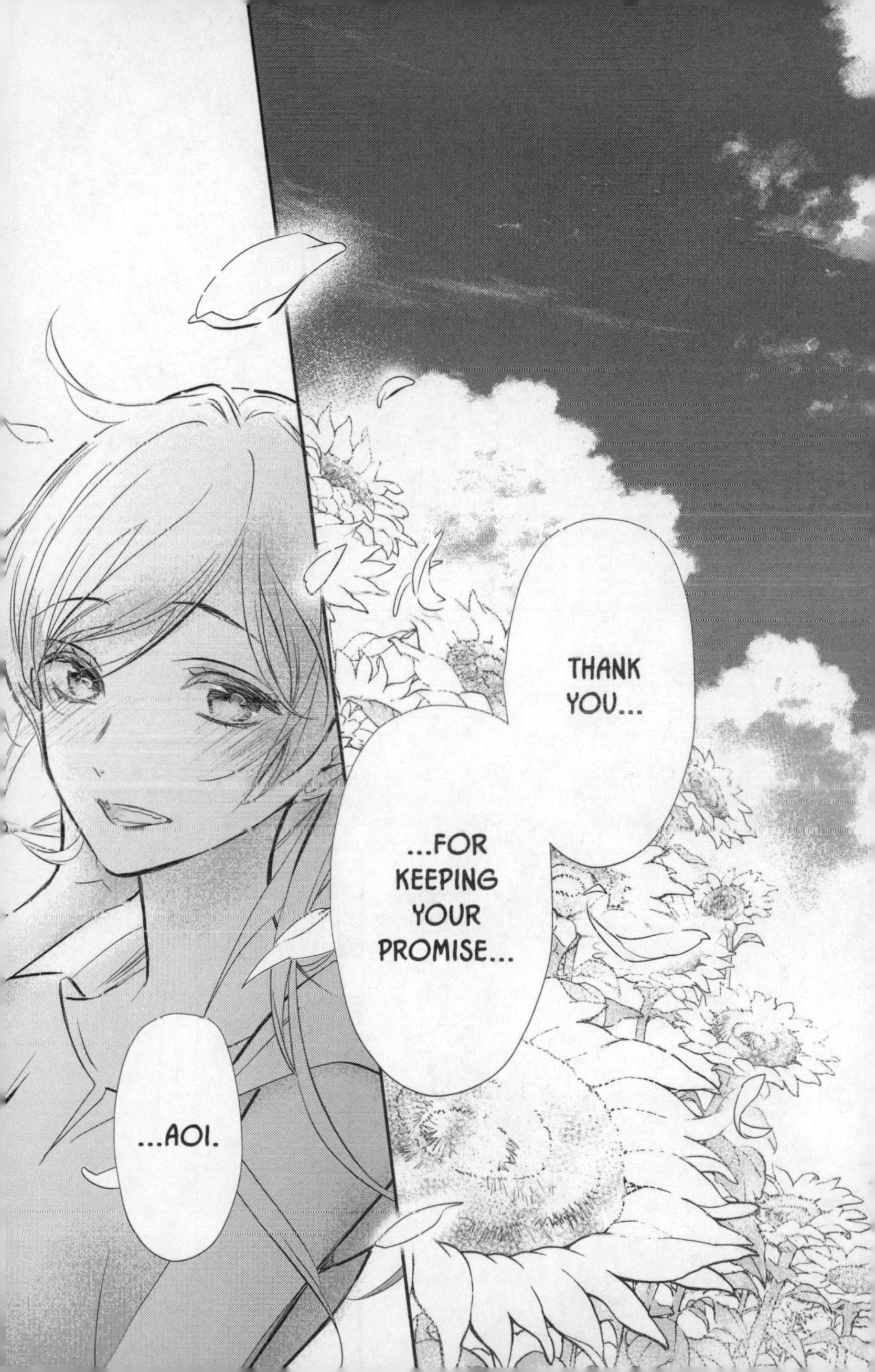
THANK YOU...
...FOR KEEPING YOUR PROMISE...
...AOI.

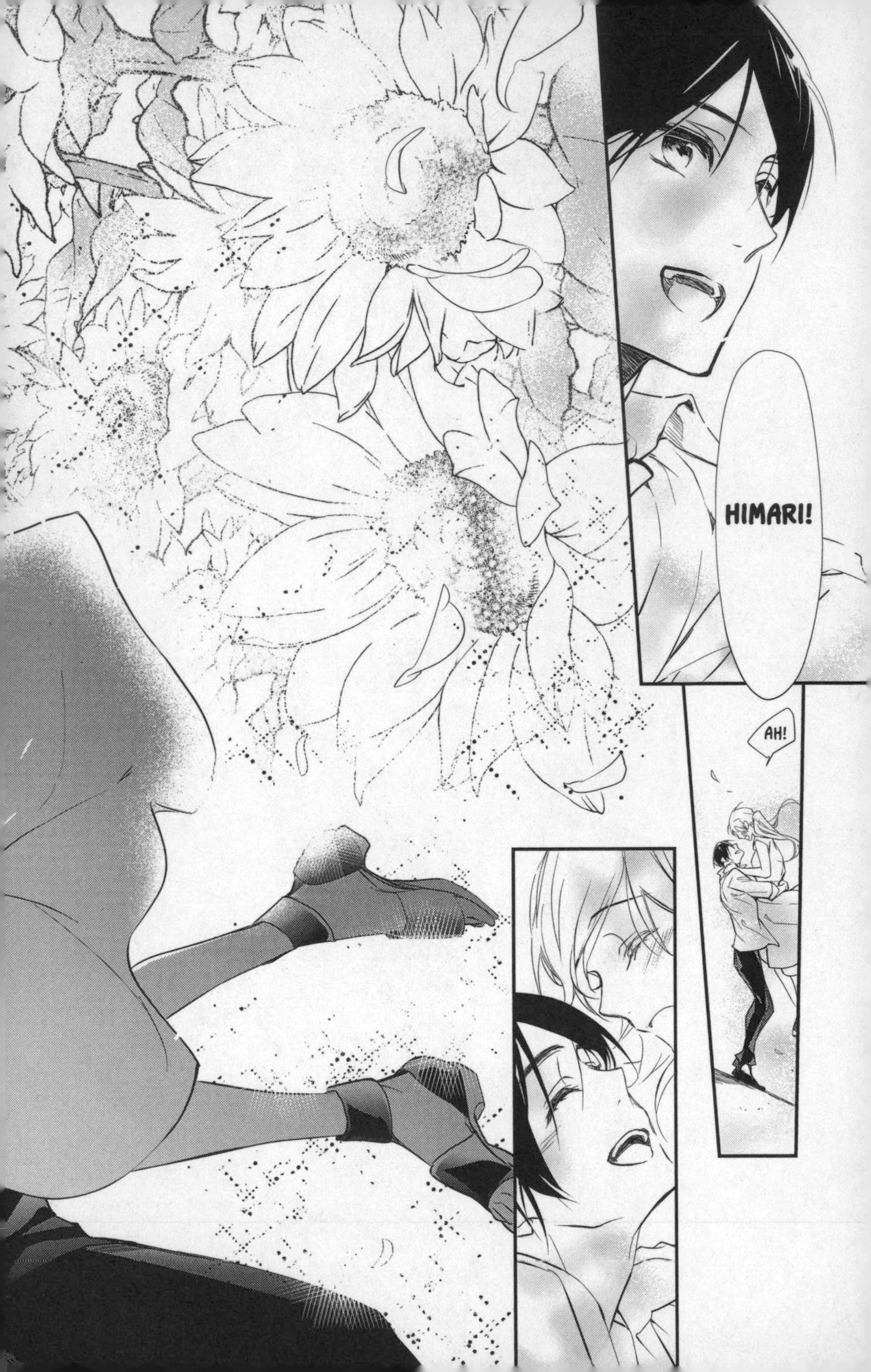
HIMARI!
AH!

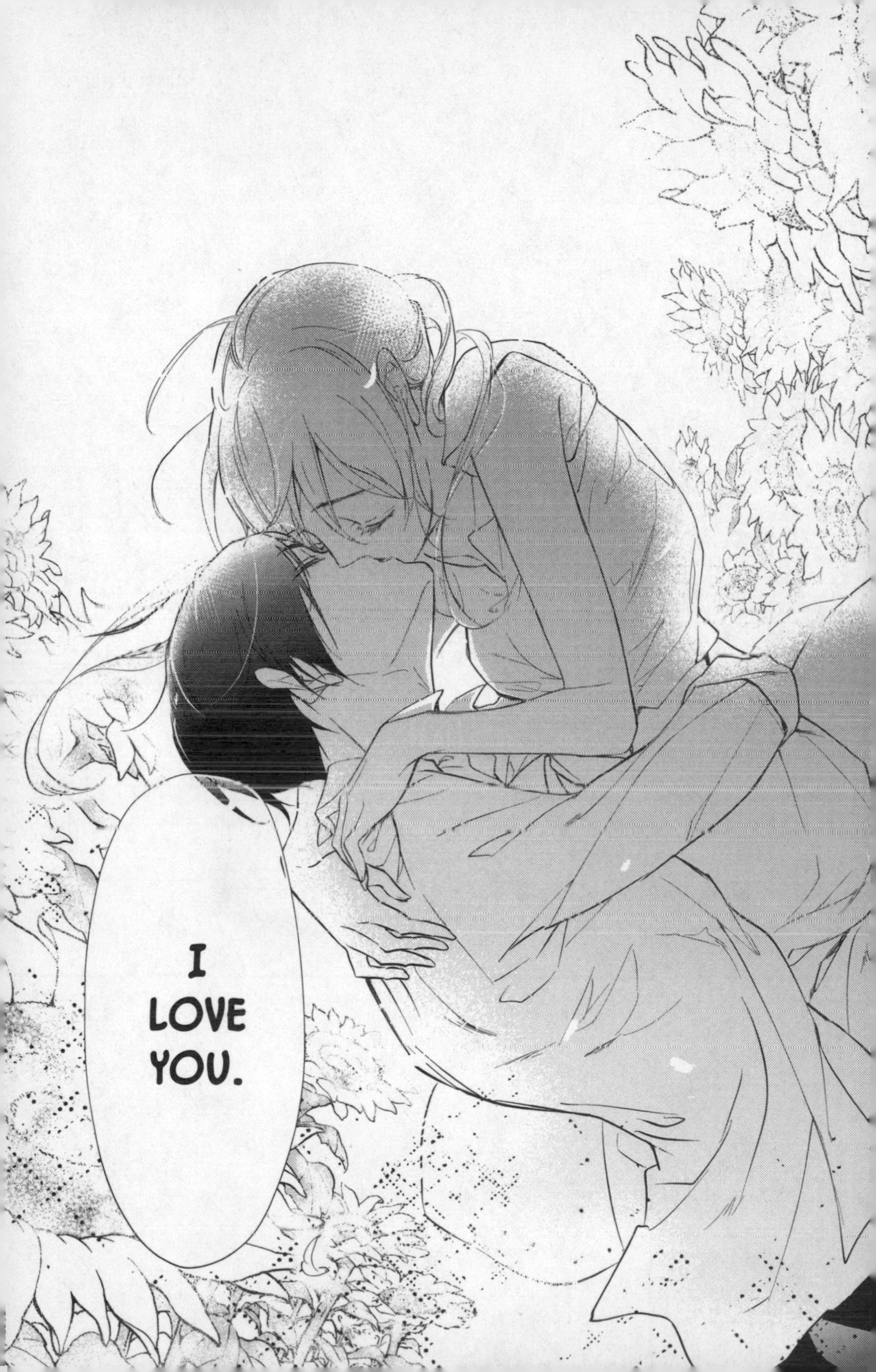
I LOVE YOU.

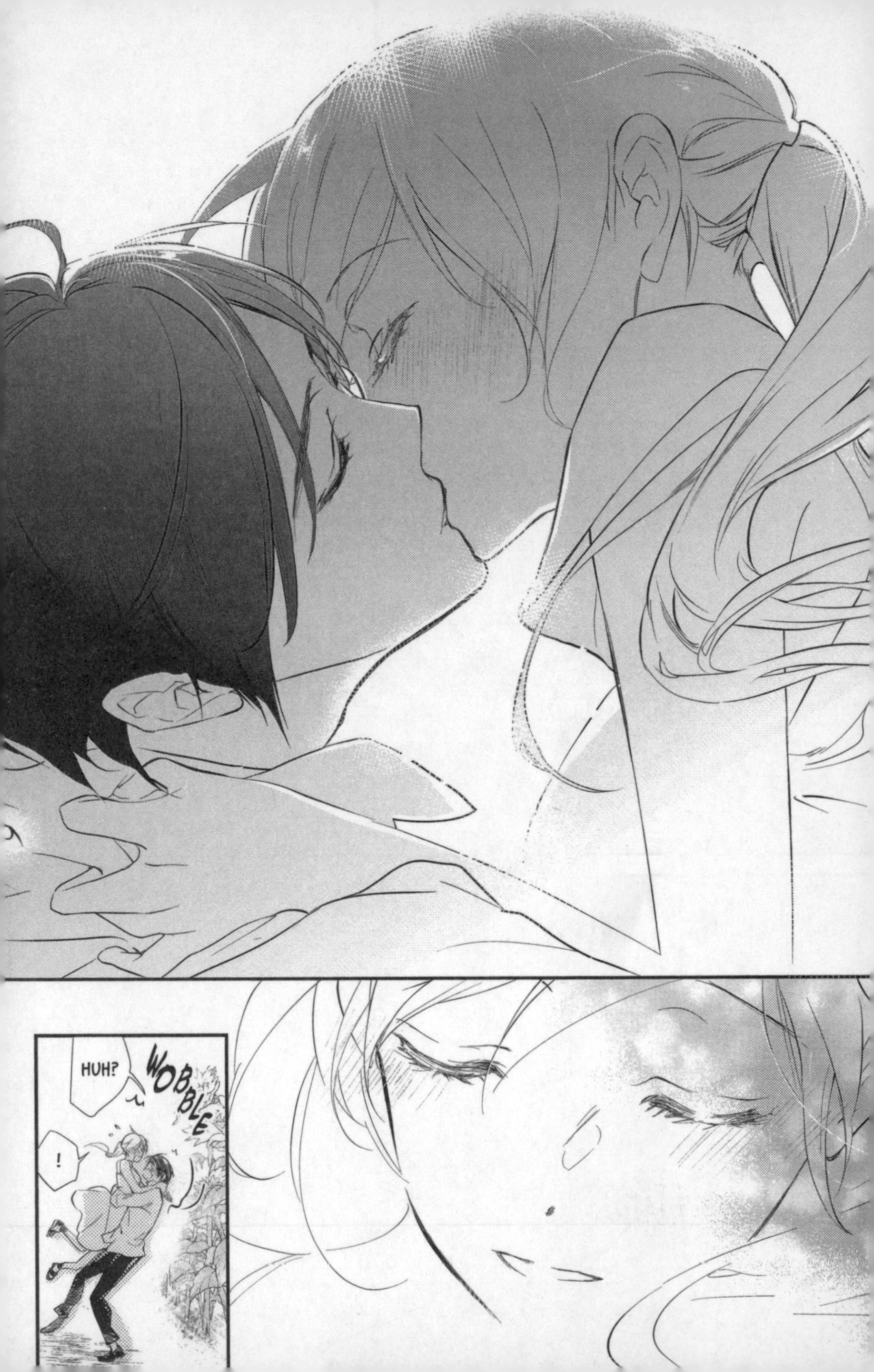
WOBBLE
HUH?
!

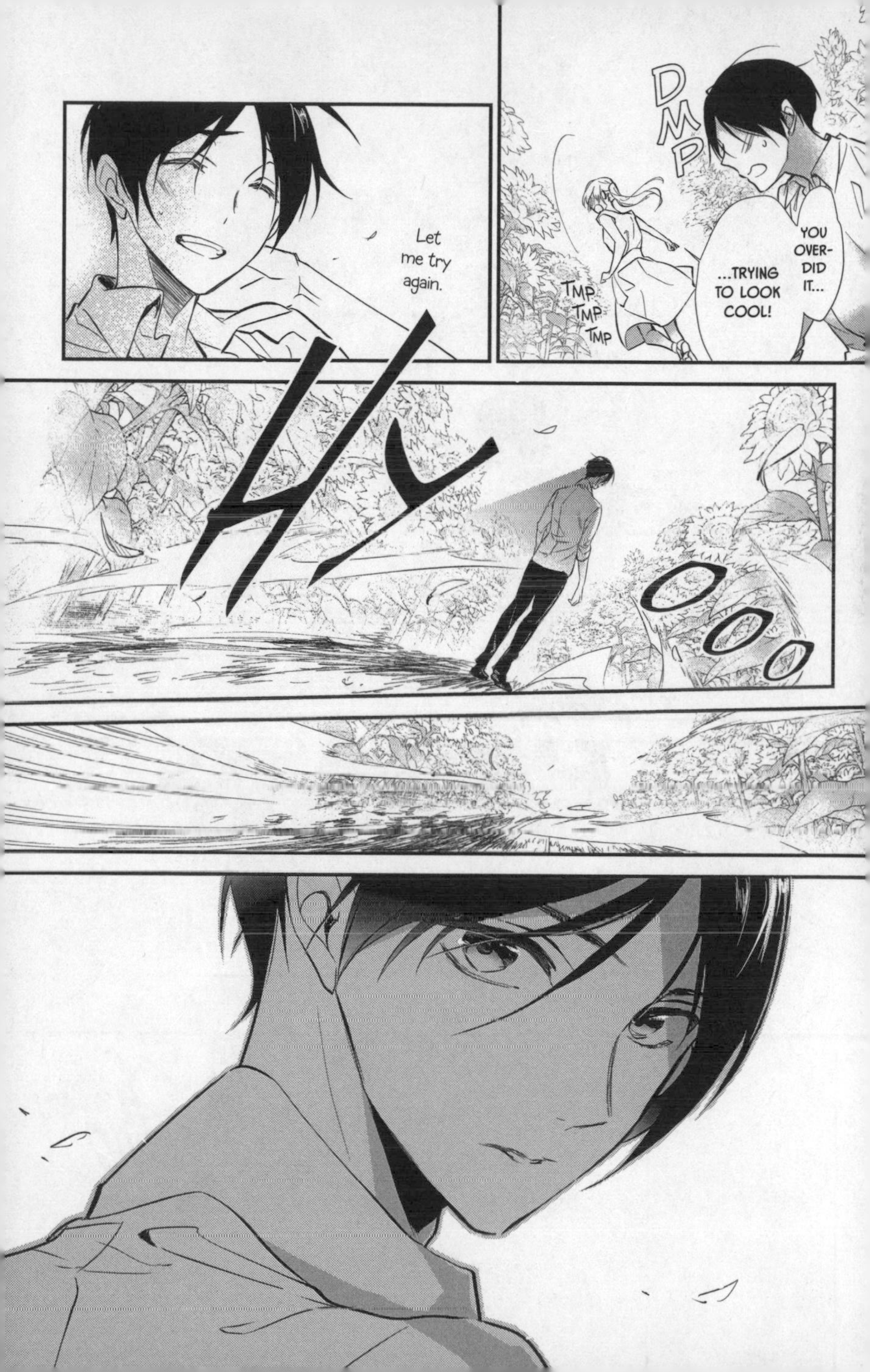
DMP
YOU OVER-DID IT...
...TRYING TO LOOK COOL!
TMP TMP TMP
Let me try again.
HYOOO

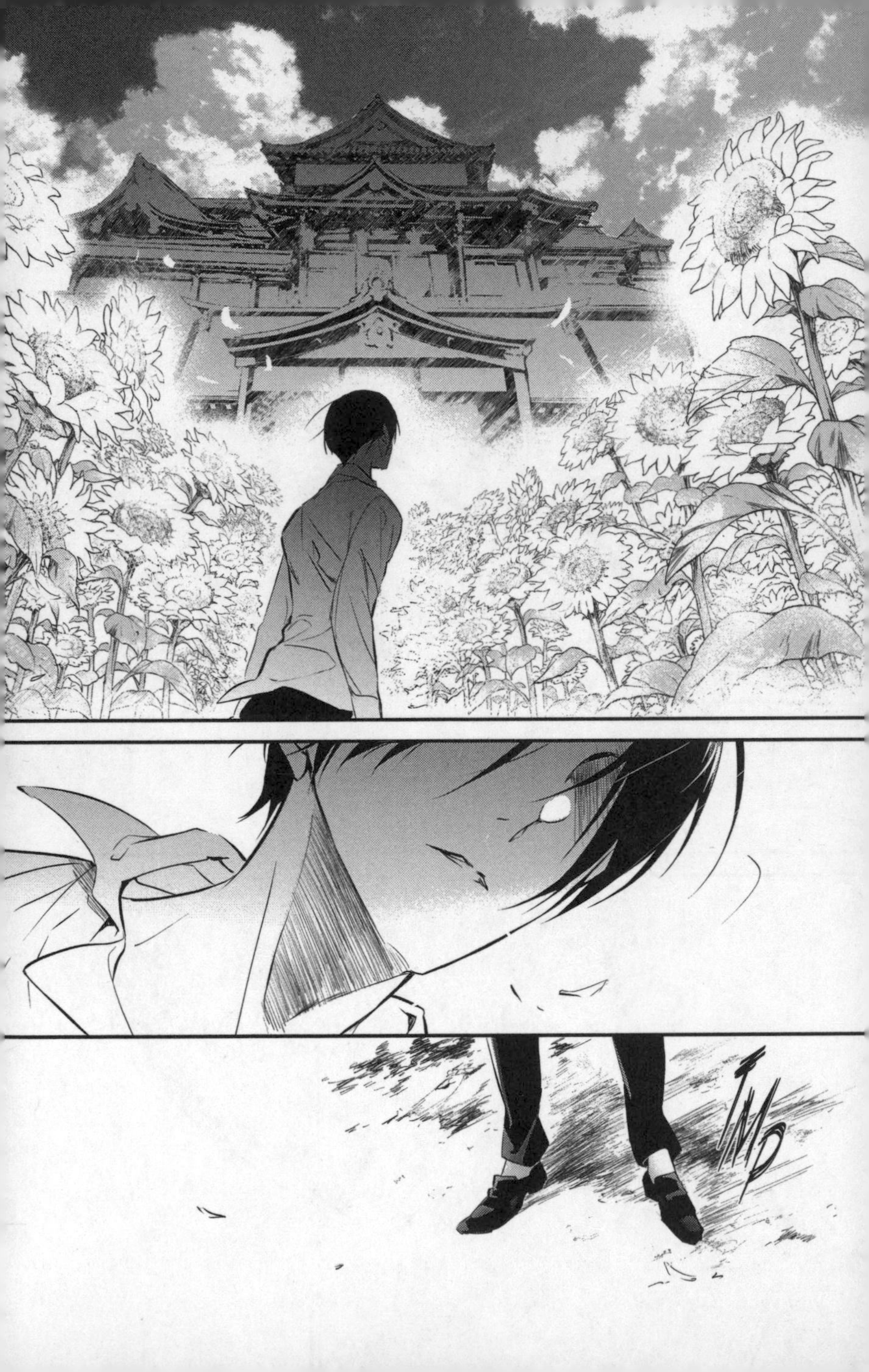
TMP

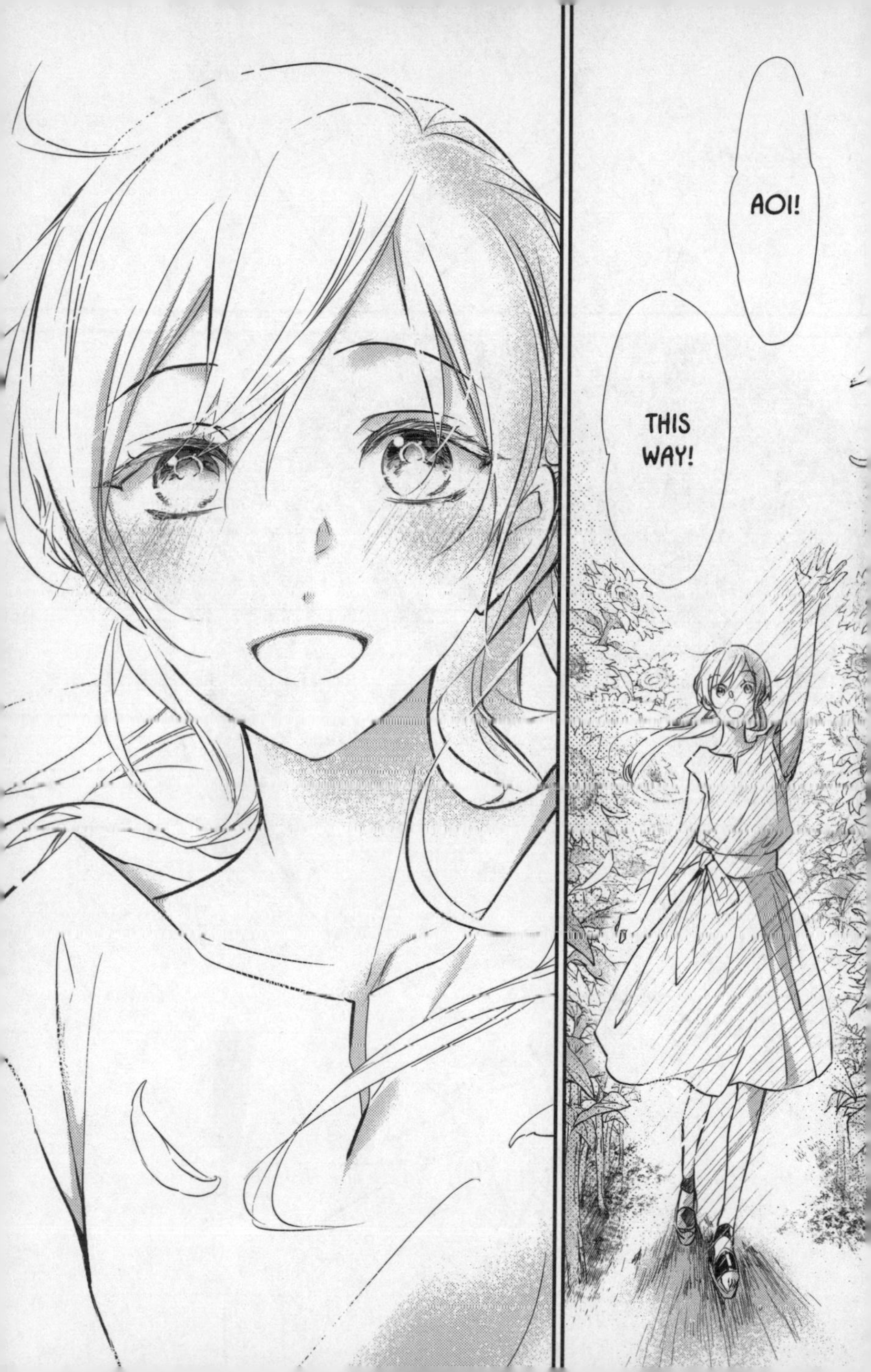
AOI!
THIS WAY!

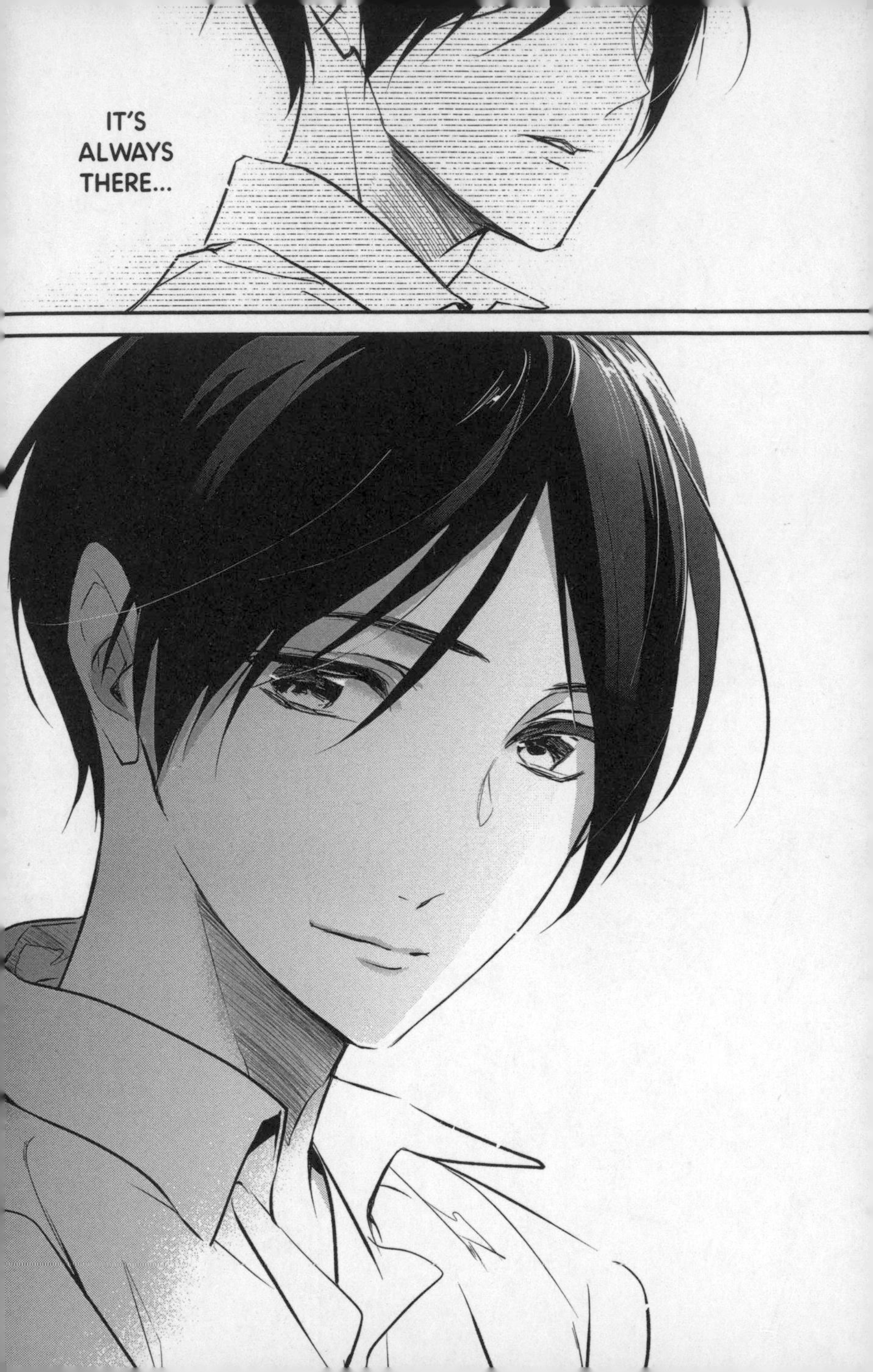
IT'S ALWAYS THERE...

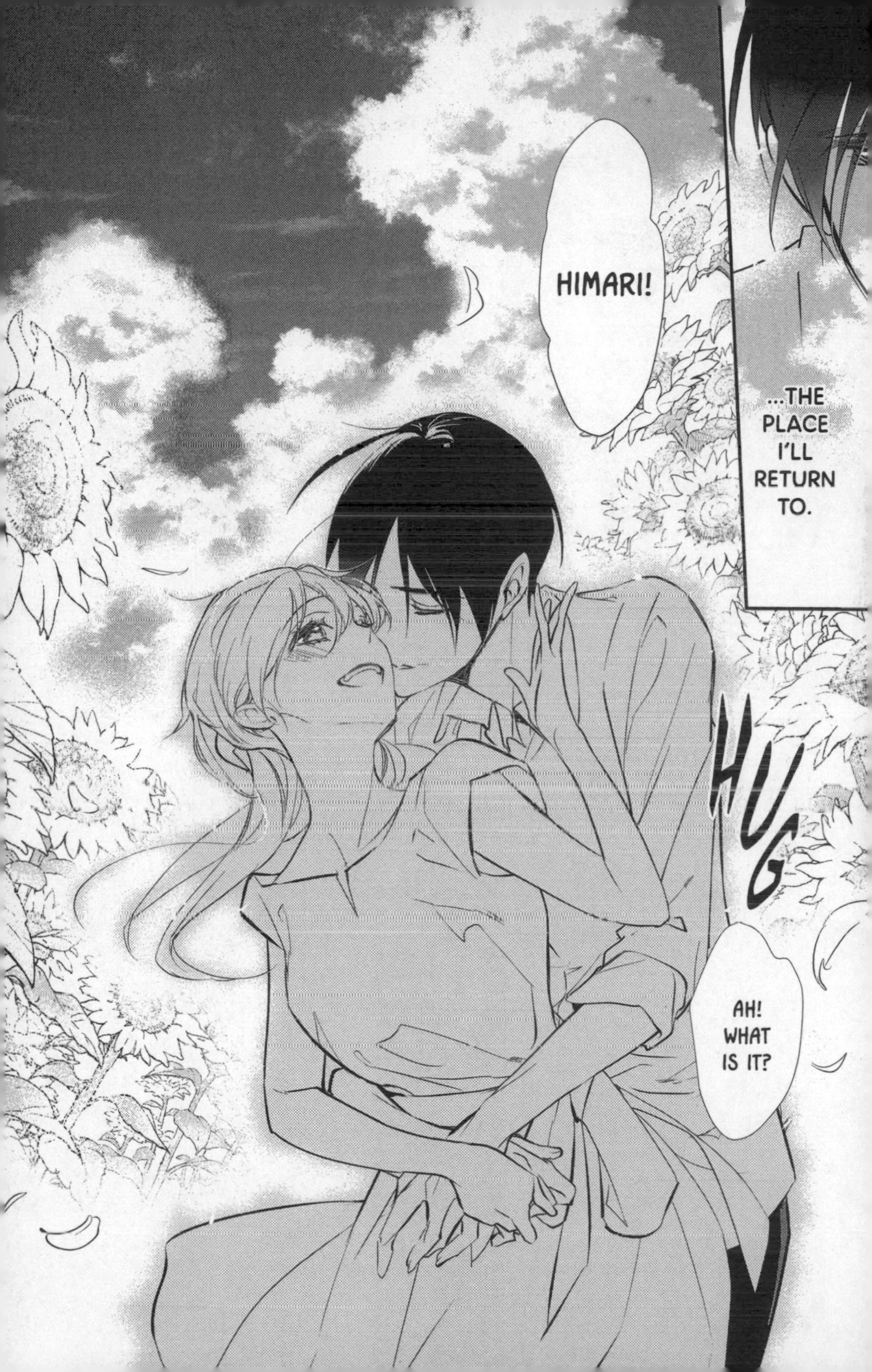
...THE PLACE I'LL RETURN TO.
HIMARI!
HUG
AH! WHAT IS IT?

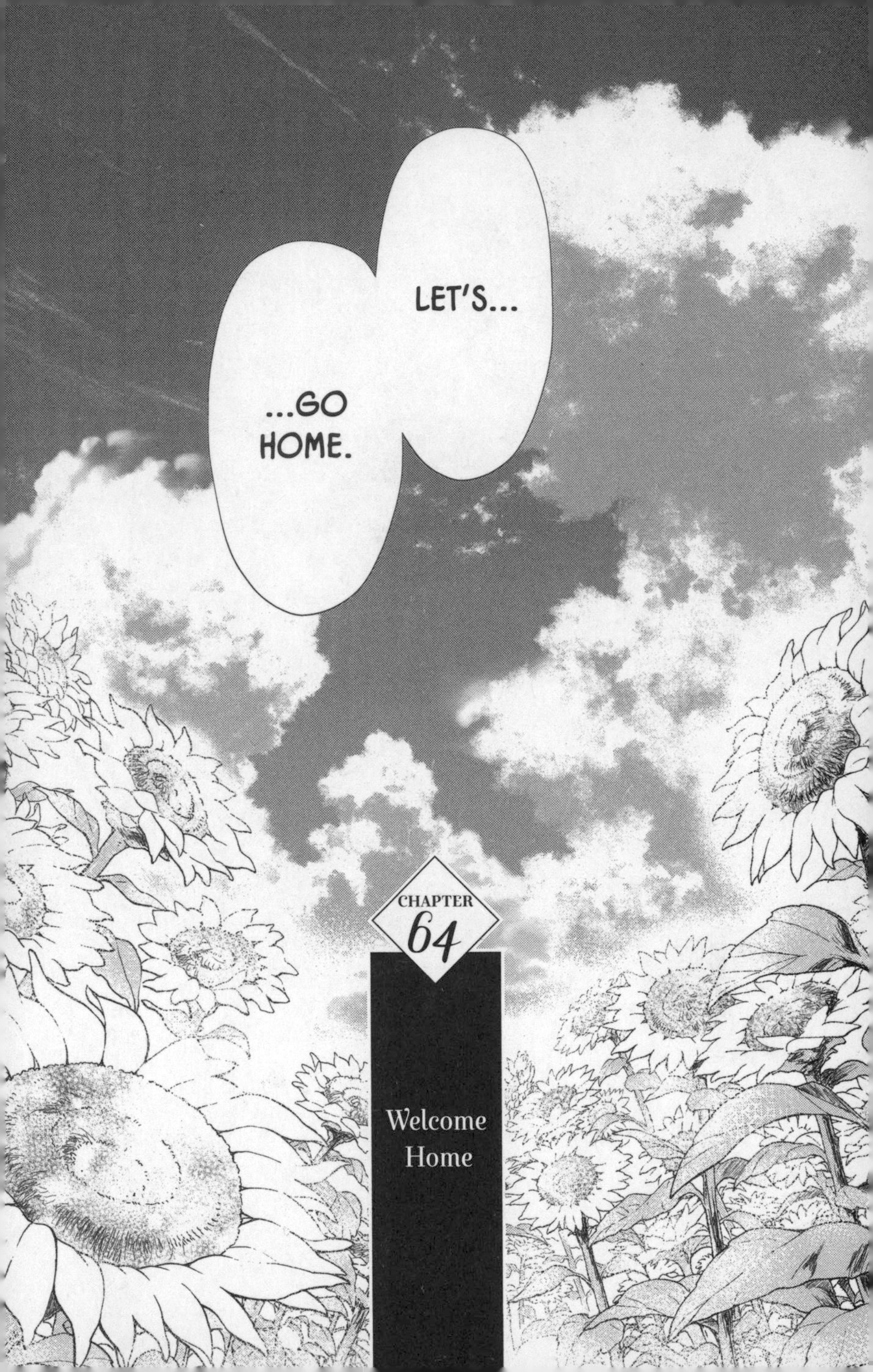
LET'S...
...GO HOME.
CHAPTER 64
Welcome Home

The DEMON PRINCE of MOMOCHI HOUSE

AYA SHOUTO PRESENTS

End

Thank you for

being together...

...
...
YEAH.
UH-HUH.
YEAH.
SEEMS EVERY-ONE'S THE SAME.

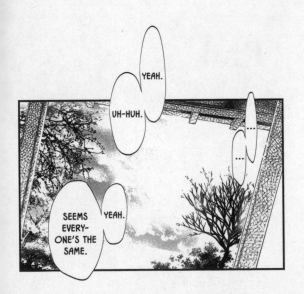

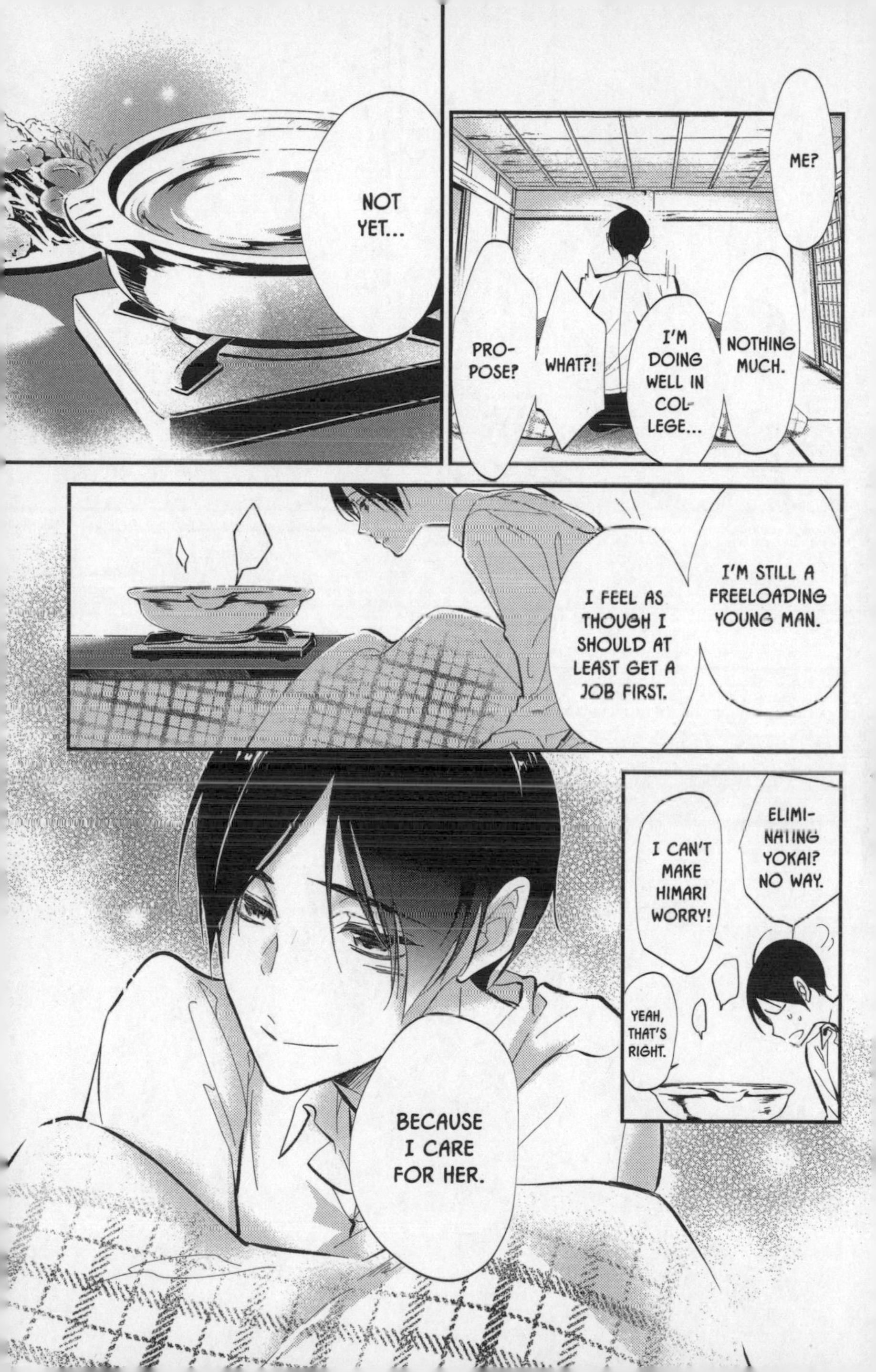
ME?
NOTHING MUCH.
I'M DOING WELL IN COL-LEGE...
WHAT?!
PRO-POSE?
NOT YET...
I'M STILL A FREELOADING YOUNG MAN.
I FEEL AS THOUGH I SHOULD AT LEAST GET A JOB FIRST.
ELIMI-NATING YOKAI? NO WAY.
I CAN'T MAKE HIMARI WORRY!
YEAH, THAT'S RIGHT.
BECAUSE I CARE FOR HER.

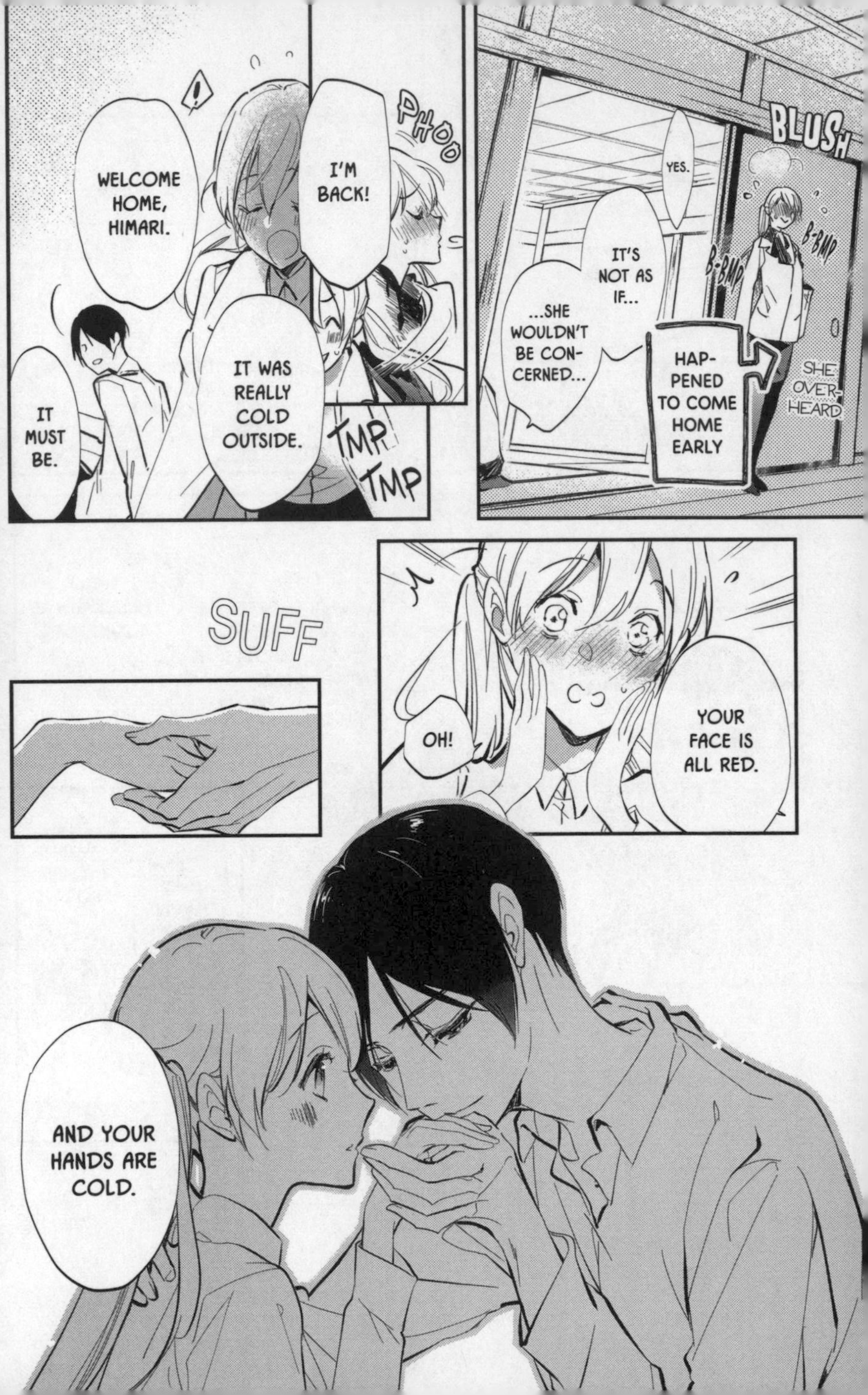
BLUSH
YES.
B-BMP
B-BMP
HAP-PENED TO COME HOME EARLY
SHE OVER-HEARD
IT'S NOT AS IF...
...SHE WOULDN'T BE CON-CERNED...
PHOO
I'M BACK!
!
WELCOME HOME, HIMARI.
TMP TMP
IT WAS REALLY COLD OUTSIDE.
IT MUST BE.
YOUR FACE IS ALL RED.
OH!
SUFF
AND YOUR HANDS ARE COLD.

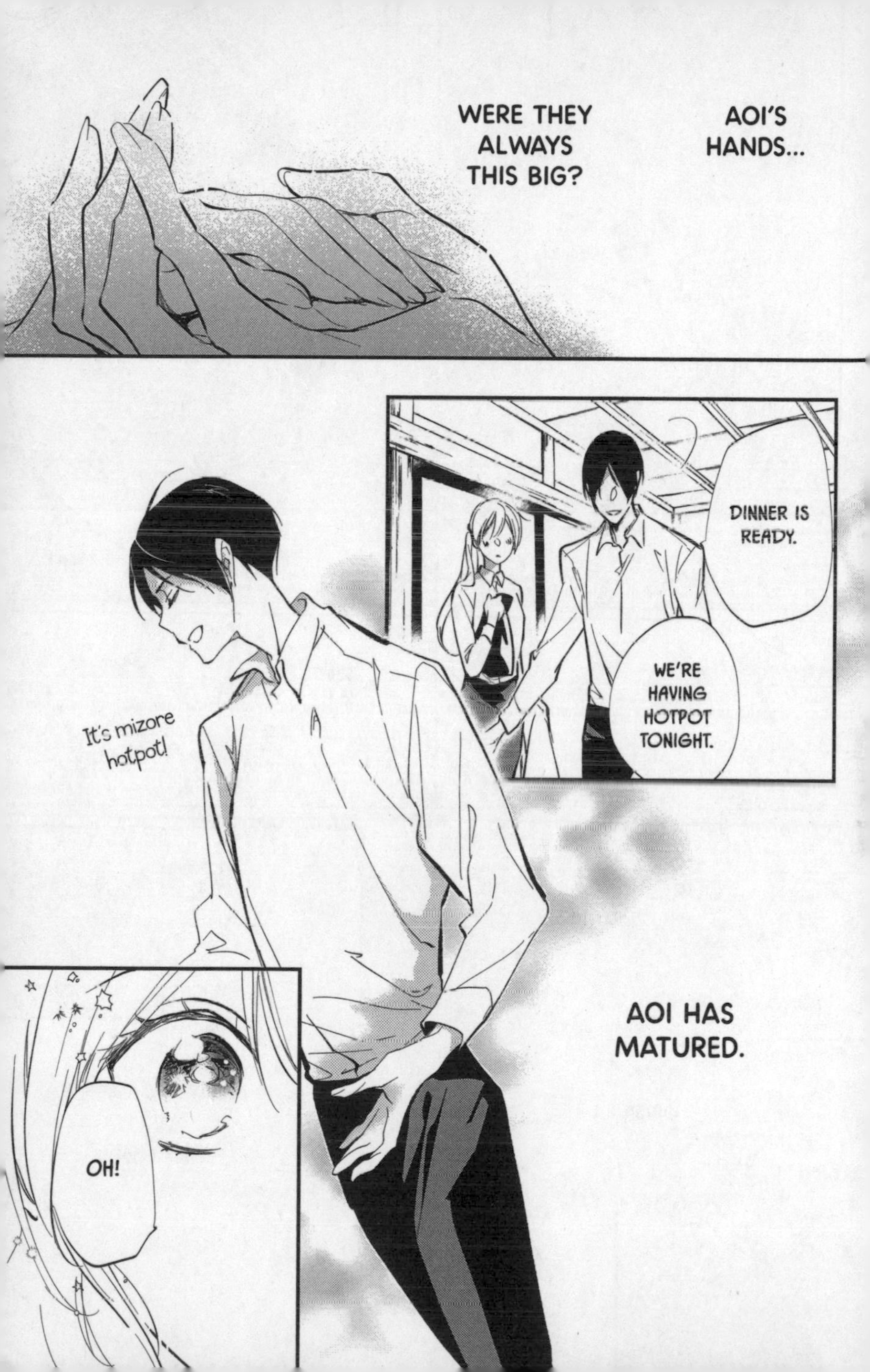
AOI'S HANDS...
WERE THEY ALWAYS THIS BIG?
DINNER IS READY.
WE'RE HAVING HOTPOT TONIGHT.
It's mizore hotpot!
AOI HAS MATURED.
OH!

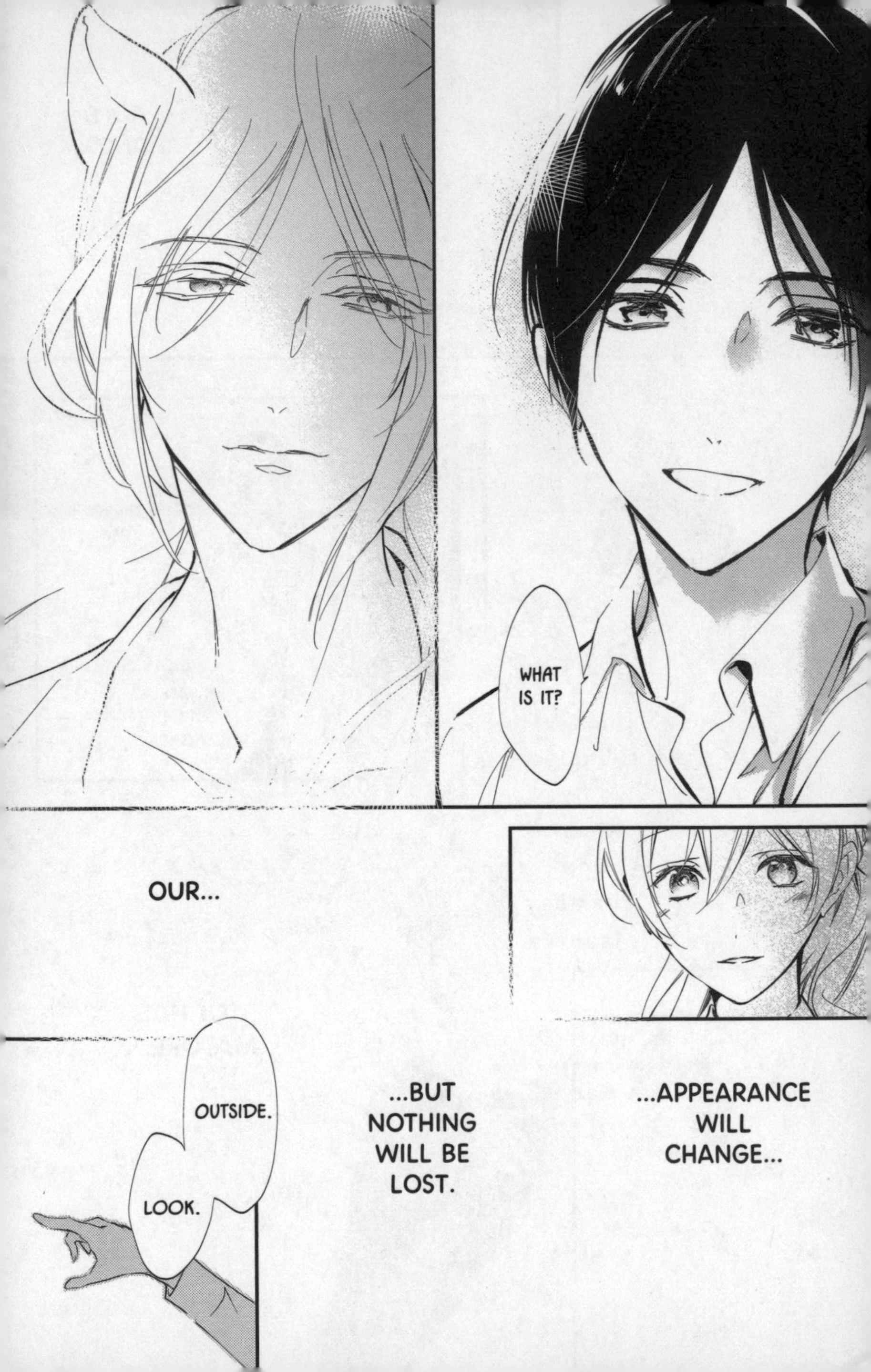
WHAT IS IT?
OUR...
...APPEARANCE WILL CHANGE...
...BUT NOTHING WILL BE LOST.
OUTSIDE.
LOOK.

IT'S
SNOWING.

Aya Shouoto

Staff

Norie Ogawa

Aya Maeda

Kazuko Mitsumata

Maiko Yoshise

Kanae Fujisawa

Naoko Kimura

Haruna Oda

Juri Kodama

Rika Kasahara

More Helpers

-Special Thanks-
Asuka, Kadokawa
Friends, Family

And
Readers

WE'LL
CONTINUE
ON.

It's been about seven years since the preview for this series came out. That's the same amount of time Aoi spent in Momochi House. Thank you for supporting me and sticking with me all this time.

-Aya Shouoto

Aya Shouoto was born on December 25. Her hobbies are traveling, staying at hotels, sewing and daydreaming. She currently lives in Tokyo and enjoys listening to J-pop anime theme songs while she works.

The Demon Prince of Momochi House

Volume 16
Shojo Beat Edition

Story and Art by Aya Shouoto

Translation JN Productions
Touch-Up Art & Lettering Inori Fukuda Trant
Design Jodie Yoshioka
Editor Nancy Thistlethwaite

MOMOCHISANCHI NO AYAKASHI OUJI Volume 16
© Aya Shouoto 2019
First published in Japan in 2019 by KADOKAWA CORPORATION, Tokyo.
English translation rights arranged with KADOKAWA CORPORATION, Tokyo.

Printed in the U.S.A.

Published by VIZ Media, LLC
P.O. Box 77010
San Francisco, CA 94107

10 9 8 7 6 5 4 3 2 1
First printing, October 2020

VIZ MEDIA

viz.com

shojobeat.com

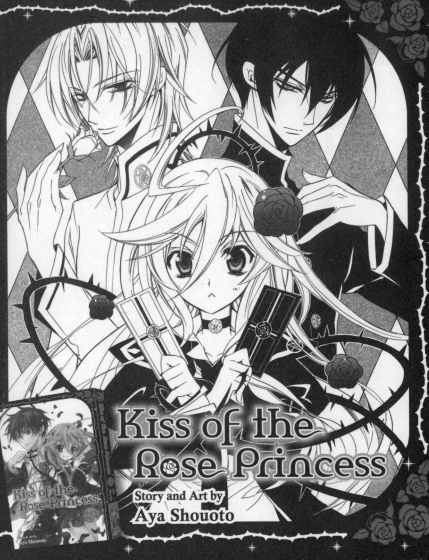

Kiss of the Rose Princess

Story and Art by
Aya Shouoto

Anise Yamamoto has been told that if she ever removes the rose choker given to her by her father, a terrible punishment will befall her. Unfortunately she loses that choker when a bat-like being named Ninufa falls from the sky and hits her. Ninufa gives Anise four cards representing four knights whom she can summon with a kiss. But now that she has these gorgeous men at her beck and call, what exactly is her quest?!

viz.com

RATED **T** TEEN

"Bloody" Mary, a vampire with a death wish, has spent the past 400 years chasing down a modern-day exorcist named Maria who is thought to have inherited "The Blood of Maria" and is the only one who can kill Mary. To Mary's dismay, Maria doesn't know how to kill vampires. Desperate to die, Mary agrees to become Maria's bodyguard until Maria can find a way to kill him.

Bloody+Mary

Story and Art by

akaza samamiya

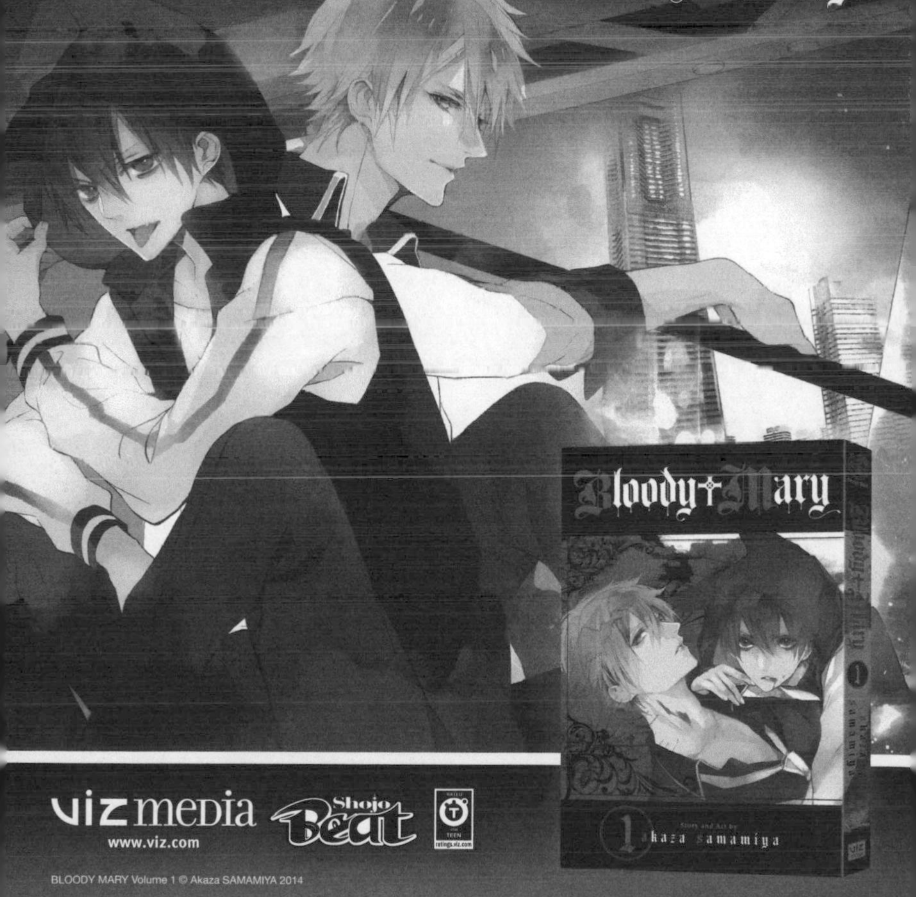
Bloody+Mary
1
Story and Art by
akaza samamiya

viz media

www.viz.com

Shojo Beat

RATED T TEEN ratings.viz.com

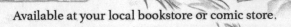

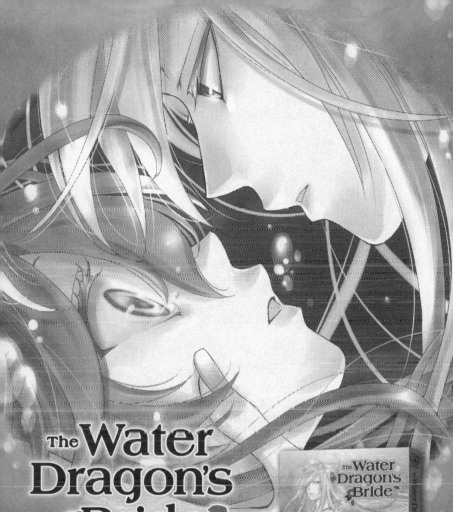

Snow White
with the Red Hair

Inspired the anime!

Snow White
with the Red Hair

SORATA 1 AKIDUKI

STORY & ART BY
SORATA AKIDUKI

Shirayuki is an herbalist famous for her naturally bright-red hair, and the prince of Tanbarun wants her all to himself! Unwilling to become the prince's possession, she seeks shelter in the woods of the neighboring kingdom, where she gains an unlikely ally—the prince of that kingdom! He rescues her from her plight, and thus begins the love story between a lovestruck prince and an unusual herbalist.

stop

You may be reading the
WRONG WAY!!

IT'S TRUE: In keeping with the original Japanese comic format, this book reads from right to left—so action, sound effects and word balloons are completely reversed. This preserves the orientation of the original artwork—plus, it's fun! Check out the diagram shown here to get the hang of things, and then turn to the other side of the book to get started!